Learners with Emotional and Behavioral Disorders

An Introduction

Anne M. Bauer
University of Cincinnati

Thomas M. Shea
University of Missouri—St. Louis

Merrill,
an imprint of Prentice Hall
Upper Saddle River, New Jersey • *Columbus, Ohio*

Library of Congress Cataloging-in-Publication Data

Bauer, Anne M.
    Learners with emotional and behavioral disorders : an introduction
/ Anne M. Bauer, Thomas M. Shea.
        p.   cm.
    Includes bibliographical references and indexes.
    ISBN 0-13-241373-6 (pbk.)
    1. Mentally ill children—Education.   2. Problem children-
Education.   3. Behavior disorders in children.   I. Shea, Thomas
M. II. Title.
LC4165.B38   1999
371.92—dc21   98-16495
                                                                              CIP

Cover art © Antonio Gore, Student—Franklin County Board MR/DD
Editor: Ann Castel Davis
Production Editor: Sheryl Glicker Langner
Photo Coordinator: Sandy Lenahan
Design Coordinator: Diane C. Lorenzo
Cover Designer: Ceri Fitzgerald
Production Manager: Laura Messerly
Director of Marketing: Kevin Flanagan
Advertising/Marketing Coordinator: Krista Groshong
Marketing Manager: Suzanne Stanton

This book was set in Bookman by Clarinda Company and was printed and bound
by Courier/Westfor, Inc. The cover was printed by Phoenix Color Corp.

©1999 by Prentice-Hall, Inc.
Simon & Schuster/A Viacom Company
Upper Saddle River, New Jersey 07458

Photo credits: pp. xiv, 30, 162, 190, 270 by Barbara Schwartz/Merrill; pp. 6, 41,
114, 147, 167 by Anne Vega/Merrill; p. 13 by Susan Burger/Lasting Impressions;
pp. 37, 143 by Tom Watson/Merrill; pp. 50, 59, 73, 79, 94, 126, 140, 174, 195,
208, 220, 228, 240 by Scott Cunningham/Merrill; pp. 55, 101, 104, 118, 252, 282
by Anthony Magnacca/Merrill; p. 68 by Michal Heron/PH College; p. 184 by Todd
Yarrington/Merrill; p. 246 by KS Studios/Merrill; p. 276 by Gilles Peress/Magnum
Photos, Inc.

Printed in the United States of America

10 9 8 7 6 5 4 3 2 1

ISBN: 0-13-241373-6

Prentice-Hall International (UK) Limited, London
Prentice-Hall of Australia Pty. Limited, Sydney
Prentice-Hall of Canada, Inc., Toronto
Prentice-Hall Hispanoamericana, S. A., Mexico
Prentice-Hall of India Private Limited, New Delhi
Prentice-Hall of Japan, Inc., Tokyo
Simon & Schuster Asia Pte. Ltd., Singapore
Editora Prentice-Hall do Brasil, Ltda., Rio de Janeiro

For Dolores, Kevin,
Jane, and Keith

and

"Coach" Riley,
Demian, Tarie, CJ,
Sarah, and Mickey

◊ ◊

Preface

Special education, which strives to meet the needs of all learners with disabilities, including those identified with emotional/behavioral disorders, is rapidly changing. Teachers are attempting to serve more children who have more problems than ever before in the history of public education. They are working with families who are more challenged than in previous generations. They are working in schools that have fewer resources available to support their efforts to provide effective service. These efforts are further complicated by the fact that schools are becoming inclusive environments, trying to serve all students in general education classes. These changes are creating tension not only in the schools, but throughout the field of special education and the education of learners with emotional/behavioral disorders. These changes are challenging our perspective of learners identified as emotional/behavioral disordered.

In this book, we present a new perspective for the education of learners identified as emotional/behavioral disordered. Our goal is to provide a reader-friendly text which contains a broad range of information about learners with emotional/behavioral disorders. The text goes beyond empirical research to address the shifting paradigm in special education.

The text offers an integrated perspective to understanding working with children and youth identified with emotional/behavioral disorders. Rather than being linked to a specific conceptual model, (i.e., behavioral, psychodynamic, or biological), the text recognizes the contribution of the various conceptual models to the understanding of learners and learning and development. It emphasizes that behavior cannot be understood as a simple cause and effect relationship, but must be understood in the context in which it occurs.

Such an approach to studying emotional/behavioral disorders is grounded in several assumptions about learners, learning, and behavior:

- To be effective service providers, teachers must consider relationships within and between all of the settings in which learners act and those settings which impinge on the learner.

- There are limitations in the application of a single perspective or conceptual model.
- Interventions are determined by the demands of the various settings and the learner's needs in those settings.
- Behavior varies with the situation in which the individual finds himself or herself.
- Behaviors are sensible, purposeful, and meaningful and serve a function for the learner which can be related to his or her intent.
- Behaviors should not be eliminated, but rather shaped toward more conventional, positive, and productive behaviors.
- The social acceptability of behavior is perceived as dependent on both culture and setting.

In the text, a growth rather than a deficit paradigm is applied. Emotional/behavioral disorders are not seen as a thing, but as an identification. Each learner is an intact person who happens to require special intervention or support.

The first section of the text presents general information on working with learners identified with emotional/behavioral disorders. The authors provide introductory information to the field (Chapter One), describe the existing theoretical perspectives (Chapter Two), and present a description of the developmental contexts in which learners develop and act (Chapter Three). In the next section, the individual and his or her developmental contexts are discussed. The section includes discussion of biological and temperamental aspects of the learner (Chapter Four), learning and interactional styles (Chapter Five), family factors (Chapter Six), and classroom factors (Chapter Seven). The issues of cultural diversity and gender are discussed in Chapter Eight.

In subsequent chapters, the authors explore how learners are identified and placed in special education and related services (Chapter Nine), and behavior change intervention for application with individuals (Chapter Ten) and groups (Chapter Eleven). The text concludes with a discussion of prevention and issues related to learners considered to be "at risk" (Chapter Twelve). The text includes a variety of pedagogical supports to assist the reader. Each chapter includes an advance organizer, learning objectives, key words and phrases, self-evaluation questions, application activities, and exercises on "making the language your own."

The authors appreciate the help and support received during the writing of this text, especially from those closest to us: our spouses, Riley and Dolores, and our children, Demian, Tarie, CJ, and Sarah, and Mickey and Kevin, Keith, and Jane. We also wish to thank the many students and teachers who have taught us over the years.

Special thanks to Ann Davis, who supported this project, and Sheryl Langner, who remembered all the details. Also thanks to our reviewers who made this a better text with constructive comments and criticisms: Karenlee Alexander, Bemidji State University; Lisa Bloom, Western Carolina University; Ellen Paula Crowley, Illinois State University; Beth Fouse, The University of Texas at Tyler; Elizabeth D. Heins, Stetson University; Jack Hourcade, Boise State University; James Krouse, Clarion University; Maureen R. Norris, Bellarmine College; and Kathy L. Ruhl, Penn State.

Anne M. Bauer
Thomas M. Shea

Contents

Contents

3 The Social Systems Perspective and Developmental Context   50

4 Biological Factors and Temperament   68

7 Classroom Factors

8 Cultural Diversity and Gender   162

9 Screening to Placement   184

1 An Introduction to Emotional/Behavioral Disorders

TO GUIDE YOUR READING

After you complete this chapter, you will be able to answer these questions:

- Who are the learners identified as emotionally/behaviorally disordered?
- How are learners identified as emotionally/behaviorally disordered?
- How did services for these learners evolve?
- What are the current definitions of "emotional/behavioral disorders"?
- How many learners are identified as emotionally/behaviorally disordered?
- Where are learners identified as emotionally/behaviorally disordered served?
- What is the situational nature of emotional/behavioral disorders?

◊ *Matthew is 5 years old. On his first day of kindergarten, he bit a student who reached across his paper for the glue. On the playground playing dodgeball, when he was struck by the ball, he grabbed the ball, ran up to the student who "got him out," and threw the ball into his face. During lunch, he stabbed with his plastic fork a student who bumped him while he was eating. By noontime, he was in the office, with the principal frantically trying to find his parents to come pick him up.*

◊ *Sam is 8 years old. During class he fidgets and squirms in his seat. When called on he rarely knows the problem the class is working on or the page they are reading. His pencils are all chewed, and he has chewed the top button off of most of his shirts. His folder contains several papers, all of which are partially completed. The teacher can't remember the last time he turned in a completed paper or a piece of homework. His parents, who are exasperated, have made an appointment to have him evaluated by a child psychologist.*

◊ *Suzanne is 14 years old. She is described by her teacher as a loner. She completes all of her work, yet says nothing in class. During lunch she sits alone, and speaks only when spoken to. Her classmates call her "Spook" and often ignore her. When teased or taunted she simply gazes past the other students or walks away. Last weekend she ate a bottle of aspirin with beer, and had to have her stomach pumped. She was hospitalized for three days, given medication for depression, and sent back to school.*

This introductory chapter presents a variety of topics basic to an understanding of learners identified as emotionally/behaviorally disordered. The chapter begins with a discussion of the diverse characteristics of these learners, including the number of such learners, their gender, age, intelligence, achievement and educational status, secondary needs and disabilities, social skills and interpersonal interactions, family, ethnicity, and economic and other demographic characteristics. Consideration is given to the identification and classification of these learners and the evolution of the services they require. In addition, the current definitions and the situational nature of emotional/behavioral disorders are discussed.

◊◊ Who Are the Learners Identified as Emotionally/Behaviorally Disordered?

Each of us can close our eyes and form a picture of "learners identified as emotionally/behaviorally disordered." We may imagine the bully who taunted us in the fourth grade, the sad sophomore who attempted suicide, or the hyperactive first grader who was always in trouble in the classroom for not sitting still or not doing his work. The vignettes presented at the beginning of this chapter demonstrate the diversity that exists among learners identified as emotionally/behaviorally disordered and their presenting behaviors.

In this section, some of the common characteristics of learners identified as emotionally/behaviorally disorders are described. Although there are some similarities between learners identified as emotionally/behaviorally disordered, individuals within this group vary a great deal. The reader is encouraged to focus attention on the diversity between learners identified as emotionally/behaviorally disordered.

They Are More Likely To Be Boys than Girls

Four times as many boys as girls are identified as emotionally/behaviorally disordered. (Singth, Landrum, Donatelli, Hampton, & Ellis, 1994; Wagner et al., 1991). In a large national sample of adolescents identified as emotionally/behaviorally disordered, only 21% were female (Cullinan, Epstein, & Sabornie, 1992). Boys far outnumbered girls among learners identified and served as emotionally/behaviorally disordered in public school programs and among learners both identified as emotionally/behaviorally disordered in public schools and receiving mental health services outside of the schools (Caseau, Luckasson, & Kroth, 1994).

Girls outnumbered boys, however, among learners not identified as emotionally/behaviorally disordered by the public schools but receiving mental health services outside of the school (Caseau et al., 1994). It appears that, compared to boys, girls were more likely to have serious problems with depression, family conflict, suicidal ideation, and suicide attempts. Apparently, these girls had problems severe enough to warrant identification as emotionally/behaviorally disordered at home and in the community, but not of the type that would warrant such identification at school. The girls who did receive services in public schools exhibited acting out behaviors similar to those of boys.

The long-term postschool outcomes of girls and boys identified as emotionally/behaviorally disordered also differ. Levine and

Edgar (1995) reported that becoming pregnant and parenting were serious problems confronting girls. Girls with disabilities are five times more likely than their counterparts without disabilities to be parenting. Parenting had a significant impact on the ability of girls to participate in postsecondary education programs.

They Usually Have Difficulty Achieving in School

Almost half (44.6%) of learners identified as emotionally/behaviorally disordered in the United States in the 1989–90 school year failed one or more courses in the previous year of high school, far more than students with communication disorders (35%) or learning disabilities (34.8%) (U.S. Department of Education, 1992). The reading achievement of learners identified as emotionally/behaviorally disordered has been reported to be significantly lower (1.5 to 2 grade levels) than that of their peers in elementary school, and even lower by the time they reach high school (3.5 grade levels) (Coutinho, 1986).

Learners identified as emotionally/behaviorally disordered receive lower grades than any other disability group and are retained at grade level more often. In addition, they fail minimum competency examinations more frequently than learners with other disabilities. Of those students identified as emotionally/behaviorally disordered taking minimum competency tests (22% were exempted), 63% failed some part of the examination (U.S. Department of Education, 1994). High school students identified as emotionally/behaviorally disordered have a mean grade point average of 1.7 (on a 4-point scale), compared to 2.0 for all learners with disabilities, and 2.6 for all students (Wagner et al., 1991).

Learners identified as emotionally/behaviorally disordered are the most likely of all learners with identified disabilities to drop out of school. The percentage of learners identified as emotionally/behaviorally disordered, 14 years and older, graduating with a high school diploma or certificate has decreased from 8.82% of all learners in the 1988–89 school year to 7.84% in 1992–93. Fifty percent of learners identified as emotionally/behaviorally disordered drop out of school, most by the 10th grade. Fifty-eight percent leave school without graduating (Wagner, 1991). Among learners identified as emotionally/behaviorally disordered, 42% graduate as compared to 56% of all learners with disabilities and 71% of all learners (Wagner et al., 1991).

The National Longitudinal Transition Study of Special Education Students (NLTS) reported similar results. The graduation rate for students identified as emotionally/behaviorally disordered is second lowest; only learners with multiple disabilities have a lower rate.

The dropout rate of students identified as emotionally/behaviorally disordered is the highest among the disability groups; learners with learning disabilities have the next highest dropout rate at 32.3%. Among students with disabilities, the percentage of students identified as emotionally/behaviorally disordered who age out of school is relatively low, but is the highest in suspension and expulsion. According to NLTS dropping out of school is the culmination of a cluster of school performance problems, including high absenteeism and poor grade performance. Students identified as emotionally/behaviorally disordered had the highest rate of absenteeism among all learners with disabilities (17.7 days a year) and the highest likelihood of failing a course (43.9%) (U.S. Office of Education, 1992).

They May Have Learning Problems or Communication Disorders

Many learners identified as emotionally/behaviorally disordered may have learning problems or communication disorders. Although the early work of Morse, Cutler, and Fink (1964) suggested that learners identified as emotionally/behaviorally disordered had above average cognitive ability, more recent studies indicate that these learners exhibit average or lower than average measured cognitive abilities when compared to their typical peers (Coleman, 1986). Learners with more severe behavioral disorders exhibit intelligence quotients in the mentally retarded range (Freeman & Ritvo, 1984).

In one study, 97% of the learners identified as demonstrating mild to moderate emotional/behavioral disorders fell more than one standard deviation below the mean on an individually administered test of language (Camarata, Hughes, & Ruhl, 1988). The pattern of these learners' language problems was consistent with the pattern of learners identified as learning disabled. After studying the communication performance of adolescents identified as emotionally/behaviorally disordered and their nonidentified peers, Rosenthal and Simeonsson (1991) suggested that communication deficits may be a central feature of emotional/behavioral disorders.

Fessler, Rosenberg, and Rosenberg (1991) reported that more than 37% of learners in their sample were identified as both learning disabled and emotionally/behaviorally disordered. Teachers rated the academic achievement of learners identified as emotionally/behaviorally disordered at a level equal to that of learners identified as learning disabled (Luebke, Epstein, & Cullinan, 1989).

Many learners identified with a primary disability other than emotional/behavioral disorders, such as mental retardation, orthopedically impaired, and visually impaired, often demonstrate

It is important to include all learners in activities.

challenging behaviors. Identification as having a primary disability, however, precludes identification as "emotionally/behaviorally disordered" according to current definitions.

Their Social Skills and Interactions Vary from Those of Their Peers

The most frequently stated reasons for learners to be identified as emotionally/behaviorally disordered are (a) poor peer relationships, (b) frustration, (c) low academic achievement, (d) shy and withdrawn behavior, (e) disruptive behavior, (f) fighting, (g) refusal to work, and (h) short attention span. Poor peer relationships was the most frequent reason for referral among both boys and girls (Hutton, 1985).

Learners identified as emotionally/behaviorally disordered vary from their counterparts with disabilities in terms of social interactions. In a full-inclusion setting, Sale and Carey (1995) documented that students with physical disabilities received significantly more "liked-most" nominations than any other group of students. Learners identified as emotionally/behaviorally disordered, however, had the lowest "liked-most" scores, being the least frequently nominated in positive situations and the most frequently nominated in negative situations.

One pervasive problem of learners identified as emotionally/behaviorally disordered, which may contribute to their being "least-liked," is *aggression* (Hughes, 1985). In their study, Epstein, Kauffman, and Cullinan (1985) found the most persistent pattern of behavior reported among the learners identified as having emotional/behavioral disorders to be aggression.

aggression physical or verbal behavior against another individual

They Are Less Likely To Live with Both Parents

In a large national sample, Cullinan et al. (1992) found that one third of adolescents identified as emotionally/behaviorally disordered lived with both parents, whereas two thirds of adolescents not identified as emotionally/behaviorally disordered lived with both parents. Students identified as emotionally/behaviorally disordered have a higher rate of living in one-parent families than students of any other disability classification (Wagner & Shaver, 1989).

Other Demographic Characteristics

Demographic and economic factors may influence the number of students identified as emotionally/behaviorally disordered (Wagner et al., 1991; Oswald & Coutinho, 1995). In school districts, the amount of per pupil revenue was the strongest single predictor of the rate at which learners were identified as emotionally/behaviorally disordered. As district revenue increased, the likelihood of identification increased. State and local evaluation and multidisciplinary team procedures may also have an impact on identification rates, as well as the availability of both a full continuum of placement settings and of comprehensive services offered by mental health service providers (Oswald & Coutinho, 1995).

One would assume that learners admitted to a psychiatric hospital for service would be identified as emotionally/behaviorally disordered by their schools. However, in a study by Singth et al. (1994), almost half—46%—of the learners receiving inpatient psychiatric services and partial hospitalization were *not* identified as emotionally/behaviorally disordered by their schools. These non-identified learners were served in general education classrooms. Ten percent of these learners were found to have other disabilities. Their average age of hospital admission was 11.6 years. African American students were *overrepresented* in the sample of non-identified students, with only 56% of the learners admitted to hospitalization being Caucasian. Significant issues for these learners were alcohol abuse (80%) and drug abuse (85%).

overrepresented in greater proportion than anticipated from the general population

Cultural differences may have an impact on the identification of learners with emotional/behavioral disorders, working against some children in opposite ways. On the one hand, many professionals are unaware of the impact of culture on behavior and may mistake cultural differences for emotional/behavioral disorders. On the other hand, learners from diverse cultural, ethnic, or linguistic groups may not be identified as emotionally/behaviorally disordered when they are in need of services. McIntyre (1993) found that learners may risk being denied special education support as emotionally/behaviorally disordered if they are members of an historically oppressed minority (African American, Hispanic American) or from low income households. Under the original federal definition (discussed later in this chapter) groups were mislabeled due to cultural differences and home circumstances; under the current definitions culturally diverse students will be provided extra safeguards against incorrect identification (McIntyre, 1993).

African American learners are also overrepresented among learners identified as emotionally/behaviorally disordered. This continues to be a concern for special education. The overrepresentation of African Americans as emotionally/behaviorally disordered has been found to occur when there was also overrepresentation of African Americans as learning disabled and underrepresentation of African Americans as "gifted" (Sewartka, Deering, & Grant, 1995).

The rate of identification of learners as emotionally/behaviorally disordered varies across racial, cultural, gender, and socioeconomic lines. African American and Caucasian students are overrepresented: they represent 16% and 68% of school age enrollment respectively, and 22% and 71% of the students classified as emotionally/behaviorally disordered. On the other hand, Hispanic American and Asian American students represent 12% and 3% of the school-age population respectively, but only 6% and 1% of the students classified as emotionally/behaviorally disordered (U.S. Department of Education, OCR, 1993)

Finally, students identified as emotionally/behaviorally disordered have significant involvement with the juvenile justice system. Twenty percent are arrested at least once before they leave school and 35% are arrested within a few years of leaving school (Wagner et al., 1991).

◊◊ How Are Learners Identified as Emotionally/Behaviorally Disordered Classified?

Several systems are used to classify learners identified as emotionally/behaviorally disordered. Three systems frequently used in special education and the education of learners identified as emotionally/behaviorally disordered are reviewed in this section: American

Psychiatric Association's *Diagnostic and Statistical Manual of Mental Disorders* (1994), Edelbrock's *Child Behavior Checklists* (1984), and Quay's and Peterson's *Behavior Problem Checklist* (1979).

The *Diagnostic and Statistical Manual of Mental Disorders* (4th ed.) (DSM-IV) (American Psychiatric Association, 1994) includes 19 major diagnostic categories, including one specifically for infants, children, and adolescents. The major syndromes and sub-syndromes of this category are presented in Figure 1.1. In the manual, each diagnostic syndrome is described in detail.

Although this system is orderly, it is not without problems. Duncan, Forness, and Hartsough (1995) reviewed the diagnostic and treatment histories of children and youth served in day treatment programs. Using the DSM IV, Duncan et al. found marked instability of psychiatric diagnoses over time. In addition, there was a lack of concordance between DSM IV diagnoses and characteristics required for special education services. Duncan et al. questioned the integrity and congruity of both psychiatric and educational diagnostic systems used by school and mental health personnel.

Edelbrock and associates (1984) developed a classification system through an analysis of behavior problems presented by learners on whom the Child Behavior Checklists were applied. As a result of the analysis, two clusters of behaviors emerged: externalizing and internalizing behaviors. **Externalizing behaviors** are those such as stealing, lying, aggression, and hyperactivity. **Internalizing behaviors** are those such as physical complaints, phobias, worrying, social withdrawal, and fearfulness. Externalizing and internalizing behaviors are presented in Figure 1.2.

As a result of a series of studies conducted using the *Behavior Problem Checklist,* Quay and Peterson (1979) concluded that behavioral disorders may be grouped into four main clusters: conduct disorders, personality disorders, inadequacy-immaturity, and socialized aggression. Students with conduct disorders are those who are perceived as nonresponsive to internal or the usual social controls. Their behaviors may include aggression, noncompliance, disruption, inattention, hyperactivity, and attention seeking. Students with personality disorders may exhibit anxiety or withdrawal and may demonstrate a sense of personal inferiority. Learners described as "inadequate-immature" may be passive, socially immature, and have difficulty making decisions. Learners who are identified as demonstrating socialized aggression tend to engage in gang behavior or some sort of organized stealing, truancy, or other rule breaking.

The *Behavior Problem Checklist* (Quay & Peterson, 1979), on which the above classification system is based, has been revised.

externalizing behaviors acting out behaviors such as stealing, lying, aggression, and hyperactivity

internalizing behaviors behaviors such as physical complaints, phobias, worrying, social withdrawal, and fearfulness

Disorders Usually First Diagnosed in Infancy, Childhood, or Adolescence

A. Mental retardation

    1. Mild mental retardation

    2. Moderate mental retardation

    3. Severe mental retardation

    4. Profound mental retardation

    5. Mental retardation, severity unspecified

B. Learning disorders

    1. Reading disorders

    2. Mathematics disorders

    3. Disorders of written expression

    4. Learning disorders, not otherwise specified

C. Motor skills disorders

    1. Developmental coordination disorder

D. Communication disorders

    1. Expressive language disorder

    2. Receptive language disorder

    3. Mixed receptive-expressive language disorder

    4. Phonological disorder

    5. Stuttering

    6. Communication disorder, not otherwise specified

E. Pervasive developmental disorders

    1. Autistic disorder

    2. Rett's disorder

    3. Childhood disintegrative disorder

    4. Asperger's disorder

    5. Pervasive developmental disorder, not otherwise specified

F. Attention-deficit and disruptive behavior disorders

    1. Combined type

    2. Predominantly inattentive type

Figure 1.1 DSM IV Classification System

3. Predominantly hyperactive-impulsive type
4. Attention-deficit/hyperactivity disorder, not otherwise specified
5. Conduct disorder (Childhood onset or adolescent onset)
6. Oppositional defiant disorder
7. Disruptive behavior disorder, not otherwise specified

G. Feeding and eating disorders of infancy or early childhood
   1. Pica
   2. Rumination disorder
   3. Feeding and eating disorder, not otherwise specified

H. Tic Disorders
   1. Tourette's disorder
   2. Chronic motor and vocal tic disorder
   3. Transient tic disorder (single episode or recurrent)
   4. Tic disorder, not otherwise specified

I. Elimination disorders
   1. Encopresis
      a. With constipation and overflow incontinence
      b. Without constipation and overflow incontinence
   2. Enuresis (not due to general medical condition)
      a. Nocturnal only
      b. Diurnal only
      c. Nocturnal and diurnal

J. Other disorders of infancy, childhood, or adolescence
   1. Separation anxiety disorder (specify if early onset)
   2. Selective mutism
   3. Reactive attachment disorder of infancy or early childhood
      a. Inhibited type
      b. Disinhibited type
   4. Stereotype movement disorder (specify if with self-injurious behavior)
   5. Disorder of infancy, childhood, or adolescence, not otherwise specified

Figure 1.2
Externalizing and
Internalizing
Behaviors

> ## Internalizing Behaviors
>
> Social withdrawal
>
> Depression
>
> Immaturity
>
> Somatic complaints
>
> Uncommunicative behaviors
>
> Obsessive-compulsive behavior
>
> ## Externalizing Behaviors
>
> Aggression
>
> Delinquency
>
> Sexual acting out
>
> Hyperactivity
>
> Cruelty
>
> Lying
>
> Stealing

The four major clusters are now conduct disorders, socialized aggression, attention problems-immaturity, and anxiety-withdrawal. Two additional clusters—psychotic behavior and motor tension-excess—are also used (Quay, 1983).

Considerable effort has been devoted to classifying learners identified as emotionally/behaviorally disordered; however the actual application of classification systems to teaching and supporting these learners is limited. In some situations, classification systems have actually been used to prevent learners from receiving services, as in the case of classifying those with conduct disorders as "socially maladjusted" and thereby excluding these learners from the federal definition. Rather than trying to categorize learners identified as emotionally/behaviorally disordered, efforts to work with them should be based on each learner's needs.

◊◊ How Did Services for These Learners Evolve?

Throughout history, services for learners identified as emotionally/behaviorally disordered have depended on the existence of some guiding theory. As Brendtro and Van Bockern (1994) suggest, without a guiding theory to support professionals in their work, a "try anything"

It hurts to be left out.

eclecticism prevails, which is, as they suggest, "choosing a potluck meal with a blindfold." Without a theory to guide them, professionals working with these challenging children and youth are likely to fall into "folk psychology," contradict themselves in the methodology they implement, have difficulty functioning as members of a treatment team, and be inconsistent in their treatment of the children and youth with whom they are working (Brentro & Van Bockern, 1994). In recent times, however, all of the models for serving learners identified as emotionally/behaviorally disordered became more eclectic. In addition, cross-fertilization has increased across all theory bases, as professionals use what is most effective within their own perception of "emotional/behavioral disorders."

Services for learners identified as emotionally/behaviorally disordered have evolved from internment or exclusion to inclusion. Prehistoric societies, in which survival depended on the fitness of each member, ostracized or killed those who did not contribute to society. Some ancient people, believing that mental disorders were the result of demonic possession, rejected, punished, or killed individuals who varied from their peers. In medieval times, individuals identified as emotionally/behaviorally disordered were often objects of amusement, or imprisoned or executed. During this period, the Roman Catholic Church began to foster what was then considered humane care, by providing asylums.

With the emergence of the Renaissance and a greater belief in the value of human life, interest in the struggles confronted by individuals with disabilities—including those identified as emotionally/behaviorally disordered—increased. Phillipe Pinel (1745–1826) was one of the first physicians to attempt to treat rather than confine persons identified as mentally ill. As the chief physician at two mental hospitals in France, the Salpatriere and the Bicetre, Pinel was convinced that mental illness was not the result of demonic possession, but of some sort of brain dysfunction. Consequently, he removed the chains that confined his patients and discontinued the use of bleeding as a form of treatment.

A few decades later in 1843, Dorothea L. Dix studied and reported on the conditions of the mentally ill in Massachusetts. Her descriptions, including the use of chains for restraints, and her argument that persons with mental illness could be properly treated and cared for only in hospitals, resulted in enlargement of the state hospital in Worcester, Massachusetts, which was one of only eight mental hospitals in the United States at the time. Dix worked in other places and was responsible for the construction of 32 hospitals in the United States, Canada, Europe, and Japan.

Late in the 19th century, a few schools in the United States began to make formal provisions for learners identified as emotionally/behaviorally disordered. In 1871 in New Haven, Connecticut, the public schools established classes for learners exhibiting unmanageable behaviors. Classes for "unruly boys" were formed in New York City's public schools in 1874. In fact, the first public school special education classes were those for learners with unmanageable behaviors (Kanner, 1970).

Although the first scientific study of childhood psychosis was published in 1838 by Jean Etienne Esquirol (1774–1840) in *Des Maladies Mentales,* it was not until the 1920s and 1930s that, through the work of Lauretta Bender and Anna Freud, children with severe emotional/behavioral disorders were systematically studied. As a senior psychiatrist at Bellevue Hospital in New York City during the 1930s, Bender studied the role of brain pathology in the development of childhood schizophrenia and other forms of emotional/behavioral disorders in children. She developed the Bender-Gestalt test to measure visual-motor maturation and applied it to screening for and measurement of brain dysfunction in children (Bender, 1938). In 1927 Anna Freud published *Introduction to the Techniques of Child Analysis,* an elaboration of the work of her father, Sigmund Freud, on ego defenses and identification. From this effort, the psychodynamic perspective of working with learners identified as emotionally/behaviorally disordered arose. Her work stimulated others, including Erik Erikson, who elaborated on the psychodynamic perspective and added the element of the impact of society and culture on the individual and behavior.

In 1947, Strauss and Lehtinen published *Psychopathology and Education of the Brain-Injured Child,* describing a structured, directive approach for teaching learners with "brain disorders." Strauss and Lehtinen believed that brain injury caused these learners to have difficulties in perception, concept formation, and mental organization, all of which interfered with learning processes. This work led directly to research related to learners identified as having learning disabilities. The central notion of this physiological perspective is that learning disabilities arise from perceptual-motor dysfunction of neurological origin (Cruickshank, 1972). As a result of the research, remedial programs, such as those described by Kephart (1960) and Frostig (1961) began to emphasize gross and fine motor training as prerequisite to more direct teaching of academics. By the mid-1970s, however, the research on which this theory was based was questioned. New research indicated that there was a verbal origin for learning disabilities.

Also during the early 1960s, Nicholas Hobbs (1982) developed "Project Re-Ed" as a cooperative program of George Peabody College for Teachers and the states of Tennessee and North Carolina. The objective of Project Re-Ed was to provide therapeutic support for the learner identified as emotionally/behaviorally disordered, and his or her family and community. These residential programs adapted schoolwork to meet the student's individual needs, and used the school setting to socialize the child to more productive ways of interacting. These small schools (typically no more than 40 children in five classrooms) provided short-term services, with the child returning home each weekend to reconnect with family and community. School personnel were assigned to work with the children's family and community.

In the mid-1960s, a group of researchers began applying the learning principles identified in the laboratory and based on the learning of animals to methods for learning or changing behavior in children. B. F. Skinner (1965) proposed that responses that were reinforced, or followed by pleasurable consequences, could be strengthened, and those followed by unpleasant consequences would be weakened. Premack (1965) applied this work to activities and demonstrated that an individual may be willing to do a relatively unpleasant activity if it is followed soon thereafter by a pleasurable activity. Bandura (1969) emphasized the role of modeling and vicarious learning to promote the development of competent behavior. As a result of these and similar efforts, behavior modification and other behavior therapy techniques emerged as the primary means of addressing emotional/behavioral disorders during the 1970s and much of the 1980s.

As behavior modification became more pervasive, issues regarding the external nature of its interventions arose. Parents and advocates expressed the concern that behaviors were controlled, rather than more productive behaviors and interactions learned. Problems of *generalization,* that is, applying a skill learned in one setting to another setting(s), emerged. In addition, research was beginning to demonstrate the situational nature of emotional/behavioral disorders, and the role of cultural mismatch in identifying learners as emotionally/behaviorally disordered. As a result, practice moved away from the rigid application of behavioral principles as the primary thrust of programming; in meeting the complex needs of learners identified as emotionally/behaviorally disordered, efforts often incorporated learning principles, counseling interventions, and medication.

Brendtro and Van Bockern (1994) describe this incorporation of various methodologies as a cross-fertilization between various models and theory bases, as professionals applied what worked and tinkered with once pure models. As we move toward the inclusion of learners identified as emotionally/behaviorally disordered in the general education setting, a learner may indeed be engaged in interventions from various conceptual bases. Any individual student may have a behavior contract (behavior modification), use medication to increase his or her ability to focus (biophysiological), and receive psychotherapy (psychodynamic).

In this text, we use a social systems perspective to facilitate the integration of several perspectives for working with learners identified as emotionally/behaviorally disordered. By considering the learner's personal characteristics and the settings in which the learner functions, an integrated effort to support his or her learning effective ways of interacting is enhanced. We will provide a detailed discussion of the social systems perspective in Chapter 2.

◊◊ What Are the Current Definitions of Emotional/Behavioral Disorders?

In 1961, Lambert and Bower developed a definition for "emotionally handicapped," which was used as the basis for the definition of "seriously emotionally disturbed" in Public Law 94-142, The Education for All Handicapped Children Act (1975). In this law, *seriously emotionally disturbed* is defined as:

generalization applying a skill learned in one setting to another setting(s)

seriously emotionally disturbed the federal definition used to describe learners identified as emotionally/behaviorally disordered

"1. . . . . a condition exhibiting one or more of the following characteristics over a long period of time and to a marked degree,
   which adversely affects performance:

   a. an inability to learn which cannot be explained by intellec-
      tual, sensory, and health factors;

   b. an inability to build and maintain satisfactory interpersonal
      relationships with peers and teachers;

   c. inappropriate types of behavior and feelings under normal
      circumstances;

   d. a general pervasive mood of unhappiness or depression; or

   e. a tendency to develop physical symptoms or fears associated
      with personal and school problems.

2. The term includes children who are schizophrenic or autistic.
   The term does not include children who are socially maladjusted unless it is determined that they are seriously emotionally disturbed (*Federal Register,* 1977, 42, 163)."

Learners with autism were excluded from the definition of seriously emotionally disturbed by regulation in 1981 and reclassified
as "other health impaired." In 1990 in Public Law 101-456 (Individuals with Disabilities Education Act), a separate category of disability for autism was delineated.

   The use of term "seriously emotionally disturbed" in the federal
law has caused considerable controversy. The Council for Children
with Behavioral Disorders (CCBD) has offered a series of arguments against both the label and the definition used in Public Law
94-142. In 1985, the CCBD argued that the term "seriously emotionally disturbed" should be replaced by the term "behaviorally
disordered" because the latter term is less associated with a particular theory or intervention techniques. In addition, it was argued that "behaviorally disordered" was far less stigmatizing, more
representative of the actual problem, and focuses on the educational responsibility delineated in the law (Huntze, 1985).

   Eli Bower (1982), one of the authors of the definition on which the
federal definition is based, questioned its use in the context of law.
He contends that the clinical aspects of the disability present in the
original, research-based definition limit services to learners who are
seriously troubled. The differentiations required in the definition
are, in his opinion, psychologically and educationally untenable.

   The Council for Children with Behavior Disorders, the largest educational professional organization related to learners identified as
emotionally/behaviorally disordered, has worked consistently to
change the definition for more than a decade. In 1986, the Executive Committee of the Council for Children with Behavior Disorders

issued a position paper urging the revision of the "seriously emotionally disturbed" category from the existing definition to an educational
definition. The Executive Committee asked that the new definition focus on gathering and content of data needed before the decision of
behavioral disorders can be made. In addition, it was argued that attempts to modify the behavior within the general education setting
should also be documented. The Committee also urged that "socially
maladjusted" children not be excluded from the definition.

In 1990, the National Mental Health and Special Education
Coalition (CCBD Newsletter, 1990) developed a new definition that
it is promoting as a substitute for the present federal definition.
This definition includes the following points:

- "Emotional/behavioral disorders" are identified when the behavioral or emotional responses of the individual are so different
  from his or her generally accepted, age-appropriate, ethnic, or
  cultural norms as to result in significant impairment in self-
  care, social relationships, educational progress, classroom behavior, or work adjustment.

- Learners with depression, anxiety disorders, attention-deficit
  disorders, or other sustained disturbances of conduct or adjustment are all included in emotional/behavioral disorders.

- Emotional/behavioral disorders are more than a transient, anticipated response to stressors in the individual's environment
  and persist despite individualized intervention and/or modification in the educational environment.

- Multiple sources of data must be used to determine eligibility.
  The disorder must be exhibited in at least two different settings,
  at least one of which is educational.

Although agreed upon by 11 national organizations, this definition
has not yet been included in any federal legislation.

McIntyre (1993) suggests that although learners who are socially
maladjusted would be able to receive the services they need under
this definition, other learners from diverse cultural groups may
not. He contends that looking at cultural norms is extremely challenging due to *ethnocentricity;* most individuals only fully understand their own culture and find it difficult to fully understand or
appreciate behavior that is culturally different from their own.

ethnocentricity see-
ing other individuals
through the values, be-
haviors, and beliefs of
one's personal culture

The "Exclusion Clause"

One of the most controversial aspects of the current federal definition
is the exclusion of learners who are socially maladjusted. The
whole issue of determining whether learners are either emotionally/

behaviorally disordered or socially maladjusted is a difficult one. In one study with a relatively large sample (118 school psychologists, 119 principals, and 108 special educators) groups disagreed on both behavioral and background descriptors of learners in distinguishing between emotional/behavioral disorders and social maladjustment (Stein & Merrell, 1992). "Social maladjustment" is not defined in Public Law 94-142, nor have there been any federal policy opinions or court decisions defining the term (Weinberg & Weinberg, 1990).

A prevalent view related to the difference between emotional/ behavioral disorders and social maladjustment is that learners who are socially maladjusted choose their behavior or feelings while learners identified as emotionally/behaviorally disordered do not have control over their behavior or feelings (Weinberg, 1992). This view assumes that certain types of learners, such as those who are delinquent and those diagnosed as exhibiting a conduct disorder, choose to engage in their deviant behavior. Weinberg argues that current empirical evidence on the causes of conduct disorders suggests that at least some of the individuals exhibiting behavior congruent with conduct disorders may not be engaging in that behavior on a completely voluntary basis. Although they are acting as if they are "socially maladjusted," these learners would qualify for services if choice were used as a criteria.

Forness (1992) suggests that the socially maladjusted exclusion clause must be considered within its historical context. Administrators and school district officials argued for the need to limit services to learners identified as emotionally/behaviorally disordered. In addition, there has been a long-standing underidentification of these learners. However, attending to specific child-centered characteristics rather than looking at behavior in the context of the learner's development will not resolve the question of whether the learner is socially maladjusted or emotionally/behaviorally disordered in a society with little tolerance for "deviant" behavior and "bad kids" (Maag & Howell, 1992).

◊◊ How Many Learners Are Identified as Emotionally/Behaviorally Disordered?

According to the U.S. Department of Education (1997), the percentage of children ages 6–21 served as seriously emotionally disturbed during the 1993–94 school year was 0.71%. The percentage rates range from a low of .04% in Mississippi to a high of 1.70% in Connecticut. In one study, 32% of the variance between states in identification rates for the 1983–84 school year was accounted for by states' definitions, and two thirds of the variation in identification rates remained unexplained (Wright, Pillard, & Cleven, 1990).

The national rate of less than 1% of the school population represents only one third to one half of the anticipated prevalence of children and youth identified as emotionally/behaviorally disordered (Knitzer, Steinberg, & Fleisch, 1990).

During the 1994–95 school year, 428,168 children and youth were identified and served in special education as "seriously emotionally disturbed" or as emotionally/behaviorally disordered. This is an increase over the previous school year of 12,620, or 3.1%. The seriously emotionally disturbed accounted for 9.6% of all children receiving special education services (U.S. Department of Education, 1997). Between school years 1990–91 and 1994–95, the number of students identified as "seriously emotionally disturbed" increased 9.6%. Whereas the incidence of other disabilities has fluctuated, the rate at which children and youth identified as emotionally/behaviorally disordered are served has remained fairly stable since child count data has been collected.

◊◊ Where Are Learners Identified as Emotionally/Behaviorally Disordered Served?

Learners identified as emotionally/behaviorally disordered are served in a variety of settings. The specific setting tends to vary with the severity of the disability and the availability of services in the school and community.

During the 1993–94 school year, 21.98% children 6 to 11 years old, 19.65% of learners 12 to 17 years old, and 19.42% of students between 18 and 21 who were identified as seriously emotionally disturbed were served in general education classrooms. These percentages were far lower than that of all learners with disabilities, and were most significantly depressed when compared to learners with learning disabilities, hearing impairments, speech or language impairments, orthopedic impairments, other health impairments, and visual impairments (U.S. Department of Education, 1997). Only students with mental retardation, multiple disabilities, autism, or dual sensory impairments were served less frequently in the general classroom.

Of the remaining students identified as emotionally/behaviorally disordered, 13.4% were served in special schools, 3.2% in residential facilities, and 1.8% in home or hospital (U.S. Department of Education, 1997).

◊◊ What Is the Situational Nature of Emotional/Behavioral Disorders?

As early as the 1960s, there were concerns that emotional/behavioral disorders were not within the child, but rather within the interaction between the learner and the setting. Rhodes (1967) indicated that emotional/behavioral disorders are as much a function of where and with whom the learner interacts as the learner's behavior itself. Kauffman (1981) indicates that a particular set of characteristics that make a learner an individual results in different reactions from others within the learner's ecosystem, rather than the level and type of behavior that the learner exhibits. A behavior may be appropriate in one setting and inappropriate in another simply because of expectations in the settings (Kauffman, 1981).

In discussing the situational issues related to emotional/behavioral disorders, it is useful to describe behaviors as "disturbed" or "disturbing." ***Disturbed behaviors*** are those that occur in many settings and are a part of the individual's typical behavior pattern. ***Disturbing behaviors*** may occur at a certain place and time or in the presence of only specific individuals. For example, if a student who is usually productive and cooperative causes serious problems for a substitute teacher, he or she is not disturbed, but is acting in a way that is disturbing to the substitute. However, if a student has difficulty focusing to the extent that he or she is unable to complete a task at school, home, or in the community, even when he or she is enjoying the activity, then the student is perceived as disturbed.

Another issue that emerges in the situational nature of emotional/behavioral disorders is in the area of survival skills. There is often a serious mismatch between the classroom, in which the teacher makes statements such as "people don't hit other people" and the student's walk home from school, during which he or she may have to physically defend himself or herself in order to arrive home safely. In this situation, the student's best survival skill, physical aggression, may be totally out of synchrony with the classroom and school rules. In order to succeed, students must learn to shift their behavioral standards among those expected by school, home, and community.

Culture also contributes to the situational nature of emotional/behavioral disorders. For example, an Anglo American principal may demand that an Asian American student look him in the eye when he is talking to him; however, to the Asian American student, looking an adult in the eye may be a sign of flagrant disrespect. Or for example, sharing solutions and cooperative problem solving may be perceived as cheating in an Anglo American culture but as acceptable behavior in the Hispanic American culture. In

disturbed behaviors behaviors that call attention to the learner and occur across settings; part of the emotionally/behaviorally disturbed individual's typical behavior pattern

disturbing behaviors behaviors that, while calling attention to the learner, occur at a certain time and place and/or in the presence of specific individuals

conventional shared
or traditional under-
standing of behavior in
the community; the
generally accepted way
of behaving

identifying learners as emotionally/behaviorally disordered, it may
be most helpful to identify behaviors that are not conventional rather
than appropriate or inappropriate. ***Conventional*** refers to "the degree to which the meaning of signals is shared or understood by the
social community" (Prizant & Wetherby, 1987, p. 474). It is far less
judgmental to refer to a learner's struggle to adhere to the participation structure in the classroom as having difficulties with conven-
tions rather than as being "inappropriate" or "disordered." Through
targeting conventional behaviors, teachers support students in per-
forming to their potential while avoiding the imposition of our culturally induced rules or constructions (Bauer & Sapona, 1991).

◊◊ Summary Points

- Learners identified as emotionally/behaviorally disordered are
  more likely to be males who have difficulty achieving in school.
- Learners identified as emotionally/behaviorally disordered often
  have learning or communication disorders.
- The actual application of classification systems for learners identified as emotionally/behaviorally disordered is limited.
- Throughout history, services for learners identified as emotion-
  ally/behaviorally disordered have evolved from internment to inclusion.
- The social systems perspective allows for the integration of several
  perspectives for working with learners identified as emotionally/
  behaviorally disordered.
- There is general agreement that the federal definition of seriously
  emotionally disturbed is problematic both to learners and professionals.
- Emotional/behavioral disorders occur within the learner's developmental context.

Self-Evaluation   ◊

Select the most appropriate response.
1. Girls identified in school as emotionally/behaviorally disordered are
   likely to
   a. regress rather than act out.
   b. behave in a way similar to boys identified as emotionally/behaviorally
      disordered.
   c. have difficulty identifying with male teachers.

2. Learners identified as emotionally/behaviorally disordered are
   a. more likely to fail proficiency tests than other learners with disabilities.
   b. more academically able than other learners with disabilities.
   c. more intellectually capable than other learners with disabilities.
3. Communication deficits may be
   a. underidentified among learners identified as emotionally/behaviorally disordered.
   b. a central feature of emotional/behavioral disorders.
   c. more common among girls than boys.
4. Demographic and economic differences
   a. are irrelevant in regard to learners identified as emotionally/behaviorally disordered.
   b. contribute to differences in parent involvement.
   c. may influence identification as emotionally/behaviorally disordered.
5. Of learners admitted to psychiatric hospitalization,
   a. almost all are identified as emotionally/behaviorally disordered.
   b. about half are identified as emotionally/behaviorally disordered.
   c. the males are usually identified as emotionally/behaviorally disordered.
6. The American Psychiatric Association is responsible for
   a. the *Child Behavior Checklist.*
   b. the *Behavior Problem Checklist.*
   c. the *Diagnostic and Statistical Manual of Mental Disorders.*
7. In recent times, the models for serving learners identified as emotionally/behaviorally disordered have become
   a. more distinct.
   b. more eclectic.
   c. empirically based.
8. According to the federal definition, learners who are socially maladjusted
   a. receive other services.
   b. are identified as other health impaired.
   c. are excluded from services.
9. "Socially maladjusted" is defined
   a. by Public Law 94-142.
   b. by policy opinions.
   c. nowhere.
10. Most learners identified as emotionally/behaviorally disordered are served
    a. in separate schools.
    b. in psychiatric hospitals.
    c. in general education classes.

Making the Language Your Own

Match each key word or phrase to its definition.

_____ 1. aggression   _____ 6. overrepresented

_____ 2. disturbing behaviors   _____ 7. internalizing

_____ 3. seriously emotionally   _____ 8. externalizing
         disturbed
                                       _____ 9. ethnocentricity
_____ 4. conventional

_____ 5. disturbed behaviors

a. occurring at a certain time and place and/or in the presence of specific individuals
b. physical or verbal behavior against another individual
c. the generally accepted way of behaving
d. behaviors that call attention to the learner and occur across settings
e. federal term describing individuals who are emotionally/behaviorally disordered
f. seeing other individuals through one's own personal culture
g. stealing, lying, aggression, and hyperactivity
h. physical complaints, phobias, fearfulness
i. in greater proportion than anticipated from the general population

Theory into Practice

1. Interview two teachers, one who was prepared during the 1970s and one who was prepared during the 1990s. Compare and contrast the strategies in which they received instruction. How do these strategies reflect the evolution of services for learners identified as emotionally/behaviorally disordered?
2. Observe a classroom of learners identified as emotionally/behaviorally disordered. How do these learners compare with the general traits depicted in this chapter?

◊◊ References

Algozzine, B. (1980). The disturbing child: A matter of opinion. *Behavioral disorders, 5*(2), 112–115.

American Psychiatric Association (1994). *Diagnostic and statistical manual of mental disorders* (4th ed.). Washington, DC: Author.

Bandura, A. (1969). *Principles of behavior modification.* New York: Holt, Rinehart, & Winston.

Bauer, A. M., & Sapona, R. H. (1991). *Managing classrooms to facilitate learning.* Upper Saddle River, NJ: Prentice Hall.

Bender, L. (1938). *A visual motor gastalt test and its clinical uses.* New York: Americal Orthopsychiatric Association.

Bower, E. M. (1982). Defining emotional disturbance public policy and research. *Psychology in the Schools, 19,* 55–60.

Brendtro, L. K., & Van Bockern, S. (1994). Courage for the discouraged: A psychoeducational approach to troubled and troubling children. *Focus on Exceptional Children, 26*(8), 1–14.

Camarata, S. M., Hughes, C. A., & Ruhl, K. L. (1988). Mild/moderately behaviorally disordered students: A population at risk for language disorders. *Language, Speech, and Hearing Services in the Schools, 19*(2), 191–200.

Caseau, D. L., Luckasson, R., & Kroth, R. L. (1994). Special education services for girls with serious emotional disturbances: A case of gender bias? *Behavioral Disorders, 20*(1), 51–60.

Coleman, M. C. (1986). *Behavior disorders: Theory and practice.* Upper Saddle River, NJ: Prentice Hall.

Coutinho, M. J. (1986). Reading achievement of students identified as behaviorally disordered at the secondary level. *Behavioral Disorders, 11,* 200–207.

Cruickshank, W. M. (1972). Some issues facing the field of learning disability. *Journal of Learning Disabilities, 5,* 380–383.

Cullinan, D., Epstein, M. H., & Sabornie, E. J. (1992). Selected characteristics of a national sample of seriously emotionally disturbed adolescents. *Behavioral disorders, 17*(4), 273–280.

Duncan, B. B., Forness, S. R., & Hartsough, C. (1995). Students identified as seriously emotionally disturbed in school-based day treatment: Cognitive, psychiatric, and special education characteristics. *Behavioral Disorders, 20,* 238–252.

Edelbrock, C. (1984). Developmental considerations. In T. H. Ollendick & M. Herson (Eds.), *Child behavioral assessment principles and procedures* (pp. 230–237) New York: Pergamon.

Editor (1990). Coalition finalized definition. *CCBD Newsletter,* August, 1990, 1.

Epstein, M. H., Kauffman, J. M., & Cullinan, D. (1985). Patterns of maladjustment among the behaviorally disordered, II: Boys aged 6–11, Boys aged 12–18, Girls aged 6–11, Girls aged 12–18. *Behavioral Disorders, 10,* 125–135.

Executive Committee of the Council for Children with Behavioral Disorders (1987). Position paper in definition and identification of students with behavioral disorders. *Behavioral Disorders, 13,* 9–19.

Federal register (August 23, 1977), 42 (163), 478.

Fessler, M. A., Rosenberg, M. S., & Rosenberg, L. A. (1991). Concomitant learning disabilities and learning problems among students with behavioral/emotional disorders. *Behavioral Disorders, 16*(2), 97–106.

Forness, S. R. (1992). Broadening the cultural-organizational perspective in exclusion of youth with social maladjustment: First invited reaction to the Maag and Howell paper. *Remedial and Special Education, 13*(1), 55–59.

Freeman, B. M., & Ritvo, E. R. (1984). The syndrome of autism: Establishing the diagnosis and principles of management. *Pediatric Annals, 13,* 284–296.

Freud, A. (1927). *Introduction to the techniques of child analysis.* London: Hampstead Child Therapy Clinic.

Frostig, M. (1961). *The Marianna Frostig developmental test of visual perception.* Palo Alto, CA: Consulting Psychologists.

Hobbs, N. (1982). *The troubled and troubling child.* San Francisco: Jossey Bass.

Huntze, S. L. (1985). A position paper of the Council for Children with Behavioral Disorders. *Behavioral Disorders, 10,* 167–174.

Hutton, J. B. (1985). What reasons are given by teachers who refer problem behavior students? *Psychology in the Schools, 22,* 79–82.

Kanner, L. (1970). Emotionally disturbed children: A historical review. In L. A. Faas (Ed.), *The emotionally disturbed child: A book of readings* (pp. 47–93). Springfield, IL: C. C. Thomas.

Kauffman, J. M. (1981). *Characteristics of children's behavior disorders* (2nd ed.). Columbus, OH: Merrill.

Kephart, N. (1960). *The slow learners in the classroom.* Columbus, OH: Merrill.

Knitzer, J., Steinberg, Z., & Fleisch, B. (1990). *At the schoolhouse door: An examination of programs and policies for children with behavioral and emotional problems.* New York: Bank Street College of Education.

Lambert, N. M., & Bower, E. (1961). *A process for in-school screening of children with emotional handicaps: A manual for school administrators and teachers.* Sacramento, CA: California Department of Education.

Levine, P. & Edgar, E. (1995). An analysis of gender of long-term postschool outcomes for youth with and without disabilities. *Exceptional Children, 61*(3), 282–300.

Luebke, J., Epstein, M. H., & Cullinan, D. (1989). Comparison of teacher-rated achievement levels of behaviorally disordered, learning disabled, and nonhandicapped adolescents. *Behavioral Disorders, 15,* 1–8.

Maag, J. W., & Howell, K. W. (1992). Special education and the exclusion of youth with social maladjustment: A cultural-organizational perspective. *Remedial and Special Education, 13*(1), 47–54.

McIntyre, T. (1993). Reflections on the new definition for emotional and behavioral disorders: Who still falls through the cracks and why. *Behavioral Disorders, 18*(2), 148–160.

Morse, W. C., Cutler, R. L., & Fink, A. H. (1964). *Public school classes for the emotionally handicapped.* Washington, DC: Council for Exceptional Children.

Oswald, D. P., & Coutinho, M. J. (1995). Identification and placement of students with serious emotional disturbance. Part I: Correlates of state child-count data. *Journal of Emotional and Behavioral Disorders, 3,* 224–229.

Premack, D. (1965). Reinforcement therapy. In D. Levine (Ed.), *Nebraska symposium on motivation* (pp. 307–324). Lincoln: University of Nebraska Press.

Prizant, B. M., & Wetherby, A. M. (1987). Communicative intent: A framework for understanding social-communicative behavior in autism. *Journal of the American Academy of Child and Adolescent Psychiatry, 26,* 472–479.

Quay, H. C. (1983). A dimensional approach to behavior disorders: The Revised Behavior Problem Checklist. *School Psychology Review, 12,* 244–249.

Quay, H. C., & Peterson, D. R. (1979). *Behavior problem checklist.* Miami, FL: Authors.

Rhodes, W. C. (1967). The disturbing child: A problem of ecological management. *Exceptional children, 33,* 449–455.

Rosenthal, S. L., & Simeonsson, R. J. (1991). Communication skills in emotionally disturbed and nondisturbed adolescents. *Behavioral Disorders, 16*(3), 191–199.

Ruhl, K. L., & Hughes, C. A. (1985). The nature and extent of aggression in special education settings serving behaviorally disordered students. *Behavioral Disorders, 10,* 95–104.

Sale, P., & Carey, D. M. (1995). The sociometric status of students with disabilities in a full-inclusion school. *Exceptional Children, 62*(1), 6–19.

Sewartka, T. S., Keering, S., & Grant, P. (1995). Disproportionate representation of African Americans in emotionally handicapped classes. *Journal of Black Studies, 25*(4), 492–506.

Singth, N., Landrum, T. J., Donatelli, L. S., Hampton, C., & Ellis, C. R. (1994). Characteristics of children and adolescents with serious emotional disturbance in systems of care. Part I: Partial hospitalization and inpatient psychiatric services. *Journal of Emotional and Behavioral Disorders, 2*(1), 13–20.

Skinner, B. F. (1965). *Science and human behavior.* New York: Free Press.

Stein, S., & Merrell, K. W. (1992). Differential perceptions of multi-disciplinary team members: Seriously emotionally disturbed vs. socially maladjusted. *Psychology in the Schools, 29*(4), 320–331.

Strauss, A. A., & Lehtinen, L. E. (1947). *Psychopathology and education of the brain-injured child* (Vol. 1). New York: Greene and Stratton.

U.S. Department of Education (1992). *Fourteenth annual report to Congress on the implementation of the Individuals with Disabilities Education Act.* Washington, DC: Author.

U.S. Department of Education (1994). *Sixteenth annual report to Congress on the implementation of the Individuals with Disabilities Education Act.* Washington, DC: Author.

U.S. Department of Education (1995). *Seventeenth annual report to Congress on the implementation of the Individuals with Disabilities Education Act.* Washington, DC: Author.

U.S. Department of Education (1997). *Eighteenth annual report to Congress on the implementation of the Individuals with Disabilities Education Act.* Washington, DC: Author.

U.S. Department of Education, OCR (Office of Civil Rights) 1993. *Revised data circulated to individuals who attended The Forum of Disproportionate Participation of Students from Ethnic and Cultural Minorities in Special Education.* Convened by Project FORUM at NASDSE, Alexandria, VA, July.

Wagner, M. (1991). *Dropouts with disabilities: What do we know? What can we do?* Menlo Park, CA: SRI International.

Wagner, M., Newman, L., D'Amico, R., Jay, E. D., Butler-Nalin, P., Marder, C., & Cox, R. (1991). *Youth with disabilities: How are they doing? The first comprehensive report for the National Longitudinal Transition Study of special education students.* Menlo Park, CA: SRI International.

Wagner, M., & Shaver, D. M. (1989). *Educational programs and achievement of secondary special education students: Findings from the national longitudinal transition study.* Paper presented at the annual meeting of the American Educational Research Association, San Francisco.

Weinberg, L. A. (1992). The relevance of choice in distinguishing seriously emotionally disturbed from socially maladjusted students. *Behavioral Disorders, 17*(2) 99–106.

Weinberg, L. A., & Weinberg, C. (1990). Seriously emotionally disturbed or socially maladjusted? A critique of interpretations. *Behavioral Disorders, 15*(3), 149–158.

Wright, D., Pilliard, E. D., & Cleven, C. A. (1990). The influence of state definitions of behavior disorders on the number of children served under PL 94-142. *Remedial and Special Education, 11*(5), 17–22.

2 Theoretical Perspectives of Emotional/Behavioral Disorders

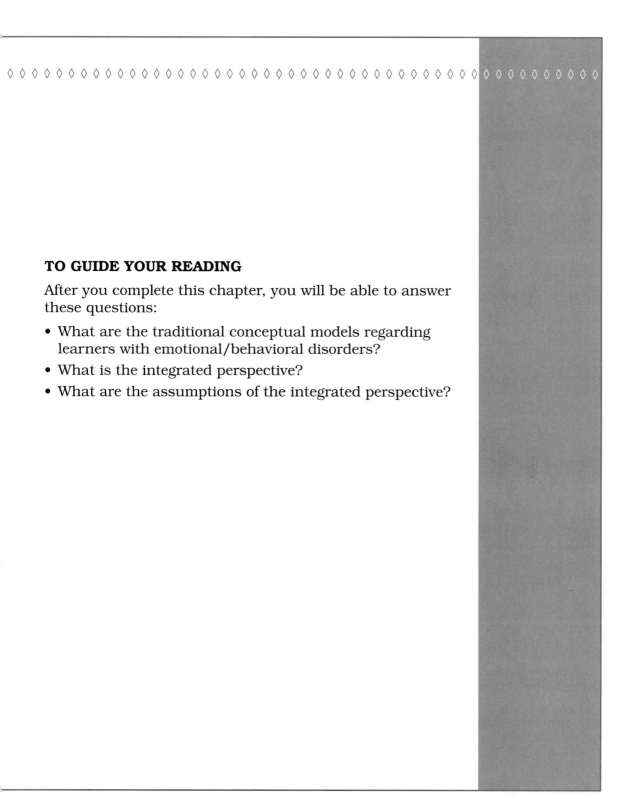

TO GUIDE YOUR READING

After you complete this chapter, you will be able to answer these questions:

- What are the traditional conceptual models regarding learners with emotional/behavioral disorders?
- What is the integrated perspective?
- What are the assumptions of the integrated perspective?

◇ *Joel, a sixth grader, was not turning in his homework. Ms. Fanicetta, his teacher, asked him to remain after class. She described to Joel a plan to increase his homework production. For each assignment he turned in on time and completed correctly, Joel would earn 1 point. After Joel accumulated 10 points, he would earn a "free pass," which allowed him to not complete one homework assignment. Joel's point totals would be recorded on a chart on the front of his loose-leaf binder.*

◇ *Joel, a sixth grader, was not turning in his homework. Mr. Francis, his teacher, asked Joel's mother to meet with him to discuss the situation. He described to her a plan to increase Joel's homework production, which included reducing the stimuli in the environment that he thought were distracting Joel. He suggested that Joel work in a quiet, stimulus-free setting, in which he was less likely to be distracted. In addition, Mr. Francis outlined a repetitive routine that would provide structure and consistency to "homework time."*

◇ *Joel, a sixth grader, was not turning in his homework. Ms. Friend, his teacher, sat down with Joel and interviewed him regarding the situation. Ms. Friend provided Joel emotional support, as they explored his feelings about homework and his perception about turning in work on time. Joel said that he felt doing homework was a waste of time and not helpful to him. Ms. Friend discussed her rationale for assigning homework, and together they agreed to explore ways to make homework meaningful for Joel. Joel was asked to begin by committing to complete one assignment that he found meaningful and helpful each evening, and to meet with Ms. Friend again in a week to discuss the situation further.*

In the preceding vignettes, the same child with the same problem is offered three different solutions, all based on different assumptions about the nature of emotional/behavioral disorders.

In this chapter, three factors essential to the understanding of the nature and treatment of emotional/behavioral disorders are discussed, and the theoretical perspective applied in this text is presented. The chapter begins with a discussion of the interrelationship of theory, intervention, and results of intervention. It continues with an examination of the four theories traditionally applied in the education of learners identified as emotionally/ behaviorally disordered. Next comes a discussion of an integrated perspective that allows and encourages the appropriate implementation of individualized interventions from each of the traditional perspectives. The chapter concludes with a discussion of the assumptions made in this text with regard to learners identified as emotionally/behaviorally disordered.

◊◊ What Is the Relationship Between Ideas, Actions, and Outcomes in Work with Learners Identified as Emotionally/Behaviorally Disordered?

Ideas are theories or ways of looking at the *etiology,* or causes, of human behavior, actions are interventions or ways of changing behavior, and outcomes are the results of intervention. If we recognize that ideas, actions, and outcomes are all interrelated, it becomes apparent that some sort of conceptual framework must be available to professionals in their work with learners identified as emotionally/behaviorally disordered. A *conceptual framework* is the cognitive structure from which interventions are derived, or the beliefs followed as a basis of intervention. Without such a foundation, actions would be too chaotic to be effective in meeting desired intervention outcomes. Each of us relates to others based on some personal theory or theories of human behavior that are products of our unique life experiences as well as our innate human universal behavioral response tendencies. We apply these personal theories to make sense of our social world (Brendtro, Brokenleg, & Van Bockern, 1990). Our thoughts, guided by our feelings, provide motivation and direction to our behavior (Weiner, 1980).

> *etiology* cause

> *conceptual framework (theory, model, perspective):* the cognitive structure from which interventions are derived; beliefs followed as the basis of intervention

Rhodes (1972) suggested that in work with learners identified as emotionally/behaviorally disordered, ideas, actions, and outcomes are all interrelated and have significant effects on each other. Rhodes proposes that a conceptual framework (ideas) directs intervention (action), by providing an analysis of the problem and potential (outcomes) results of intervention. He suggests that the same intervention, implemented by two individuals using different conceptual frameworks, may have vastly different meanings and lead to vastly different experiences and outcomes for the participants.

In the classroom, our personal theory of human behavior, our interactions and those of others, and the existing emotional/behavioral disorders are combined into what is called "teacher stance." *Teacher stance* is the teacher's personal posture toward self and others, as well as his or her theoretical orientation and instructional and management methods (McGee, Menolascino, Hobbs, & Menousek, 1987). Teacher stance guides the decision-making and design processes necessary in the planning of instruction. In addition, it permits the improvisation that evolves from interactions between learners and instructional and management problems (Bauer & Sapona, 1991).

> *teacher stance* a teacher's personal posture toward self and others, including his or her theoretical orientation and instructional and management methods

The methods that a teacher employs make a difference not only in terms of what is learned, but also in how it is learned. Learners identified as emotionally/behaviorally disordered react differently to teachers acting from various stances, and no two learners react the same way to any one stance (Joyce & Weil, 1980). A student who prefers predictability may interact well with a highly-structured, sequentially-oriented teacher, whereas a creative child who prefers a more fluid turn of events may function most effectively under a teacher who offers little formal structure and encourages individual exploration and initiative in the classroom.

Educators' perceptions of children and the behavior children exhibit in large part determine the interventions or treatments selected and imposed. These perceptions may be grouped by the conceptual frameworks that have emerged in the education of learners identified as emotionally/behaviorally disordered.

◊◊ What Are the Various Conceptual Models Regarding Learners Identified as Emotionally/Behaviorally Disordered?

The four primary conceptual frameworks that have emerged in work with learners identified as emotionally/behaviorally disordered are psychodynamic, biophysical, behavioral, and ecological. Brendtro and Van Bockern (1994) maintain that although each conceptual framework has continued to develop with a separate tradition and literature, they have all become more eclectic over time. In practice, each framework has become more comprehensive. Cross-fertilization has occurred as practitioners pragmatically apply interventions that have emerged from once pure models.

To work without one of these conceptual frameworks while trying to develop interventions for learners identified as emotionally/behaviorally disordered, Brendtro and Van Bockern (1994) suggest, is like choosing what to eat at a potluck dinner while blindfolded. Figure 2.1 offers the reader a visual picture of the relationship between these conceptual frameworks and human behavior and misbehavior. In this figure, conceptual frameworks are depicted simply as eyes with different ways of looking at the etiology of human behavior and its expression in the environment. The essential characteristics of these models are presented in Table 2.1.

psychodynamic theory
the perspective that perceives behavior as determined by dynamic intrapsychic relationships

The Psychodynamic Perspective

The **psychodynamic perspective** emerged out of the work of Sigmund Freud and, as it relates to children, Anna Freud. In this conceptual framework, behavior is said to be determined by dynamic

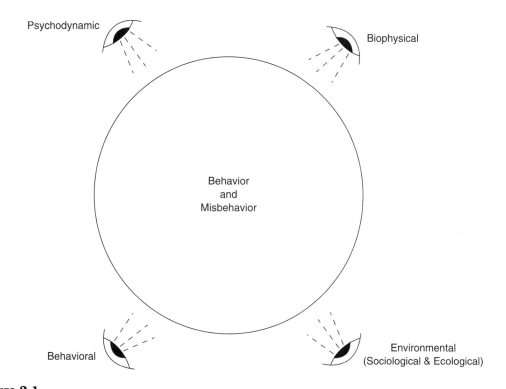

Figure 2.1

Source: J. E. Walker & T. M. Shea, *Behavior Management: A Practical Approach for Educators,* 1995, Upper Saddle River, NJ: Merrill/Prentice Hall.

intrapsychic relationships. The teacher using psychodynamic theory would view the causes of behavior as being within the individual. Early life experiences, specifically traumatic experiences, may cause unresolved challenges, or conflicts, to the learner's emotional development.

In the classroom, the application of a psychodynamic perspective would be reflected in an accepting atmosphere in which the teacher tolerates and interprets the child's behavior. The educational interventions that have emerged from this perspective include the clinical teaching model developed by Berkowitz and Rothman (1967). In this model, the teacher's actions are based on "need-acceptance" during which the teacher fosters the child's individuality, security, and self-respect. Emphasis is on utilizing the child's potential to resolve his or her emotional conflicts and to support the child's movement toward emotional adjustment. The development of academics, though important, is secondary to helping the child resolve emotional conflicts in a secure, accepting environment.

Table 2.1 Summary of Conceptual Frameworks

Framework	Causes of Behavior	Nature of Emotional/ Behavioral Disorders	Common Interventions
Psychodynamic	within the learner	result from unresolved challenges to emotional development	accepting atmosphere; resolve emotional conflicts
Biophysical	organic, physical	the result of sensory or neurological deficits	diet, medication, highly structured classrooms
Behavioral	stimuli in the environment	inappropriate behaviors have been reinforced	behavior modification, token economies
Ecological	transaction of learner and multiple developmental settings	the response to settings as these interact with personal traits	supportive environment that recognizes dynamic relationships of settings

If a student in the psychodynamic classroom, has been identified as having a problem, such as being out of seat, the teacher would explore with the student why he or she feels the need to be out of seat. The student would be assured that he or she is valued and an important part of the classroom group even though appropriate in-seat behavior was difficult. The student's feeling about being in seat would be explored and validated. The teacher would then work with the student to prevent the conflict or resolve the issues related to the student being out of seat.

As more educators began applying psychodynamic principles, a "psychoeducational" approach evolved. A broad approach, the psychoeducational perspective includes a variety of psychological and educational methods to help children and youth identified as emotionally/behaviorally disordered (Nichols, 1984; Fink, 1988). Several of the operating principles that support the psychoeducational approach are presented in Figure 2.2 (Long, Morse, & Newman, 1976).

All learners can contribute to the group.

The Biophysical Perspective

The *biophysical perspective* emphasizes an organic origin of behavior. Emotional/behavioral disorders are viewed as the result of a physical deficit or malfunction and developmental challenges.

biophysical theory
the perspective that emphasizes an organic origin of behavior

Schroeder and Schroeder (1982) discussed the two primary subgroups of biophysical theory: (a) deficit and (b) developmental. The deficit subgroup includes theories related to genetics, temperament, neuropsychopharmacology, nutrition, and neurologic dysfunction. Developmental theories include neurological organization, perceptual motor learning, physiological readiness, sensory integration, and development.

Biophysical disabilities can be classified as:

• Structural defects. One or more parts of the body are defective in size or shape.

- There is a constant interaction of cognitive and affective processes.
- The psychoeducational process involves creating a special environment in which students can function successfully at their present levels.
- Given this specialized environment, each student is taught that he or she has the capacity and resources to function appropriately and successfully.
- Teachers must understand how each student perceives, feels, thinks, and behaves in this setting to facilitate optimal behavior change.
- Students in conflict can create their feelings and behaviors in others; if a student succeeds in getting the adult to act out his feelings and behavior, he succeeds in perpetuating his self-fulfilling prophecy of life, which in turn decreases the potential for change.
- Student identified as emotionally/behaviorally disordered may associate adult intervention with adult rejection. The student needs constant reassurance that adults protect students from real dangers and psychological depreciation.
- Teachers should listen to what the student says, and focus on his or her feelings.
- Teachers should expect and accept a normal amount of hostility and disappointment from students and colleagues.
- Each student's home and community is an important support that must be considered by any remedial process. However, if all attempts fail, the school becomes a safe place for the student.
- Teachers must demonstrate that fairness is treating children differently. Although group rules are necessary for organization, individualized expectations are necessary for growth and change.
- Crises provide appointments for teachers to teach and for students to learn.
- Teaching students social and academic skills enhances their capacity to cope in stressful settings.
- Students learn through identifying with significant adults. The teacher's personal appearance, attitudes, and behavior are important factors in teaching, and must be evaluated continuously.

Figure 2.2 Operating Principles of the Psychoeducational Approach (Long, Morse, & Newman, 1976)

- Functional defects. One or more parts of the body are malfunctioning.
- Inborn errors of metabolism. The body is unable to convert certain chemicals to other chemicals needed for normal body functioning.

• Blood diseases. The blood is unable to conduct normal functions. (National Foundation—March of Dimes, 1975)

Many of the direct and indirect effects of these biophysical disabilities on emotional/behavioral development are unknown. However, as information regarding the role of neurotransmitter and brain functioning expands, emphasis on the organic origins of emotional/behavioral disorders is increasing.

With increased information about the relationship between neural processing and behavior, the biophysical perspective is gaining attention. Sylwester (1997) explores the relationship between neurobiology and self-esteem. As the brain processes cognitive activity, several dozen neurotransmitters and hormonal systems are working. Neurotransmitters, substances produced within one neuron and passing over to the dendrites of the next neuron in the information-transfer sequence, have been the subject of much research and discussion. The neurotransmitter serotonin, for example, reportedly plays an important role in regulating our level of self-esteem and our position in the social hierarchy in which we live and work. High levels of serotonin are related to high self-esteem and smooth behavioral control, whereas low levels are related to low self-esteem and impulsivity, violence, and suicidal behavior. Sylwester indicates that it is possible to stimulate serotonin release when conditions are adverse and the students' self-esteem and serotonin levels are low. One medication, for example, Prozac, produced an increased serotonin level that enhances self-esteem. This positive mood leads to positive social feedback that allows the natural system to take over in time. Alcohol also increases serotonin for a brief period of time, but eventually depletes the brain's store of serotonin, even further decreasing impulse control and self-concept.

Hewett (1968) describes the teacher using this perspective in the classroom as an individual who identifies the learner's sensory and neurologically-based deficit through extensive observation and diagnostic testing. Once the deficit is identified, the teacher must train the learner to accurately perceive the task and demonstrate motor efficiency before being given more complex tasks. The class based in biophysical principles will offer structure and routine and frequent repetitions of sequential learning tasks. Extraneous environmental stimuli are minimized to avoid distraction among learners considered to be neurologically impaired.

The biophysical teacher, when presented with the student who is out of seat, would decrease the stimuli surrounding the individual, which may increase the likelihood that he or she will remain in seat. If such impulsivity fails to decrease, the biophysical teacher may request that the student be evaluated for the use of medication.

Among the many interventions derived from biophysical theory and research are prenatal and postnatal health care, nutrition, diet, megavitamin therapy, general and specific physical examinations, and medication.

The Behavioral Perspective

Whereas professionals using the psychodynamic and biophysical perspectives focus on *why* learners behave as they do, those using the behavioral perspective focus on *what* behaviors the learner demonstrates and the cues and contingencies needed to increase or decrease those behaviors. The ***behavioral theory*** suggests that behavior is controlled by stimuli in the immediate environment impinging on the behavior, and that behavior can be changed by manipulating those stimuli. In a behavioral setting, the teacher manipulates the variables that occur before and after a behavior occurs. The statement "what you do is influenced by what follows what you do" (Sarason, Glaser, & Fargo, 1972, p. 10) is an excellent summary of the essence of behavioral theory, specifically in reference to behavior modification.

behavioral theory the perspective that perceives behavior as contingent on stimuli in the immediate environment

Practitioners of behavior modification assume that all human behavior, adaptive and maladaptive, is the consequence of the lawful application of the principles of reinforcement. These principles are:

1. Reinforcement is dependent on the exhibition of the behavior of concern or interest.
2. The behavior is to be reinforced immediately after it is exhibited.
3. During the initial stages of the intervention process the behavior is reinforced each time it is exhibited.
4. When the behavior reaches a satisfactory level, it is reinforced intermittently.
5. Social reinforcers are always applied with tangible reinforcers. (Walker & Shea, 1995)

Behavior modification has been the predominant perspective taught in teacher education programs in recent decades. The simplicity of the model—identify the behavior, select the reinforcer, provide the reinforcer contingent on the behavior, evaluate the procedure—has made it pervasive in educational programs for learners identified as emotionally/behaviorally disordered. However, questions have arisen regarding the generalization of behaviors learned in this manner and the ***curriculum of control***—or a structure that emphasizes managing undesirable behaviors rather than teaching desirable behaviors (Knitzer, Steinberg, & Fleisch, 1990)—leading to questions about the strict application of behavioral interventions without consideration of the context in which the interventions are applied.

As emphasis on the student's internal control has increased, so has emphasis on cognitive behavior modification. In cognitive behavior modification, the student uses self-talk to modify his or her behavior. This self-talk behavior modification strategy has provided an alternative to extrinsic reinforcers and reinforcement schedules that are not portable from one environment to another.

When confronted with the student who leaves his or her seat, the behavioral teacher would first take a baseline count, charting the frequency at which the student leaves the desk. The teacher would then consistently reinforce an incompatible alternative, that is, provide a reward to the student after a specific period of in-seat

curriculum of control
a structure found in classrooms for learners with emotional/behavioral disorders that emphasizes managing undesirable behaviors rather than teaching desirable behaviors

Solving problems together.

behavior. A teacher who employs cognitive behavior modification may work with the student to have him cue himself to remain in seat, and mark on his or her own checksheet whether
or not he felt the need to get out of seat and if he or she did get
out of seat.

The Ecological Perspective

ecological theory the
perspective that per-
ceives behavior as a
product of the individ-
ual's response to his or
her social system

Ecology is the study of the interrelationships between an organism
and its environment. As presented in this text, the *ecological perspective* maintains that the child is an inseparable part of a social
system, which is made up of the learner and his or her school,
family, neighborhood, and community (Bronfenbrenner, 1979;
Hobbs, 1966). From this perspective, the emotional/behavioral
disorder is a product of the child's response to the settings in
which he or she functions as these interact with the child's personal traits and experiences.

A teacher applying ecological theory would be aware of the impact of the environment on the individual or group and carefully
manage the classroom to provide a supportive environment. In addition, the ecological teacher would remain aware of the dynamic,
reciprocal relationships that exist between the individual or group
and the environment, managing these behaviors for the benefit of
the individual or group.

The ecological teacher would analyze the context in which a student leaves his or her seat. After identifying the variables that appear related to being out of seat, the ecological teacher would provide supports in the environment that would increase the
likelihood that the student would stay in seat.

◊◊ What Is the Integrated Perspective?

**integrated perspective
(social systems per-
spective)** the perspec-
tive that emphasizes
that behavior cannot be
understood as a cause
and effect relationship,
but must be viewed in
the context in which it
occurs

In this text, we offer an **integrated perspective** to understanding
the nature and treatment of children and youth identified as emo-
tionally/behaviorally disordered. This approach recognizes the
contribution of each of the conceptual models described above to
working with learners identified as emotionally/behaviorally disordered. It emphasizes that behavior cannot be understood simply
as a cause and effect relationship, but must be understood in the
context in which it occurs.

From this perspective, development is the result of a series of
transactions between the individual and the environment.
Sameroff (1975) suggests that each action by an individual has an
impact on the following action. Consider the example of a junior

high school student who blurts out answers without raising his hand and being called on by the teacher. The teacher ignores the answer the student blurted out and asks him to raise his hand if he wishes to be called on. Frustrated in his effort to respond, the student may then both raise his hand and blurt out the answer. As the teacher becomes increasingly impatient, she may send him to the back of the classroom, where he disengages from the activity.

The usual response to such behavior is to determine that the student has difficulty paying attention. However, if the behavior is taken in context, we posit that the student is not responding as the teacher expects, that is, not meeting the teacher's expectations.

Such an approach to the emotional/behavioral disorders of learners is based on several assumptions about learners and their behavior.

What Are the Assumptions of the Integrated Perspective?

Bronfenbrenner (1979) suggests that *development* is the growth and change that is the result of transactions between the individual and the environment. Development is affected by relations between these settings, and by the larger contexts in which the settings are embedded. To effectively intervene in the learning of students identified as emotionally/behaviorally disordered, we must consider relationships within and between all of the settings in which these learners act and those settings that impinge on the learner.

development growth and change that is the result of transactions between the individual and the environment

When behavior is taken in this context, the following assumptions emerge:

- There are limitations in the application of a single perspective. Through considering the contexts in which the learner develops, we may recognize the potential of applying interventions grounded in the various frameworks. For example, a learner may have a behavior contract, take medication, and attend a play therapy group. The intervention is determined by the demands of the various settings and the learner's needs in those settings.

- Behavior varies with the situation in which the individual finds himself or herself. A learner may behave one way for his or her parents, another way for teachers, and yet another way for the principal.

- Behaviors are sensible, purposeful, and meaningful. Behaviors serve a function for the individual that can be related to his or her intent. For a young child with limited verbal skills, for example, throwing his lunch on the floor may be a very effective way of communicating, "I don't want anymore."

- Negative Behaviors should not be eliminated, but rather shaped toward more conventional, positive, and productive behaviors. It does little good to decrease a learner's aggression toward other children if we do not support him or her in learning other more positive, productive ways to interact with others.

- The social acceptability of behavior is dependent on both culture and setting. Fighting that could be the most essential survival skill for the learner on the walk home after school may be the very behavior that causes him or her to be suspended or expelled from school if exhibited in the classroom or hallway, or on the playground or school bus. We must recognize that the demands of school are unique, and the behavioral standards of school may not be those of any other environment in which the learner interacts.

Table 2.2   Growth Versus Deficit Paradigms (Armstrong, 1994)

Growth Paradigm	Deficit Paradigm
Labels are avoided; the individual is an intact person who just happens to have a need for supports.	Individuals are diagnosed and labeled.
The needs of each individual are assessed in the natural context, focusing on strengths.	Specific impairments are identified using a battery of standardized tests.
Varied and rich interactions are used to assist the person in learning and growing.	Specialized treatment strategies, often removed from real-life context, are used to remediate impairments.
Individuals are maintained with their peers to pursue as normal a life pattern as possible.	The individual is separated for specialized treatment.
Materials, strategies, and activities used are good for all students.	Terms, tests, programs, kits, materials, and workbooks are different from those found in general education.
The individual is a whole human being whose program toward goals must be viewed as a whole.	The individual's life is broken into specific behavioral/educational objectives that are individually monitored, measured, and modified.
General educators and special educators work hand in hand.	Special educators work in settings that are parallel to general education.

In the next chapter we will more fully explore the developmental contexts of learners identified as emotionally/behaviorally disordered.

In addition, in this text, we use a growth rather than deficit paradigm of individuals with disabilities. Whereas the deficit paradigm labels individuals with impairments, the growth paradigm avoids labeling, putting the person first, and viewing the individual as an intact person who happens to have a special need. Rather than remediating deficits, we believe that each learner should be provided supports to enhance his or her opportunity for success. The growth and deficit paradigms are further contrasted in Table 2.2.

◊◊ Summary Points

- The four primary conceptual frameworks that have emerged in work with learners identified as emotionally/behaviorally disordered are psychodynamic, biophysical, behavioral, and ecological.

- An integrated perspective recognizes the contributions of each of the conceptual models in working with learners identified as emotionally/behaviorally disordered.

- The integrated perspective assumes that development is affected by relations among the various settings in which individuals interact. Behavior is taken in context.

- The growth paradigm assumes that each learner should be provided supports to enhance his or her success.

◊ **Self-Evaluation**

Select the most appropriate response.
1. When working with learners with emotional/behavioral disorders, an intervention
   a. is usually effective or ineffective for most students with emotional/behavioral disorders.
   b. may be implemented very differently by two individuals with different conceptual frameworks.
   c. is the result of the teacher's stance.
2. Conceptual frameworks
   a. have become more eclectic over time.
   b. have generated very different bodies of professional literature.
   c. are formulated through intrapsychic relationships.

3. In the psychodynamic perspective, the cause of behavior
    a. is in the environment.
    b. is organic.
    c. is within the individual.
4. An example of a biophysical intervention is
    a. a token economy.
    b. medication.
    c. resolution of emotional conflicts.
5. The predominant perspective in teacher education programs is
    a. psychoeducational.
    b. ecological.
    c. behavioral.
6. In a behavioral setting, the teacher
    a. manipulates the variables before and after a behavior occurs.
    b. minimizes extraneous environmental stimuli.
    c. provides opportunities for the student to meet social-emotional needs.
7. Development
    a. is a cause and effect relationship to experiences.
    b. depends on appropriate stimuli.
    c. results from transactions between the individual and the environment.
8. To effectively intervene on behalf of learners identified as emotionally/behaviorally disordered, we must
    a. identify the cause within the learner.
    b. rule out organic causes.
    c. consider relationships between all of the settings in which the learner acts.
9. In this text, we assume that behavior
    a. is purposeful and meaningful.
    b. is a result of stimuli in the environment.
    c. judged unproductive should be decreased.
10. In this text, we assume that behavioral standards
    a. are determined by age.
    b. are related to achievement.
    c. are dependent on culture and setting.

Making the Language Your Own

Match each word with the appropriate phrase.

———— 1. behavioral theory   ———— 6. etiology

———— 2. biophysical theory   ———— 7. integrated perspective

———— 3. conceptual framework   ———— 8. psychodynamic theory

———— 4. curriculum of control   ———— 9. teacher's stance

———— 5. development   ———— 10. ecological theory

a. perspective that behavior is organic in origin
b. an emphasis on decreasing undesirable behavior
c. occurs as a result of transactions
d. perspective that behavior cannot be understood out of context
e. personal posture towards self and others
f. perspective that behavior is determined by intrapsychic relationships
g. cause
h. perspective that behavior is the individual's response to the social
   system
i. cognitive structure from which interventions are derived
j. perspective that behavior is contingent on stimuli in the environment

Theory into Practice

1. Observe a teacher who works with learners with emotional/behavioral
   disorders. Based on your observations, describe what you think the
   teacher's stance and conceptual framework are?
2. Interview the teacher you observed. Ask his or her perception of the
   cause of behavior and the nature of intervention. Compare the results of
   this interview with your observations.

◊◊ References

Armstrong, T. (1994). *Multiple intelligences in the classroom.*
   Alexandria, VA: ASCD.

Bauer, A. M., & Sapona, R. H. (1991). *Managing classrooms to facilitate learning.* Upper Saddle River, NJ: Prentice Hall.

Berkowitz, P. H., & Rothman, E. P. (1967). *Public education for disturbed children in New York City.* Springfield, IL: C. C. Thomas.

Brendtro, L. K., Brokenleg, M., & Van Bockern, S. (1990). *Reclaiming youth at risk: Our hope for the future.* Bloomington, IN: National Educational Service.

Brendtro, L. K., & Van Bockern, S. (1994). Courage for the discouraged: A psychoeducational approach to troubled and troubling children. *Focus on Exceptional Children, 26*(8), 1–14, 16.

Bronfenbrenner, U. (1979). *The ecology of human development.* Cambridge, MA: Harvard University Press.

Fink, A. H. (1988). The psychoeducational philosophy: Programming implications for students with behavioral disorders. *Behavior in Our Schools, 2*(2), 8–13.

Hewett, F. M. (1968). *The emotionally disturbed child in the classroom: A developmental strategy for educating children and maladaptive behaviors.* Boston: Allyn & Bacon.

Hobbs, N. (1966). Helping disturbed children: Psychological and ecological strategies. *American Psychologist, 21,* 1105–1115.

Joyce, B., & Weil, M. (1980). *Models of teaching.* Upper Saddle River, NJ: Prentice Hall.

Knitzer, J., Steinberg, Z., & Fleisch, B. (1990). *At the schoolhouse door: An examination of problems and policies for children with behavioral and emotional problems.* New York: Bank Street College of Education.

Long, N. J., Morse, W. C., & Newman, R. G. (1976). *Conflict in the classroom* (3rd ed.). Belmont, CA: Wadsworth.

McGee, J. J., Menolascino, F. J., Hobbs, D. C., & Menousek, P. E. (1987). *Gentle teaching.* New York: Human Service Press.

National Foundation—March of Dimes (1975). *Birth defects: The tragedy and the hope.* White Plains, NY: Author.

Nichols, P. (1984). Down the up staircase: The teacher as therapist. In J. Grosenick, S. Huntze, E. McGinnis, & C. Smith (Eds.), *Social/affective intervention in behavioral disorders* (pp. 43–66). DesMoines: State of Iowa Department of Public Instruction.

Rhodes, W. C. (1972). Overview of interventions. In W. C. Rhodes & M. L. Tracy (Eds.), *A study of child variance* (Vol. 2). Ann Arbor: University of Michigan Press.

Sarason, I. G., Glaser, E. M., & Fargo, G. A. (1972). *Reinforcing productive classroom behavior.* New York: Behavioral Publications.

Sameroff, A. (1975). Transactional models in early social relations. *Human Development, 18,* 65–69.

Schroeder, S. R., & Schroeder, C. (1982). Organic factors. In J. L. Paul & B. Epanchin (Eds.), *Emotional disturbance in children.* Columbus, OH: Merrill.

Sylwester, R. (1997). The neurobiology of self-esteem and aggression. *Educational Leadership, 54*(4), 75–79.

Walker, J. E., & Shea, T. M. (1995). *Behavior management: A practical approach for educators.* Upper Saddle River, NJ: Merrill/Prentice Hall.

Weiner, B. (1980). A cognitive (attribution)-emotion-action, model of motivated behavior: An analysis of judgments of help-giving. *Journal of Personality and Social Psychology, 39,* 186–200.

3 The Social Systems Perspective and Developmental Context

TO GUIDE YOUR READING

After completing this chapter, you will be able to answer these questions:

- What is the social systems perspective?
- What is the transactional nature of development?
- What are the assumptions regarding emotional/behavioral disorders that emerge if one assumes a social systems perspective?

◊ *Joshua's fifth birthday occurred in early August. Late the same month he began kindergarten. His teacher, who believed in a strong academic program emphasizing readiness for first grade, was concerned about his activity level and inability to complete work. She felt his fine motor skills were poor, that he was "just too young for kindergarten" and that he was becoming a behavior problem. If he continued in her class, she felt he would have to be evaluated for special education services.*
After 3 weeks in the program, his parents acquiesced and withdrew him from kindergarten. They indicated that they would enroll Joshua again next year after he had matured.

◊ *Jason's fifth birthday occurred in early August. Late in the same month, he began kindergarten. His teacher, who believed in developmentally appropriate practice, guided Jason toward the more active learning centers that allowed him to be engaged physically. When Jason was frustrated by paper with lines for writing, she provided him with large sheets of paper without lines and indicated that he didn't need lines to write stories. After 3 weeks his parents were surprised at his increased attention span and the language he used to describe his activities in kindergarten.*

These two vignettes depict how the social system in which each child was expected to function had an impact on his development. Both children have similar issues and abilities. However, the way in which the first classroom "worked" helped to identify the student as having a behavior problem. The teacher perceived the challenges Joshua presented as *his* problems, rather than *her* problems or *their* problems. In that Joshua didn't fit into her program, he would need to be evaluated for special education.

In the second vignette, the child is viewed as a contributor to the problem and provided a supportive developmental context. Jason's activity level is directed toward exploring and learning. His frustrations are met by accommodations by the teacher. As Lovitt (1996) suggests, the lenses are reversed: instead of focusing on deficits and disabilities, in this vignette the focus is on strengths and successes.

The social systems perspective contributes two primary assumptions to our work with learners identified as emotionally/behaviorally disordered. The first assumption is that if one wishes to change an individual's behavior, one must first change the environment in which the individual functions. The second assumption is that an individual can be affected by events occurring in settings in which that individual is not present. For example, a learner identified as emotionally/behaviorally disordered and his or her family are influenced by the extended family's beliefs about the cause of that emotional/behavioral disorder, the neighborhood's tolerance of difference, the community's mental health policy, and society's perception of "good" or "bad" children. This may be true even if the child himself or herself has very little contact with each of these systems. Unlike other developmental perspectives, the core of the social systems perspective is concern with the progressive accommodation (relationship) between the growing organism (the individual) and forces in the larger social and physical environment.

In this chapter, the social systems perspective is presented and discussed in detail. Examples for each of the contexts within this perspective are provided. The distinction between social maladjustment and emotional/behavioral disorders is used to enhance the discussion of the various contexts. The second section of the chapter is devoted to an explanation of the transactional nature of development. The chapter concludes with the assumptions regarding emotional/behavioral disorders that emerge if one assumes a social systems perspective.

◊◊ What Is the Social Systems Perspective?

As discussed in the previous chapter, ideas, actions, and outcomes are all interrelated. A conceptual framework must be available to each of us as we work with learners identified as emotionally/ behaviorally disordered. As Pagano (1991) suggests, "To act is to theorize." We act as we do because of our beliefs and we judge others because of our beliefs about persons and the freedoms and constraints on their actions. The social systems perspective provides such a framework and is applied in this text.

The social systems perspective sees each individual as developing in dynamic relationships with, and as an inseparable part of, the several social contexts or settings in which the individual either functions directly or is affected by, throughout his or her life span. Bronfenbrenner (1979) viewed this as an "ecology of human development," a way of looking at the individual as interacting within several nested environments. He used the term *ecology* in its strictest sense, that is, the study of the relationship of humans with their environment. This relationship involves both the environment and the individual as both actors and reactors (Thomas & Marshall, 1977).

ecology the study of the relationship of humans with their environment

development the progressive, mutual accommodation between an acting and reacting individual and the ever-changing settings in which the individual functions, as well as the relationships between those settings and the broader contexts in which they are embedded

accommodation adaptation and adjustment

behavior the expression of the dynamic relationship between the individual and the environment

congruence match or goodness of fit

role a set of activities and relations expected of a person occupying a particular position in society, and of others in relation to that person

In the social systems perspective, development is a lifelong process of continual adaptation or adjustment of the individual within the environment. Development is based on each individual's evolving in, and his or her relationship to the environment, as well as the individual's ability to discover, sustain, or change the characteristics of the environment. Learning and development are facilitated by the developing individual's participation in progressively more complex patterns of reciprocal activities with someone with whom the person has developed a strong and enduring emotional attachment, as well as when the balance of power gradually shifts in favor of the developing person (Bronfenbrenner, 1979).

Development, then, is the progressive, mutual *accommodation* or adaptation and adjustment, between an acting and reacting individual and the constantly changing settings in which the individual functions, as well as the relationships between those settings and the broader contexts in which they are embedded. Using this broad concept of development, when discussing behavior we must take into account more than those aspects of the environment in the immediate setting.

In the social systems perspective, *behavior* is viewed as the expression of the dynamic relationship between the individual and the environment. Behavior occurs in a setting that includes specific time, place, and objects as well as previously established patterns of behavior (Scott, 1980). These "previously established patterns of behavior" are ways of behaving that are characteristic of an individual and that he or she develops over time and brings to the setting in which the behavior is occurring.

One major factor in the social systems perspective that influences the identification of an individual as emotionally/behaviorally disordered is congruence. *Congruence* is the match or goodness of fit between an individual and his or her environment. Individuals we judge to be "normal" are those whose behavior is congruent or in harmony with the norms, or standards, of their environment. Those judged to be deviant or incompetent are individuals who are not congruent with their environment. These individuals may be either out of harmony with the norms of the environment or lack the skills necessary to perform effectively in the environment (Thurman, 1977).

Another important concept of the social systems perspective is that of roles. A *role* is a set of activities and relations expected of a person occupying a particular position in society, and of others in relation to that person (Bronfenbrenner, 1979). An individual acting in a role tends to elicit perceptions, actions, and interpersonal relationships consistent with the expectations of the role from both the person occupying the role and others with respect to that person. As the role becomes more established in the institutional structure of society, and consensus regarding the expectations of the role is achieved, the tendency to evoke perceptions, actions, and interpersonal relationships is enhanced. For example, parents are "expected" to keep their children "under control" in a supermarket. The institutionalized role of "good parent" is one whose child sits in the shopping cart, keeps his or her hands in the cart, and remains quiet and still. The parent whose child is in and out of the cart, skidding up and down the aisles on his or her knees, or screaming evokes a very different set of perceptions, actions, and interpersonal relationships.

The social system perspective is unique in its concern with the ongoing and progressive accommodation between the growing individual and his or her ever-changing or dynamic environment, and the way in which this relationship is formed and reconciled by forces from the individual's various impinging social contexts. These social contexts include (a) one-to-one relationships; (b) interactions between contexts; (c) community, work, and school; and (d) society. At the core of these social contexts is (e) the self or the individual. The nested aspect of these contexts is depicted in Figure 3.1 and discussed in the remainder of this section.

To demonstrate how the social system perspective can be applied to organize information around a concept, we have chosen to discuss a controversial issue that was introduced in the first chapter: the distinction between "social maladjustment" and "emo-

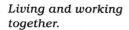

Living and working together.

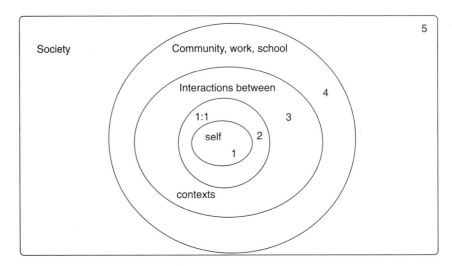

Figure 3.1 Developmental Contexts

tional/behavioral disorders." The application of the social systems perspective to this controversy will enhance not only our understanding of this complex issue but also of the social systems perspective itself.

Self

Bronfenbrenner was concerned primarily with ecological contexts (areas 2 through 5 in Figure 3.1). Belsky (1980), however, suggested that using only these contexts failed to take into account the individual differences (area 1 in Figure 3.1) that each individual brings to his or her ecological contexts.

According to Belsky, the self includes the personal characteristics of each individual. These include the cognitive, communicative, social, physical, and personality characteristics that the individual brings to his or her relationships in the ecological contexts. In addition, each individual brings previously learned personal skills, abilities, and competencies for dealing with the environment.

With regard to the issue of identifying social maladjustment versus emotional/behavioral disorders, a primary concern is the assumptions underlying the label, "social maladjustment," at the level of "self." The most prevalent view regarding distinguishing between individuals with emotional/behavioral disorders and individuals labeled socially maladjusted, is whether or not the individual chooses his or her behavior (Weinberg, 1992). Some authorities suggest that socially maladjusted students, including those who are delinquents and those identified as having conduct disorders, choose to engage in inappropriate behavior. In other words, this learner knows how to behave appropriately but chooses to act inappropriately. Viewing individuals identified as socially maladjusted at the level of "self" alone leads to little sympathy for them and, as a consequence, results in few interventions to support them in their efforts to behave appropriately. This position tends to lead to the conclusion that such students should be punished for their inappropriate behavior.

One-to-One Relationships

All individuals engage in multiple one-to-one relationships or interpersonal relationships. In the home, there are relationships with parents, sisters and brothers, and other individuals. At school, there are relationships with peers, teachers, administrators, and staff. All of these relationships have an impact on individual functioning and development. Bronfenbrenner (1978) suggests that "in order to develop, a child needs the nurturing, rational involvements of one or more adults in care and joint activity with the child" (p. 773). In other words, "Somebody has got to be crazy about that kid!" (Bronfenbrenner, 1978, p. 774).

In these one-to-one relationships, Bronfenbrenner suggests that learning is facilitated when two individuals regard themselves as doing something together. In addition, greater learning and joint activity takes place when the relationship is characterized by positive feeling, whereas mutual antagonism interferes with learning. The developmental potential of a pair of individuals is further enhanced when a third person outside of the original pair demonstrates positive feelings and support of the developmental activities (Bronfenbrenner, 1979).

In one-to-one relationships, learners who are classified as socially maladjusted would be oppositional simply for the sake of being oppositional, and therefore would not engage in the mutual attention and joint activity necessary for learning. A learner identified as emotionally/behaviorally disordered, however, would not consciously choose to be deviant, but would interact without conscious understanding of the inappropriateness of his or her behavior. In addition, these individuals would lack the ability to act and react differently. Caspi, Bem, and Elder (1989) suggest that humans engage in interactional continuity; an individual's interaction style evokes reciprocal, sustaining responses from others during interaction and, consequently, reinforces the behavior pattern throughout the individual's life whenever relevant interactions are replicated. Individuals identified as emotionally/behaviorally dis-ordered would exhibit inappropriate interactional continuity. Learners identified as socially maladjusted, on the other hand, would not exhibit interactional continuity, but would choose to act and react differently across various interactions.

In addition, individuals identified as socially maladjusted may have fewer third-party relationships that include mutual positive feelings and support. As such, the developmental potential of their relationships is limited.

Interactions Between Contexts

Interactions between contexts may include interactions between school and home, home and service agency, home and church, home and neighborhood, and school and peer group. Bronfenbrenner de-scribes four general kinds of interconnections between settings:

1. multisetting participation, in which the same person engages in activities in more than one setting, for example, when a learner spends time both at home and at school;

2. indirect linkage, when the same person does not actively partic-ipate in both settings, yet a third party serves as an intermedi-ate link between persons;

3. intersetting communication, in which messages are transmit-ted from one setting to another using face-to-face interaction, telephone conversations, correspondence or announcements, or chains in the social network; and

4. intersetting knowledge, in which information or experience about one setting exists in another.

Bronfenbrenner (1979) suggests that the developmental poten-tial of interrelated settings is increased when the learner enters the new setting in the company of one or more persons with whom he has participated in prior settings, such as when a parent accom-panies a child to school on the first day. In addition, transitions are enhanced if role demands in the different settings are compat-ible, and if the individuals engage in mutual trust, a positive orien-tation, and goals consensus between settings.

To continue our extended example of learners identified as so-cially maladjusted, these learners may be a member of a gang, that is, a group that chooses to position itself in opposition to generally accepted rules regarding appropriate behavior. The learner identi-fied as socially maladjusted may not share mutual trust, positive orientation, or goal consensus with individuals in the school or in the home, yet may have great trust and goal consensus with fellow gang members. Learners identified as emotionally/behaviorally disordered would not consciously choose to be a member of a gang, and would perhaps have the same difficulties with goal consensus across settings.

This context includes, at a practical level, parent-teacher collaboration and family–community service involvement. Also included are the transitions or movements of an individual between various environments.

The Community, Work, and School

The community, work, and school settings affect or are affected by what happens in other settings in which the individual functions. Such settings do not involve the individual directly. However,

Parents are the first teachers

events occurring in these settings are affected by or may affect the individual. The community, work, and school context includes the availability of special education programs, the goals of educational programs in the community, school-system wide disciplinary plans, and so on. Dudley-Marling and Dippo (1996) suggest that having special education services, in fact, fulfills a need for the schools, and preserves conventional assumptions about the role of potential and effort in school achievement, by placing the responsibility of school failure within the individual student.

Bronfenbrenner (1979) suggests that the developmental potential of settings is enhanced if there are direct and indirect links to "power settings." Through power settings, individuals in the original setting can influence the allocation of resources and decision making that respond to the needs of the developing person and the efforts of those who act on his or her behalf. In addition, the developmental potential of a setting decreases as the number of links in the network chain connecting the setting to settings of power decreases.

In terms of learners who are socially maladjusted, schools may exclude them through discipline plans that include suspension and expulsion. If the learner's family has few resources, the school system will be even less responsive and provide the family with fewer choices. The community may react to them through juvenile justice system. With regard to students who are identified as emotionally/behaviorally disordered, the school will react to them by providing counseling services, special education programs, and various related services.

Society

In society there is a general cultural belief system, made up of society's general social values, that is applied to judge individuals whose behavior varies from that of their peers. The direction and growth of an individual are governed by the extent to which opportunities to enter settings conducive to development are open to the learner (Bronfenbrenner, 1979). Society may close doors to an individual because of his or her behavior and society's belief about "good children" and "good families."

To continue our extended example, factors in society may contribute to excluding learners who are socially maladjusted from being identified as emotionally/behaviorally disordered. Among these factors may be financial concerns, such as the need to limit services and related costs of services to children (Forness, 1992). Excluding socially maladjusted learners from the classification emotionally/behaviorally disordered may also be a result of society's lack of tolerance for "deviant" behavior, and the school's need to maintain popular support from the community (Maag & Howell, 1992). Society's response to learners who are emotionally/behaviorally disordered is generally one of concern and the provision of needed services.

Denti and Katz (1996) contend that special education has constructed a reality in society that supports society's vision of the purposes of education. The field of special education in our society has acquired an intellectual and institutional life of its own. A culture of special education has emerged, with beliefs, values, and rituals passed on to future generations of special educators.

◊◊ What Is the Transactional Nature of Development?

The social systems perspective assumes that behavior is not linear, that is, behavior is not the result of a simple cause and effect relationship. Behavior is viewed as composed of "transactions" among the individual and his or her environment (contexts). Sameroff (1975) contends that the contact between the individual and the environment is a *transaction* in which each is altered by the other. For example, the behaviors of students in a classroom are influencing their teacher's behavior while the teacher's behaviors are influencing students' behaviors. Teachers with similarly behaving students respond differently to different students and thus cause different developmental outcomes. A child's development cannot be explained entirely by either biological or environmental factors. Rather, developmental and behavioral outcomes are a result of the ongoing reciprocal interactions between the individual and the environment (Sameroff & Chandler, 1975).

transactions contacts between two individuals or an individual and the environment in which each is altered by the other

An example of the way in which teacher-student interaction molds subsequent interaction is provided in Figure 3.2. In both situations, the student is demonstrating the same behavior: squirming in his seat. In the first situation, the teacher responds by telling the student to sit still. The student, concentrating on sitting still, is distracted from his or her work. Because the task isn't completed, the teacher reprimands the student. The student, now anxious about squirming, becomes even more fidgety, again evoking the teacher's response.

In the second situation, the teacher responds to the squirming student by asking him or her if he or she needs to stand up and stretch. After stretching, the student returns to the task and completes it.

The transaction model of development forces teachers into social constructivism. In *constructivism,* each individual is viewed

constructivism the belief that each individual learns through interaction with the environment and that as this learning occurs, the individual constructs his or her own knowledge

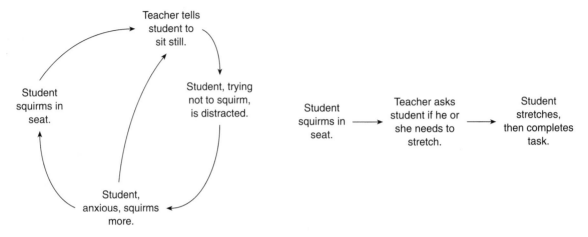

Figure 3.2

as a transactive participant, constructing knowledge and information about each interaction. The role of the teacher in social constructivism is that of a capable individual, responsible for learning about the children within his or her care, and utilizing this knowledge to construct developmentally and situationally appropriate practices (Mallory & New, 1994).

◊◊ What Are the Assumptions Regarding Emotional/Behavioral Disorders that Emerge Through a Social Systems Perspective?

The social systems perspective provides a framework for this text. The remaining sections describe various aspects of the developmental contexts, including the individual, the family and classroom, and school and society. These descriptions are based on several assumptions from the social systems perspective about learners identified as emotionally/behaviorally disordered.

First, it is assumed that in order to change the learner's behavior, you must change the environment. Even settings in which the individual does not directly engage may have an impact on the learner's behavior. For example, stress on a parent's job may increase tension in the home, which in turn affects the learner's behavior.

The social systems perspective also assumes that because of the nature of the nested context in which the individual is developing, linear, cause and effect relationships between events and behavior can rarely be identified. The social systems perspective recognizes the complexity and multiple variables that impact on the individual's behavior.

Just as complex as the development and maintenance of behavior is the selection of interventions. The social systems perspective assumes that there is no "cookbook," with "recipes" of interventions for each type of behavior. Rather, any development of interventions must involve a careful study of the situation in which the behavior occurs, including all of the personal, temporal, and physical variables within that setting. When asked, "How do you deal with a certain behavior?" the proponent of the social systems perspective responds, "It all depends."

Although the social systems perspective is apparently far more complex than linear theories of human development and behavior, it celebrates the incredible diversity among human learners and the uniqueness of each individual. We hope as you work through this text you marvel with us at the complexity of each of the issues and characteristics of learners identified as emotionally/behaviorally disordered.

◊◊ Summary Points

- Each individual develops in dynamic relationships with, and as an inseparable part of, several social contexts.
- The social systems perspective is unique in its concern with the ongoing and progressive accommodation between the individual and the dynamic environment.
- Each individual develops within a series of nested contexts, including (a) one-to-one relationships, (b) interactions among contexts, (c) community, work, and school, and (d) society.
- At the core of these social contexts is the individual.

◊ **Self-Evaluation**

Select the most appropriate response.
1. In the social systems perspective, development is
    a. the individual's adaptation to the environment.
    b. mutual accommodation.
    c. grounded in the interactions within systems.
2. In the social systems perspective, individuals judged incompetent
    a. have deviations in development.
    b. are not congruent with the environment.
    c. have inappropriate transactions in the environment.

3. All relationships
   a. form the individual's ecology.
   b. impact on individual functioning and relationships.
   c. support accommodation.
4. Society's general social values
   a. have little impact on individuals judged to be socially maladjusted.
   b. are used to judge individuals whose behavior varies from their peers.
   c. support strong special education programs.
5. Behavior is composed of
   a. actions and reactions in the environment.
   b. the reinforcement of appropriate responses to the context.
   c. transactions among the individual and his or her environment.
6. Each interaction
   a. molds subsequent interactions.
   b. can be analyzed in terms of competence.
   c. depends on the context.

Making the Language Your Own

Match each key word or phrase to its definition.

_____ 1. constructivism   _____ 5. role

_____ 2. behavior   _____ 6. transactions

_____ 3. accommodation   _____ 7. ecology

_____ 4. congruence   _____ 8. development

a. adaptation and adjustment
b. the expression of the dynamic relationship between the individual and the environment
c. match or goodness of fit
d. the belief that each individual learns through interaction with the environment and that as this learning occurs, the individual constructs his or her own knowledge
e. the progressive, mutual accommodation between an acting and reacting individual and the ever-changing settings in which the individual functions, as well as the relationships between those settings and the broader contexts in which they are embedded
f. the study of the relationship of humans with their environment
g. contacts between two individuals or an individual and the environment in which each is altered by the other
h. a set of activities and relations expected of a person occupying a particular position in society

Theory into Practice

Review the social contexts in which you interact. Describe the relationships in each of the social contexts that have an impact on your daily functioning, the decisions you make, and the choices you have made professionally. What are the strengths that are present in each of these contexts?

◊◊ References

Belsky, J. (1980). Child maltreatment: An ecological integration. *American Psychologist, 35,* 320–335.

Bronfenbrenner, U. (1979). *The ecology of human development.* Cambridge, MA: Harvard University.

Bronfenbrenner, U. (1978). "Who needs parent education?" *Teachers College Record, 79,* 773–774.

Caspi, A., Bem, D. J., & Elder, G. H. (1989). Continuities and consequences of interactional styles across the life course. *Journal of Personality, 57*(2), 375–406.

Denti, L. G., & Katz, M. S. (1996). Escaping the cave to dream new dreams: A normative vision for learning disabilities. In M. S. Poplin & P. T. Cousin (Eds.), *Alternative views of learning disabilities: Issues for the 21st century* (pp. 59–76). Austin: Pro-Ed.

Dudley-Marling, C., & Dippo, D. (1996). What learning disabilities do: Sustaining the ideology of schooling. In M. S. Poplin & P. T. Cousin, (Eds.), *Alternative views of learning disabilities: Issues for the 21st century* (pp. 45–57). Austin: Pro-Ed.

Forness, S. R. (1992). Broadening the cultural-organizational perspective in exclusion of youth with social maladjustment: First invited reaction to the Maag and Howell paper. *Remedial and Special Education, 13* (1), 55–59.

Lovitt, T. (1996). Foreword. In M. S. Poplin & P. T. Cousin, (Eds.), *Alternative views of learning disabilities: Issues for the 21st century* (pp. viii-xii). Austin: Pro-Ed.

Maag, J. W., & Howell, K. W. (1992). Special education and the exclusion of youth with social maladjustments: A cultural-organizational perspective. *Remedial and Special Education, 13,*(1), 47–54.

Mallory, B. L., & New, R. S. (1994). Social constructivist theory and principles of inclusion: Challenges for early childhood special education. *The Journal of Special Education, 28,* 322–337.

Pagano, J. A. (1991). Moral fictions: The dilemma of theory and practice. In C. Witherell & N. Noddings (Eds.), *Stories lives tell: Narrative and dialogue in education* pp. 193–206. NY: Teachers College Press.

Sameroff, A. (1975). Transactional models in early social relations. *Human Development, 18,* 65–79.

Sameroff, A., & Chandler, M. J. (1975). Reproductive risk and the continuum of care-taking causality. In F. D. Horowitz, M. Heatherington, S. Scarr-Salaptatek, & G. Siegel (Eds.), *Review of child development research* (Vol. 4, pp. 103–197). Chicago: University of Chicago Press.

Scott, M. (1980). Ecological theory and methods of research in special education. *Journal of Special Education, 4,* 279–294.

Thomas, E. D., & Marshall, M. J. (1977). Clinical evaluation and coordination of services: An ecological model. *Exceptional Children, 44,* 16–22.

Thurman, S. K. (1977). Congruence of behavioral ecologies: A model for special education programming. *Journal of Special Education, 11,* 329–333.

Weinberg, L. A. (1992). The relevance of choice in distinguishing seriously emotionally disturbed from socially maladjusted students. *Behavioral Disorders, 17,* 99–106.

4

Biological Factors and Temperament

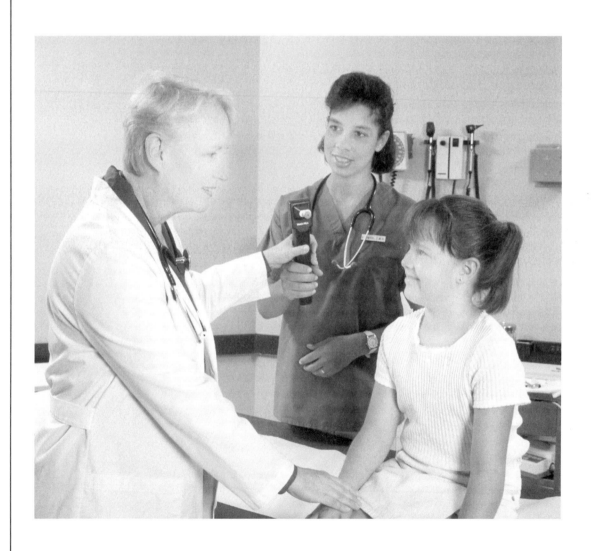

TO GUIDE YOUR READING

After you complete this chapter, you will be able to answer these questions:

- What are some of the biological issues related to emotional/behavioral disorders?

- What are some of the issues related to temperament and emotional/behavioral disorders?

- What are some of the more common biological disorders with which learners may be identified as emotionally/behaviorally disordered?

- What are the interventions related to the biological bases of emotional/behavioral disorders?

- What is the role of the teacher in biological intervention?

◊ *Chris, a seventh grader, had to leave his classroom at 10:00 a.m. and 1:00 p.m. each school day to take his medication. He was extremely preoccupied with these times, wearing four watches to school: two watches on his right wrist with alarms set for 10:00 a.m. and two watches on his left wrist with alarms set for 1:00 p.m. Frequently throughout the day Chris would push his sleeves up to check the time first on his "morning watches" and then on his "afternoon watches." At 10:00 a.m. and 1:00 p.m. the class would hear Chris' alarms signaling that it was time for his medication.*

When the teacher asked Chris not to let his alarms sound during class time because they were disturbing others, he became upset, and was unable to complete any work. He spent all of his time staring at the wall clock.

◊ *Susan, a third grader, was described by her teacher as "often wandering around the room." When the school psychologist visited the classroom to observe Susan, she noted the following behaviors: Susan dropped her pencil, breaking the point. She raised her hand to ask her teacher if she could sharpen it, and was granted permission. Susan got out of her seat, walked toward the pencil sharpener, which was by the window, and stopped to pet the class gerbil. Noticing the gerbil was out of food, she took the food box from under the counter and sprinkled food into the cage. Observing that the gerbil's water seemed murky, Susan took the water dish over to the sink, rinsed it out, filled it with fresh water, and returned it to the cage. Next, she noticed the paper towel dispenser was almost out and refilled it from the stack of towels under the sink. While the sink cabinet was open, Susan saw a can of cleanser, picked it up, sprinkled some in the sink and began to clean it. At this point, the teacher called, "Susan, what are you doing, and where is your pencil?" Susan looked at the teacher with a puzzled expression on her face.*

A t the core of the developmental contexts is the self—the learner (See Figure 3.1). In recent years, there has been growing evidence that some emotional/behavioral disorders may be related to biological variations within the individual. In addition, research has lent credibility to the concept of a temperamental predisposition, suggesting that some children are simply born more difficult to raise and teach than others.

In this chapter, we discuss the learner and biological factors that may contribute to emotional/behavioral disorders. Issues related to temperament are also discussed. The chapter concludes with a discussion of various means of addressing these biological factors, such as medication and diet. The role of the teacher in bio-physical intervention is also discussed.

◊◊ What Are Some of the Biological Issues Related to Emotional/Behavioral Disorders?

The consideration of biological issues related to emotional/behavioral disorders is the basis of the biophysical perspective. This view of the individual emphasizes neurologic and other organic factors as the cause of behavior. If the cause of behavior is organic, then it would follow that the ways of dealing with emotional/behavioral disorders would include nutrition, medication, and other medical interventions.

Recent work in three areas has made significant contributions to the biophysical perspective. First, an analysis of risk factors has suggested a significant relationship between physical and mental health. Second, studies of families with histories of alcoholism and depression have raised questions of genetic predisposition. Finally, medical technology has provided far greater insight into psychoneurology and various brain functions.

Risk Factors

The prevention of placing children at risk for physical and mental health problems begins at the onset of pregnancy (Slavin, 1989). Physical problems, such as lead poisoning and poor nutrition, have been related to children's behavioral problems in school. The last decade has seen significant reversals in the general health indicators that affect children. Studies by Baumeister, Kupstas, and Klindworth (1990) suggested that without specific prevention efforts, a "biological underclass" of children, whose problems are related to poverty, a lack of prenatal care, and the prevalence of chronic illnesses such as AIDS and Hepatitis B, will emerge.

The risks to children of poverty have been described by Parker, Greer, and Zuckerman (1988) as "double jeopardy." The interaction of both biological factors and poor social support puts children at serious risk for emotional/behavioral disorders. Children living in poverty are biologically vulnerable due to prematurity, maternal depression, temperamental passivity, and inadequate early stimulation.

Genetic Predisposition

The term *genetic predisposition* is used to describe the likelihood that a particular characteristic present in the parents will be present in their child. Although the particular gene responsible for the

genetic predisposition
the likelihood that a particular characteristic present in the parents will be present in their child

trait (characteristic) has not been identified, its likelihood suggests that some emotional/behavioral disorders may be inherited, or, "run in families." For example, it is estimated that 30% of fathers and 20% of mothers of children with attention deficit hyperactivity disorder have the disorder themselves (Copps, 1992). Alcoholism and drug abuse may also be linked to genetic predisposition (Crabbe, McSwigan, & Kelknap, 1985). The occurrence of schizophrenia, a very low-incidence disorder, has been studied in families. According to Paul (1980), the children of schizophrenic individuals are far more likely to have schizophrenia, and among identical twins, even those raised apart, there is the same incidence of schizophrenia.

Psychoneurology

Using the case of Attention Deficit Hyperactivity Disorder, Copps (1992) describes the evolution of our understanding of the psychoneurological bases of some emotional/behavioral disorders.

Copps relates the history of Attention Deficit Hyperactivity Disorder as beginning in 1845, when Henrich Hoffman described "fidgety Phil," the boy who never sat still, as being naughty, rude, and wile (cunning). In 1902, George Still indicated that such children had a "deficit in moral control." However, he described a biologic deficit in "inhibitory volition" because these children often had competent parents who would not typically have had such "morally defective" children.

Following an outbreak of encephalitis in the 1940s, there were reports of children becoming disruptive, inattentive, and hyperactive as a result of being afflicted with this neurologic disease. These children were referred to as "brain damaged" or "behavior disordered"; children who did not have a physically detectable neurologic deficit were said to have "minimal brain damage." Despite intensive study of children who demonstrated these behaviors, direct evidence could not be found for minimal brain damage. Because no evidence of damage was detected, and also because the term itself was considered distasteful, the name of this condition was changed to "minimal brain dysfunction."

As the symptoms of Attention Deficit Hyperactivity Disorder became increasingly accepted as a dysfunction, rather than a damage, and as a result of a resurgence of a belief in the idea that nurture, rather than nature, determined a child's behavior, poor parenting emerged as a probable cause of this disorder. The response to medication, however, increasingly cast doubt on ineffective parenting and supported a biological cause.

With increased technology, it became possible to measure the functioning of the brain and levels of **neurotransmitters,** which

neurotransmitters chemicals in the brain that affect the efficiency with which the brain functions

Sharing thoughts and feelings.

are chemicals in the brain that affect the efficiency with which the brain functions. It became apparent that individuals with Attention Deficit Hyperactivity Disorder show a deficiency or imbalance in the chemical elements catecholamine, dopamine, and norepinephrine. Although it is not yet clear whether there is a decrease in production or excessive absorption of these neurotransmitters, a significant body of evidence indicates that inefficient transmission of neurological impulses affects the entire attention system of the brain, including attention, inhibition, and motor planning. Viewing Attention Deficit Hyperactivity Disorder in this way, children with this disorder have a deficiency in executive control, which governs the inhibition and monitoring of behavior. These students then neurologically have difficulty selecting and maintaining goals, anticipating, planning, completing tasks, and adapting plans.

Similar evolutionary paths are apparent in our understanding of pervasive developmental disorders, including autism, which was once thought to be a consequence of inadequate parenting, but is now thought, by some, to be a complex neurological disorder; Tourette's disorder; borderline personality disorder; and obsessive compulsive disorder. These disorders, with the exception of autism, will be discussed in more detail in another section of this chapter.

executive function
the processes that regulate, integrate, and coordinate various cognitive processes to support goal-directed behavior

One construct that frequently emerges in discussions of the psychoneurological bases of emotional/behavioral disorders is executive function. ***Executive function*** regulates, integrates, and coordinates other cognitive functions, such as attention, memory, language, and visual-spatial skills, toward the successful completion of goals (Welsh, 1994). Executive functioning supports successful problem solving and strategizing. Any unique academic task that requires critical thinking, judgment, planning, or self-monitoring requires executive function skills.

Executive function has great implications for behavior. Welsh (1994), using the available vast research base, suggests that executive functioning skills are mediated in the prefrontal section of the brain. The symptoms demonstrated by adult patients who have received damage to the frontal lobe suggest that this part of the brain is uniquely dedicated to support the executive function activities of insight, anticipation, planning, self-evaluation, and goal directedness (Damasio, 1985; Fuster, 1980).

Attention Deficit Hyperactivity Disorder again provides a good example of the complexity of the impact of psychoneurological processes and behavior. Studies have demonstrated that in some learners with Attention Deficit Hyperactivity Disorder, the central nervous system is underaroused (Ferguson & Rappaport, 1983). In addition, decreased cerebral blood flow has been documented in the frontal lobe of these learners, and the use of a stimulant medication, Ritalin, increased the blood flow to this area of the brain (Lou, Henricksen, & Bruhn, 1984). Ritalin released stored dopamine, a neurotransmitter, from neurons, suggesting that the level of neurotransmitters also has an effect on executive function. In a later study, Lou, Henriksen, Bruhn, Borner, and Nielsen (1989) found more specifically that the locus of the diminished blood flow was the basal ganglia, the structure in the subcortex with many dopamine receptors that connects to the frontal lobe. Neurochemical research (Shaywitz, Cohen, & Bowers, 1983) has indicated that the depletion of dopamine may underly attention deficits; Ritalin releases stored dopamine, decreases motor activity, and supports increased attention in many learners with Attention Deficit Hyperactivity Disorder (Barkley, 1977).

Glucose utilization has been related to central nervous system underarousal and Attention Deficit Hyperactivity Disorder (Pennington, 1991). Among learners identified as emotionally/behaviorally disordered, glucose underutilization has been isolated in the right frontal lobe and increased utilization in posterior brain regions (Zametkin, Nordahl, Gross, King, Semple, Rumsey, Hamburger, & Cohen, 1991). So, at least in terms of Attention Deficit Hyperactivity Disorder, the psychoneurological bases of behavior may be a complex interaction of structure, blood flow, and neuro-transmitter release.

The role of neurotransmitters in self-esteem and aggression has also been explored. The brain uses several dozen neurotransmitters and hormonal systems during information processes. Sylvester (1997) contends that fluctuations in serotonin, one of the neuro-transmitters, plays an important role in regulating self-esteem and position in the social hierarchy. High levels of serotonin are related to high self-esteem and social status and low levels to low self-esteem and social status. High levels are related to smooth control, and low levels are related to impulsive, reckless, violent, or suicidal behavior.

Sylvester (1997) suggests that it is possible to stimulate sero-tonin when conditions are adverse and self-esteem and serotonin levels are low. Administering a medication such as Prosac is one way to increase serotonin levels that enhances self-esteem. In-creased self-esteem enhances mood, leading to positive social feed-back, allowing the natural system to take over in time. Alcohol, sometimes used by individuals to deal with depression, increases serotonin short-term, but eventually depletes the store of sero-tonin, even further decreasing impulse control.

◊◊ What Are Some of the Issues Related to Temperament and Emotional/Behavioral Disorders?

An individual's temperament is his or her style; temperament de-scribes the way in which an individual behaves or does something, not the action he or she carries out. Thomas and Chess (1977), de-scribed nine factors that compose temperament: activity level, adaptability, approach/withdrawal, attention span and persis-tence, distractibility, intensity of reaction, quality of mood, regu-larity, and threshold of responsiveness.

The biological view of temperament was given greater impetus by Buss and Plomin (1984), who argued that to be considered a temperament, a behavioral predisposition must be present in adults, and must be developmentally stable, adaptive, and have a genetic component. Emotionality, activity, sociability, and impul-sivity, then, are dimensions of temperament. *Temperament* is the dimensions of an individual's personality that are largely present at birth, exist in most historical ages and most societies, are con-sistent across settings, and are stable as the individual develops (Plomin, 1983). Temperament is an individual variation that is bi-ological or constitutional, remains with the individual, and is linked to differences in behavioral or expressive style.

temperament the di-mensions of an individ-ual's personality that are largely present at birth, exist in most ages and most societies, are consistent across set-tings, and are stable as the individual develops

Temperament, as an individual variation, can be a significant factor in identification as having an emotional/behavioral disorder. Thomas and Chess (1977) suggest that the "goodness of fit" of the individual's temperament and the environment can be a major factor in problem behavior. Temperament may also affect a child's learning by determining the ease and speed with which attention and activity may be modulated and directed.

According to Martin (1992a), there is a limited, though significant, body of research on the relationship between child characteristics in the social, emotional, and attentional domains, collectively referred to as "temperamental characteristics," and the educational process and outcomes for learners with disabilities. He reviews the research in the relationships between temperament and the characteristics of learners with disabilities such as Down syndrome, neurological disabilities, learning disabilities, hyperactivity, and behavior problems; family interactions; teachability, or teacher attitudes toward learners; teacher decision making; and classroom interaction. Martin presents a model of the effects of temperament on educational outcome, mediated by their effects on parents, peers, and teachers.

In Martin's model, temperament is one of the factors that functions across home and school settings and affects learning and school behavior. A child's temperament, he suggests, is manifest in classroom behavior, which affects peer attitudes and behavior, which in turn have an additional impact on the child's educational outcome. These peer attitudes and behavior toward a learner identified as emotionally/behaviorally disordered may have additional impact because of the increased risk for social rejection (Janke & Lee, 1991). Children who are perceived to have a "difficult temperament" are particularly at risk for social relationship problems (Martin, 1992a).

Although there may be a relationship between the temperament of parent and child, Martin (1992b) suggests that parents and their children will always differ in temperament in that they are at different developmental stages, share only half of their genetic material, and are responding to different demands. The goodness of fit between the temperaments of parent and child is an important determiner of the child's development.

◊◊ What Are Some of the More Common Biological Disorders with Which Learners May Be Identified as Emotionally/Behaviorally Disordered?

As we indicated previously in this chapter, there are several disorders that have been related to a biological basis. Among the most common of these disorders are Tourette's disorder, Attention

Deficit Hyperactivity Disorder, obsessive compulsive disorder, and depression. In addition, a group of children have recently emerged whose behavior and learning are biologically related to prenatal exposure to drugs and alcohol.

Tourette's Disorder

Individuals with Gilles de la Tourette's disorder demonstrate *tics* or repetitive, recurring, and involuntary movements or sounds. Motor tics range from eyeblinks to complex muscular patterns, and vocal tics include grunts, barks, screams, or throat clearing (Anderson, 1993). These tics occur many times during the day. Generally tic-free periods are no longer than three months. In about one half of the individuals with Tourette's disorder, the tics usually begin with a single tic such as eye blinking (American Psychiatric Association, 1994). Tics occur as early as two years of age, and because Tourette's disorder is a developmental disability, must occur before the individual is 18 years of age. The "vulnerability"—or receiving genetic basis for developing a condition—to Tourette's disorder is transmitted in a dominant pattern, and the range in which this vulnerability is expressed could be from Tourette's disorder, motor or vocal tics, obsessive-compulsive disorder, or Attention Deficit/Hyperactivity Disorder.

tics repetitive, recurring, involuntary movements or sounds

Burd, Kauffman, and Kerbeshian (1992) reported that slightly more than half of the clinical files of students with Tourette syndrome they reviewed reported learning disabilities. Tourette syndrome may be highly disruptive in the classroom, and learners frequently have difficulties in social relationships. For individuals with moderate or severe tics, medication is frequently used.

Attention Deficit Hyperactivity Disorder

Attention Deficit Hyperactivity Disorder is one of the most frequently diagnosed and researched disorders among school-age children.

Reid, Maag, Vasa, and Wright (1994) examined the educational treatment of children clinically diagnosed as having Attention Deficit Hyperactivity Disorder. Among the children in the large sample, more than half were receiving special education services, with most receiving services as learners with emotional/behavioral disorders and learning disabilities. The most common special education placement was general education classrooms with resource room support. More than 90% of the students were taking medication.

One of the major controversies regarding the use of medication with learners diagnosed with Attention Deficit Hyperactivity Disorder involves the impact of medication on learning. In a study of the clinical effects of medication on behavior and cognition, Swanson, Cantwell, Lerner, Pfiffner, and Kotkin McBurnett, (1992) reported that the effects of stimulant medication on academic performance is minimal compared to its effects on behavior. They found no evidence of beneficial effects of medication on learning or academic achievement.

The dominant paradigm applied to explain Attention Deficit Hyperactivity Disorder has been psychiatric (neurological and biological). As a consequence, according to Maag and Reid (1994), other efforts to explain the disorder, such as a functional approach to assessment and treatment, have been hampered. For the purpose of the learner's education, the usefulness of accepted conceptualizations of Attention Deficit Hyperactivity Disorder should be judged from an educational perspective, that is, the conceptual model's implications for classroom intervention (Maag & Reid, 1994).

Depression

The characteristics of depression for children are similar to those for adults. A "Major Depressive Episode" for both adults and children is described as a period of at least two weeks during which there is either depressed mood or the loss of interest or pleasure in most activities. The *Diagnostic and Statistic Manual of Mental Disorders* (American Psychiatric Association, 1994) notes that in children, depression is often seen as irritation, crankiness, and sadness. The duration of symptoms required for identification is also shorter among children. Children and youth who are depressed have low self-esteem, poor social skills, and are pessimistic.

In a study of 8- to 11-year-old children identified as learning disabled, Wright-Strawderman and Watson (1992) found that more than a third scored in the depressed range on the Children's Depression Inventory. Females with learning disabilities may be even more likely to demonstrate symptoms related to depression (Maag, Behrens, & DiGangi, 1992).

Obsessive Compulsive Disorder

obsessions unwanted, intrusive, and unpleasant repeated ideas

compulsions repetitive behaviors usually involved with counting, listing, or rearranging objects

For many years, obsessive compulsive disorder was considered a rare disease. Recent research by the National Institute of Mental Health (1996), however, suggests that perhaps as many as 2% of the population may have obsessive compulsive disorder. Individuals with this disorder have **obsessions,** or unwanted, intrusive, and unpleasant ideas that occur repeatedly, which they manage through **compulsions,** or repetitive behaviors usually involved

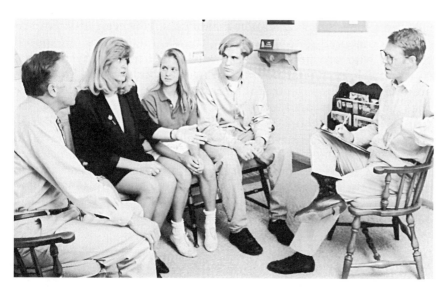

Listening is essential.

with counting, listing, or rearranging objects. The most common obsessions are thoughts about contamination; doubts, such as those concerning turning off the stove or locking a door; or a need to have things in a particular order, such as lining objects up on desks or tables. Common compulsions include handwashing, ordering, checking, or repeating words silently (American Psychiatric Association, 1994).

Individuals with obsessive compulsive disorder respond well to specific medications, supporting a neurobiological basis of the disorder. The use of positron emission tomography (PET) scanners to study the brains of individuals with obsessive compulsive disorder have demonstrated unusual neuro-chemical activity in regions known to play a role in other neurological disorders, such as Tourette syndrome (National Institute of Mental Health [NIMH] 1996).

Children Prenatally Exposed to Drugs and Alcohol

Infants who have been prenatally exposed to drugs and alcohol are at risk for physical and behavioral/emotional problems. According to Williams and Howard (1993), these children demonstrate a marked failure to adapt to the environment; difficulties in appropriate interaction with caregivers; and problems in language, learning, and motor skills. Initial follow-up on infants prenatally exposed to drugs and alcohol suggest that some will suffer long-term behavioral and education disabilities. However, little empirically documented data concerning the characteristics of exposed children who are in school is available. Although the potential causal mechanisms for neural damage to children who have been prenatally exposed to cocaine are strong, the empirical literature does not support an inevitable developmental consequence. Infants who have been exposed to cocaine in utero are similar to other children with neurological challenges, but may have an added disadvantage of a chaotic caregiving environment in which the parent focuses more on obtaining and using drugs than on caring for the child. This combination of biological problems and chaotic environment increases the probability that the child will demonstrate disabilities.

◊◊ What Are Interventions Related to the Biological Bases of Emotional/Behavioral Disorders?

The two primary interventions related to the biological bases of emotional/behavioral disorders involve the use of medication and diet control.

Medication

One of the most important concepts concerning the use of medication as treatment for biologically based emotional/behavioral disorders is that medication does not "cure" the disorder, but modifies specific symptoms of the disorder. Although medication can be effective with individuals identified as emotionally/behaviorally disordered, several logistical issues must be given consideration. Brown, Dingle, and Landau (1994) suggest that a pervasive problem is making sure that the individual is taking the medication as prescribed. Following medication schedules is complicated by the fact that medication may be prescribed for long periods of time and that parents and/or children may be ambivalent about the medication. Medications often have to be administered at school, and dispensation may be affected by school staff attitudes and availability. In addition, community attitudes and beliefs regarding the appropriateness of using drugs with children may intrude on the parents' decision-making process regarding medication.

Although the use of medication with children has increased greatly since its first use more than 60 years ago, the use of psychoactive medication for children has increased at a far slower rate than for adults (Wiener & Jaffe, 1985). The physician must not only be concerned with the individual child's personal status, but must evaluate the child's environment, potentially biased evaluations of those associated with the child, and the actual and potential effects of other interventions being applied with the child, including special education services (Shea & Bauer, 1987). Yet, among adults, medication is the primary method of therapy supplemented by other forms of treatment for some adult mental disorders (Baldessarini, 1985). Systematic research regarding the efficacy and safety of pharmacological agents in children, however, has been a recent phenomenon (Brown, Dingle, & Landau, 1994).

Several groups of medication are in general use with children and youth (Brown, Dingle, & Landau, 1994). Antidepressants are primarily used to treat depression, with target behaviors such as appetite and sleep problems, fatigue, lack of energy, and problems in attention and concentration. Antidepressants may also be used for nocturnal enuresis, sleepwalking, night terrors, school phobias, and with individuals identified as having both Attention Deficit Hyperactivity Disorder and mood or anxiety disorders. If the individual with Attention Deficit Hyperactivity Disorder has severe side effects, the antidepressant is prescribed with stimulants (Brown, Dingle, & Landau, 1994). Antidepressants are usually started at a low dose and adjusted until an optimal effect on target behaviors is attained. Throughout the time during which the antidepressant is used, both target behaviors and side effects should be monitored. The range of effective doses of antidepressants varies across medications, diagnoses, and individual differences, including the child's size and metabolism.

A less frequently used group of medications is antipsychotic drugs. However, a limited number of drug trials exists with children and adolescents using antipsychotic medication (Brown, Dingle, & Landau, 1994). Among children, antipsychotic medications are most commonly used for such developmental disorders as autism and severe aggression, with target symptoms of overactivity, aggression, hallucinations, delusions, and agitation.

The most commonly prescribed medications for children and youth identified as emotionally/behaviorally disordered are stimulants. Of these, the two most frequently prescribed are Ritalin and Dexedrine. Dexedrine is used with children who have not responded to Ritalin. The side effects of stimulants are similar and can be managed by administering the medication early in the day, after meals, and planning the time for other doses. An advantage of stimulants is that they last a short time, so may be administered when behavior is most problematic (Brown, Dingle & Landau, 1994).

There are several other medications that are used less frequently with learners identified as emotionally/behaviorally disor-

Table 4.1 Medications Used with Children and Youth with Emotional/Behavioral Disorders

Medication	Use	Common Side Effects
Antidepressants		
Tofranil (Imipramine)	enuresis, depression	sedation, dry mouth, constipation, urinary retention
Elavil (Amitriptyline)	enuresis	blurred vision, slowed cardiac conduction
Norpramin (desipramine)	Attention Deficit Hyperactivity Disorder (ADHD), depression	mild tachycardia, elevated blood pressure
Palemor (Noritriptyline)	ADHD, depression	weight gain, orthostatic hypotension
Prozac (fluoxetine)	depression, obsessive compulsive disorder	anxiety, diarrhea, drowsiness, nausea, trouble sleeping
Antipsychotics: Thorazine (chloropromazine)	acute psychotic states	sedation, orthostatic hypotention
Mellaril (thioridazine)	autism, pervasive developmental disorder	akathisia motor restlessness, Parkinsonian symptoms, cognitive blunting, photosensitivity
Stelazine (trifluperazine)	Tourette's disorder	sedation, hypotension, headache, upset stomach, insomnia
Stimulants		
Dexadrine (dextroamphetamine)	ADHD	insomnia, dysphoria, behavioral rebound
Ritalin (methylphenidate)	ADHD	loss of appetite, weight loss
Cylert (permoline)	ADHD	weight loss

dered. Antihistamines are sometimes prescribed for children and youth with insomnia. Antianxiety agents are very rarely used because few data on their efficacy and safety with children are available. These medications are reserved for times and occasions when other interventions are insufficient or inadequate (Brown, Dingle, & Landau, 1994). The use of antianxiety agents is discouraged for individuals with Attention Deficit Hyperactivity Disorder because they can produce symptoms of excitation and agitation.

Anticonvulsants are generally not the agent of choice for emotional/behavioral disorders and are typically used only when chil-

Medication	Use	Common Side Effects
Antihistamines		
Benadryl (Diphenhydramine)	anxiety, insomnia	dizziness, oversedation, agitation
Atarax (Hydroxyzine)	sleep disorders, agitation	blurred vision, abdominal pain
Inderal (Propanolol)	aggression	dry mouth
Antianxiety agents		
Valium (Diazepam)	seizures, anxiety disorders, behavioral problems	substance abuse
Anticonvulsants		
Phenobarbital	seizures	memory and attention problems, hyperactivity
Dilantin (Diphenylhydantoin)	seizures	irritability, aggression, depression
Tegretol (carbamazepine)	aggression, emotional lability, irritability, seizures	drowsiness, nausea, rash, eye problems
Depakane (valproic acid)	mania, seizures	nausea, weight gain, tremors
Other medications		
Lithium carbonate	bipolar disorders, aggression	stomach upset, tremors, headaches
Catapress (Clonidine)	Tourette's disorder, ADHD, aggression	sedation

Source: Brown, Dingle, & Landau, 1994; United States Pharmaceutical Convention, 1994

dren have not responded to other medications (Brown, Dingle, & Landau, 1994). With regard to other medications, lithium is an effective treatment of bipolar disorder, depression, and severe impulsive aggression (Bukstein, 1992). Clonidine is effective with mood and activity level in some children with Attention Deficit Hyperactivity Disorder who are highly aroused, overactive, impulsive, and defiant.

Medications commonly used with children and youth with emotional/behavioral disorders are presented and summarized in Table 4.1.

Diet

In 1980, the National Advisory Committee on Hyperkinesis and Food Additives issued a position statement that there is no evidence to support the claim that artificial food coloring, artificial flavoring, and salicylate produce hyperactivity and learning disabilities. The Committee suggested that changes that are observed in children's behavior are related to what is called a "placebo effect." Even more recent studies have demonstrated no link between food ingested and problem behavior (Pescara-Kovach & Alexander, 1994).

◊◊ What Is the Role of the Teacher in Biological Interventions?

The teacher plays an important supportive role to the medical personnel in biological interventions, including (a) referral, (b) collaboration with and reporting of observations, (c) modification of classroom structure and curricular content, (d) obtaining permission to administer medication, and (e) safeguarding and administering medication in the school (Shea & Bauer, 1987).

The teacher is not qualified to refer a child directly to a physician or to suggest the prescribing of medication. However, the educator may inform the parents of a child's behavior problem. The school may initiate contact with medical personnel on behalf of a particular child, with parental consent. It is suggested that an educator not directly involved with the child in the school serve as a contact person or intermediary between the teacher and parents during the referral process (Report of the Conference on the Use of Stimulant Drugs, 1971).

A primary role of the educator in biological interventions is to provide current and objective feedback to the physician on the observable effects of medication on the child's behavior and learning. The majority of the present-day symptom-control medications are experimental substances whose effects on a particular child cannot be predicted exactly. Consequently, feedback to the prescribing physician will assist in efforts to maximize the positive effects and minimize the side effects of the medication. Because teachers are trained observers and are with the child throughout the day, they are in an excellent position to observe the effects of the medication and report, through proper channels, to the physician.

During the biological treatment process, especially during the beginning weeks, the child's behavior and learning styles may change significantly. Thus, it may be necessary to modify both classroom structure and curricular content to respond to the child's needs. Classroom structure may have to be increased or decreased to permit the child to adjust to "new" behaviors and interests. The curriculum may have to be changed to allow the child to learn the information and skills neglected by earlier, less successful programming.

Professional school personnel must obtain permission to dispense medication in the school when medical personnel (a physician or nurse) are not available during the school day. The school should develop a policy with regard to medication in an effort to

---

Student: Birth date:

Address: Telephone:

School:

Physician's Statement
1. Name/Type of medication:
2. Dosage/Amount to be administered:
3. Frequency/Times to be administered:
4. Duration of order (week, month, indefinitely):
5. Anticipated reaction to medication (symptoms, side effects):
Physician's signature: Date:
Address:
Phone:

Parent Request
I hereby request and give my permission for the designated school staff member to administer the medication prescribed on this form to my child.
Parent's signature: Date:
Comments:

CC: Physician
     Parent
     School

Figure 4.1 Permission form for administration of medication

improve services and minimize personnel liability (Courtnage, Stainback, & Stainback, 1982). A permission form for administering medication in the school is presented in Figure 4.1.

When medication is dispensed in the school, the following guidelines should be followed.

1. Permission forms should be obtained and filed in the child's permanent record file.

2. Medication should be stored in a central location in a locked cabinet. A refrigerator may be necessary for some medications.

3. Medication must be properly labeled with the child's and physician's names. The label should include directions for use.

4. Medications should be logged in and out of the school. Medication should be inventoried daily. One professional member of the school's staff, preferably a nurse, should be appointed to inventory medication and function as a contact person in all communications with parents, physicians, pharmacists, and other medical personnel related to medication.

5. A responsible adult must be present when the child takes his or her medication.

Student			Birth date:	
Date	Time	Medication/ Dosage	Person Dispensing Medication	Notes

Figure 4.2 Medication log

6. A log, to be completed each time a child takes medication, should be maintained in the medication area or the child's record file. A sample form is presented in Figure 4.2. The completed forms should be retained in the child's file.

Children should not be dismissed from school because medical personnel are not immediately available. Following the above suggestions will prevent this from occurring.

◊◊ Summary Points

- Young children living in poverty are at risk because of the interaction of biological factors and poor social support.
- An increase in information regarding the relationships of physical and mental health, genetic predisposition, and more advanced medical technology has lent credibility to the biophysical model.
- Several common psychological disorders, including Attention Deficit Hyperactivity Disorder, Tourette's disorder, and obsessive compulsive disorder can be attributed to biological causes.
- Two primary interventions of the biophysical model are medication and diet.
- The role of teachers in medical interventions include referral, observation, modifying classroom structure and activities, and safely administering medication with permission.

◊ **Self-Evaluation**

Select the most appropriate response.
1. Alcoholism and drug abuse may be linked to
   a. genetic transmission.
   b. medication use.
   c. genetic predisposition.
2. Dopamine, catecholamine, and norepinephrine
   a. cause ADD.
   b. levels vary with genetic predisposition.
   c. affect the efficiency of brain functioning.

Chapter 4

3. Temperament varies
   a. according to the presence of certain individuals.
   b. in relationship to the context.
   c. little across settings.
4. With learners with Attention Deficit Hyperactivity Disorder, stimulant medication
   a. increases learning rates.
   b. increases manageability.
   c. increases hyperactivity.
5. Obsessive compulsive disorder is
   a. learned from compulsive parents.
   b. more common than once believed.
   c. less common than once believed.
6. The most pervasive difficulty in using medication is
   a. side effects.
   b. taking the medication as prescribed.
   c. interactions among medications.
7. The most frequently prescribed medications for children are
   a. antipsychotics.
   b. antidepressants.
   c. stimulants.
8. The role of the teacher in medical intervention is
   a. recommendations for medication.
   b. referral.
   c. modifying medication levels.
9. In children, depression is
   a. demonstrated in the same ways as depression in adults.
   b. demonstrated by irritability.
   c. rarely seen.

Making the Language Your Own

Match each key word or phrase to its definition.

_____ 1. neurotransmitters   _____ 5. compulsions

_____ 2. obsessions   _____ 6. executive function

_____ 3. genetic predisposition   _____ 7. temperament

_____ 4. tics

a. the likelihood that a particular characteristic present in the parents will be present in their child
b. chemicals in the brain that effect the efficiency with which the brain functions
c. the dimensions of an individual's personality that are largely present at birth
d. repetitive, recurring, involuntary movements or sounds
e. unwanted, intrusive, and unpleasant, repeated ideas
f. repetitive behaviors usually involved with counting, listing, or rearranging objects
g. the processes that regulate, integrate, and coordinate various cognitive processes to support goal-directed behavior

Theory into Practice

1. Interview a teacher who teaches students receiving medication. Are there any similarities between these children? What types of medication do they take?
2. Interview a principal regarding the regulations and procedures for the administration of medication in his or her school.

◊◊ References

American Psychiatric Association. (1994). *Diagnostic and statistical manual of mental disorders* (4th ed.) Washington, DC: Author.

Anderson, D. J. (1993). Identifying the child with Gilles de la Tourette syndrome. *Preventing School Failure, 32,* 25–28.

Baldessarini, R. J. (1985). Drugs and the treatment of psychiatric disorders. In A. G. Gilman, L. Goddman, T. W. Rall, & F. Murad (Eds.), *The pharmacological basis of therapeutics* (pp. 387–446). New York: Macmillan.

Barkley, R. A. (1977). The effects of methylphenidate on various types of activity levels and attention in hyperkinetic children. *Journal of Abnormal Child Psychology, 5,* 351–369.

Baumeister, A. A., Kupstas, F., & Klindworth, L. M. (1990). New Morbidity: Implications for prevention of children's disabilities. *Exceptionality, 1,* 1–16.

Brown, R. T., Dingle, A., & Landau, S. (1994). Overview of psychopharmacology in children and adolescents. *School Psychology Quarterly, 9*(1), 4–25.

Bukstein, O. (1992). Overview of pharmacological treatment. In V. B. Van Hassalt & M. Hersen (Eds.), *Handbook of behavior ther-*

apy and pharmacotherapy for children (pp. 213–232). Boston: Allyn & Bacon.

Burd, L., Kauffman, D. W., & Kerbeshian, J. (1992). Tourette syndrome and learning disabilities. *Journal of Learning Disabilities, 25*(9), 598–604.

Buss, A. H., & Plomin, R. (1984). *Temperament: Early developing personality traits.* Hillsdale, NJ: Erlbaum.

Copps, S. C. (1992). *The attention physician: Attention deficit disorder.* Atlanta: SPI Press.

Courtnage, L., Stainback, W., & Stainback, S. (1982). Managing prescription drugs in school. *Teaching Exceptional Children, 15*(1), 5–10.

Crabbe, J. C., McSwigan, J. D., & Belknap, J. K. (1985). The role of genetics in substance abuse. In M. Galizio & S. A. Maisto (Eds.), *Determinants of substance abuse* (pp. 13–54). New York: Plenum.

Damasio, A. R. (1985). The frontal lobes. In M. K. Heilman & E. Valenstein (Eds.), *Clinical neuropsychology* (pp. 339–376). New York: Oxford University Press.

Ferguson, H. B., & Rappaport, J. L. (1983). Nosological issues and biological validation. In M. Rutter (Ed.), Developmental Neuropsychiatry (369–384). New York: Guilford Press.

Janke, R. W., & Lee, K. (1991). Social skill ratings of exceptional students. *Journal of Psychoeducational Assessment, 9,* 54–66.

Lou, H. C., Henriksen, L., & Bruhn, P. (1984). Focal cerebral hypofusion and/or attention deficit disorder. *Archives of Neurology, 41,* 825–829.

Lou, H. C., Henriksen, L., Bruhn, P., Borner, H., & Nielsen, J. B. (1989). Striatal dysfunction in attention deficit and hyperkinetic disorder. *Archives of Neurology, 46,* 148–152.

Maag, J. W., Behrens, J. T., & DiGangi, S. A. (1992). Dysfunctional cognitions associated with adolescent depression: Findings across special population. *Exceptionality, 3* 31–47.

Maag, J. W., & Reid, R. (1994). Attention-deficit hyperactivity disorder: A functional approach to assessment and treatment. *Behavioral Disorders, 20*(1), 5–23.

Martin, R. P. (1992a). Child temperament effects on special education: Process and outcomes. *Exceptionality, 3,* 99–115.

Martin, R. P. (1992b). Reflections on "Child temperament effects on special education process and outcomes." *Exceptionality, 3,* 127–131.

National Advisory Committee on Hyperkinesis and Food Additives (1980). *Hyperactivity and food additives.* New York: Nutrition Foundation.

National Institute of Mental Health (1996). *Obsessive Compulsive Disorder: National Institute of Mental Health Decade of the Brain.* Washington, DC: Author.

Parker, S., Greer, S., & Zuckerman, B. (1988). Double jeopardy: The impact of poverty on early child development. *The Pediatric Clinics of North America, 35,* 1227–1240.

Paul, S. M. (1980). Sibling resemblance in mental ability: A review. *Behavior Genetics, 10*(3), 277–290.

Pennington, B. F. (1991). *Diagnosing Learning Disorders.* New York: Guilford Press.

Pescara-Kovach, L. A., & Alexander, K. (1994). The link between food ingested and problem behavior: Fact or fallacy? *Behavioral Disorders, 19,*(2), 142–148.

Plomin, R. (1983). Childhood temperament. In B. B. Lahey & A. E. Kazdin (Eds.), *Advances in clinical child psychology* (Vol 6., pp. 45–92). New York: Plenum.

Reid, R., Maag, J. W., Vasa, S. F., & Wright, G. (1994). Who are the children with attention deficit-hyperactivity disorder? A school-based survey. *The Journal of Special Education, 28*(2), 117–137.

Report of the Conference on the Use of Stimulant Drugs in the Treatment of Behaviorally Disordered Young School Children (1971). *Journal of Learning Disabilities, 4,* 523–30.

Shaywitz, B. A., Cohen, D. J., & Bowers, M. B. (1977). CSF monoamine metabolites in children with minimal brain dysfunction: Evidence of alteration of brain dopamine. *Journal of Pediatrics, 90,* 67–71.

Shea, T. M., & Bauer, A. M. (1987). *Teaching children and youth with behavior disorders.* Upper Saddle River, NJ: Prentice Hall.

Slavin, R. E. (1989). Students at risk of school failure: The problem and its dimensions. In R. Slavin, N. Karweit, & N. Madden (Eds.), *Effective programs for students at risk* (pp. 3–19). Boston: Allyn & Bacon.

Swanson, J. M., Cantwell, D., Lerner, M., McBurnett, K., Pfiffner, L., & Kotkin, R. (1992). Treatment of ADHD: Beyond medication. *Beyond Behavior, 4*(1), 13–16; 18–22.

Sylvester, R. (1997). The neurobiology of self-esteem and aggression. *Educational Leadership, 54*(9), 75–77.

Thomas, A., & Chess, S. (1977). *Temperament and development.* New York: Bruner-Mazel.

United States Pharmaceutical Convention (1994). *About your medicine: Prozac.* Washington, DC: Author.

Welsh, M. C. (1994). Executive function and the assessment of attention deficit hyperactivity disorder. In L. C. Wilkinson (Ed.), *Learning about learning disabilities* (pp. 21–42). New York: Guilford Press.

Wiener, J. M., & Jaffe, S. L. (1985). Historical overview of childhood and adolescent psychopharmacology. In J. M. Wiener (Ed.), *Diagnosis and psychopharmacology of childhood and adolescent disorders* (pp. 2–30). New York: John Wiley and Sons.

Williams, B. F., & Howard, V. F. (1993). Children exposed to cocaine: Characteristics and implications for research and intervention. *Journal of Early Intervention, 17*(1), 61–72.

Wright-Strawderman, C., & Watson, B. L. (1992). The prevalence of depressive symptoms in children with learning disabilities. *Journal of Learning Disabilities, 25*(4), 258–264.

Zametkin, A. J., Nordahl, T. E., Gross, M., King, A. C., Semple, W. E., Rumsey, J., Hamburger, S., & Cohen, R. M. (1991). Cerebral glucose metabolism in adults with hyperactivity of childhood onset. *New England Journal of Medicine, 323,* 1361–1366.

5 Learning and Interactional Styles

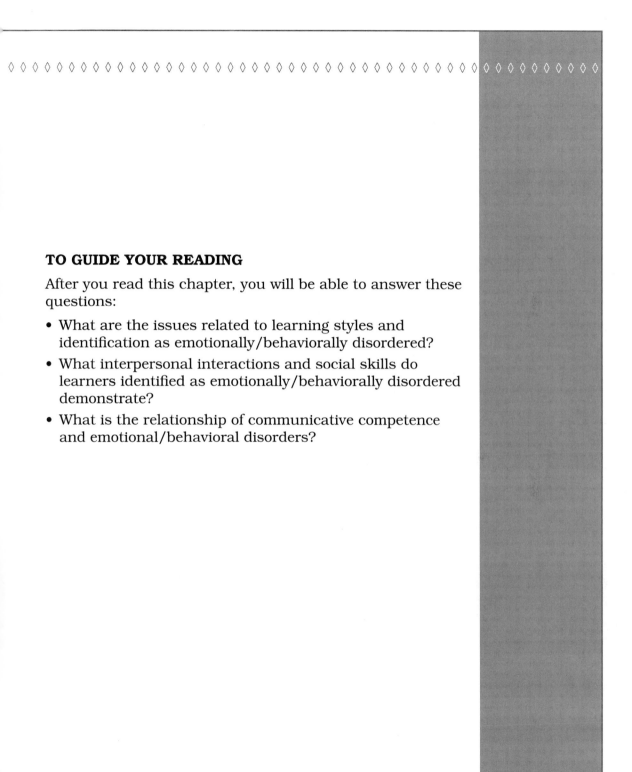

TO GUIDE YOUR READING

After you read this chapter, you will be able to answer these questions:

- What are the issues related to learning styles and identification as emotionally/behaviorally disordered?
- What interpersonal interactions and social skills do learners identified as emotionally/behaviorally disordered demonstrate?
- What is the relationship of communicative competence and emotional/behavioral disorders?

◊ *Ms. Rivers, the art teacher, was taking her students step-by-step through the process of making a coil pot. She monitored the students as they first completed their "snakes" of clay, coiled the bottoms of the pots, and continued to build their pots. Throughout these steps, Jacob simply sat back and observed. Angered by his apparent lack of interest and participation, Ms. Rivers sent him back to his desk as the others continued to work on their pots. At his desk Jacob independently completed his coil pot. Ms. Rivers was amazed that Jacob could sit there, apparently "lost in space," and then complete the project independently in such a short period of time. How did he do it?*

◊ *Eight-year-old Maryanne was a great concern for her teacher, Mr. Larsen. Mr. Larsen contended that Maryanne could do nothing quietly. Each time she was presented a task, she would mumble the steps it took to complete it and when the task was completed she would congratulate herself under her breath. When she was reprimanded for making noise, Maryanne appeared unaware that she had been talking to herself. Why did she mumble to herself?*

◊ *School learning is primarily verbal and sequential. However, not all students are verbal, sequential learners. Jacob, a visual learner, performs best by observing a task being completed before he begins it, rather than kinesthetically going through each step. Maryanne, who is very auditory, creates her own auditory stimuli when none is provided. In a classroom in which learning is primarily verbal and sequential, Jacob and Maryanne may be perceived as problem learners. However in a classroom that values each individual learner's unique style of learning, Jacob and Maryanne may be perceived as "stars."*

In this chapter, the learning and interactional styles of learners identified as emotionally/behaviorally disordered will be explored.

As in our other descriptions of characteristic and behavior patterns of learners identified as emotionally/behaviorally disordered, we must understand, as Guild (1994) suggests, that "generalizations about a group of people have often led to naive inferences about individuals within the group" (p. 16). In the discussions of this chapter, keep in mind that:

• Learners of any particular age vary in their ways of learning.
• Learning styles emerge from both nature and nurture.
• Learning styles are neutral; one learning style is not better than the other, nor are some "good" and others "bad."

- Within a group, differences are as great as similarities (Guild, 1994).

Teachers and researchers are often tempted to link a specific learning style or interaction pattern to identification as emotionally/behaviorally disordered. However, as Sameroff, Selfer, Barocas, Zax, and Greenspan (1987) discuss, no single factor enhances or limits an individual; the cumulative effects of multiple risk factors increase the probability that an individual's emotional and behavioral development will be compromised.

◊◊ What Are the Issues Related to Learning Styles and Identification as Emotionally/ Behaviorally Disordered?

The Issue of Choice

Weinberg (1992) suggested that learners are not considered emotionally/behaviorally disordered because of their beliefs or behaviors. If the learner simply disagrees with the normative values and practices of society, then he or she does not demonstrate emotional/behavioral disorders. Rather, emotional/behavioral disorders suggest a lack of freedom or an inability to choose a more productive or conventional set of behaviors. The social interactions of an individual identified as emotionally/behaviorally disordered are not immediately manageable by the individual himself or herself. For example, a child identified as emotionally/behaviorally disordered who is withdrawn may desperately want to join the activities at a birthday party, but may be unable to enter the group. With prompts from an adult, rather than feeling safer, the child may become even more withdrawn and threatened. Even though the child wishes he or she were able to enter the group, he or she is unable to choose to do so.

Responses to Interactions

Even among infants, the range of the responses to interactions may be set on a continuum; 10% to 20% of all infants are described as "easy," an additional 10% to 20% are described as "testy," and the remainder fall into the intermediate ranges (Brazelton, 1983).

Greenspan (1995) describes five different groups of children who are challenging in their interactions. The first group, "highly sensitive" children, are those who are articulate, insightful, and empathic, yet are challenging in their mercurial moods. At school age, the sensitive child may stay on the periphery of interactions on the playground, unable to enter what Greenspan refers to as the "politics" of social interactions. Sensitive children are unusually susceptible to embarrassment and humiliation. These children usually have great variations in their moods that are confusing to themselves, their peers, and the adults around them.

A second group of children include those Greenspan refers to as "self-absorbed." These children withdraw often and seem to be content to be passive. Like the highly sensitive child, self-absorbed children stay on the periphery, preferring to stay home or daydream rather than interact with peers. These children have great difficulty with interactions, and miss many of the developmental experiences of "getting out there and mixing it up."

The third group, "defiant" children, on the other hand, have a negative response to virtually everything. Defiant children tend to be concrete, with a strong desire to be organized and in control. They may isolate themselves because other children won't play the way in which they want to play. They tend to be "all-or-nothing" in their ways of thinking, and have difficulty, for example, competing and remaining friends, or having a brief argument and then becoming friends again.

"Inattentive" children, Greenspan's fourth group of difficult children, have difficulty remaining with any activity for a period of time. Inattentive school-age children have difficulty concentrating in the classroom because of the vast amount of stimuli occurring simultaneously. For example, these students are unable to listen to the teacher's voice when there are voices in the hall, an airplane is flying overhead, papers are rustling, or the hamster is spinning his treadmill. These children are very distractible; the complexities of playground games and classroom relationships are lost on them due to the amount of information they lose as a result of their distractibility.

"Active-aggressive" children are described as impulsive and constantly on the go. According to Greenspan, this pattern of behavior is particularly difficult in families in which there is emotional neglect or physical abuse. The more the impulsive, aggressive child's family is engaged in maltreatment, the more likely the child will be violent. Greenspan describes several characteristics of these children:

- They have experienced little consistent care so they have difficulty caring for others.
- They have difficulty purposefully communicating their intentions and feelings.
- They tend not to construct internal dialogue; and rather than speak, they impulsively act.

Multiple Intelligences

Gardner (1993) argues that intelligences cannot be conceptualized apart from the context in which individuals live. Rather than taking a unitary view of intelligence, Gardner and Walters (1993) propose that intelligence involves the ability to solve problems or generate products that are significant to a particular cultural setting or community. This problem-solving skill supports the learner as he or she approaches situations to obtain a goal and plan the most

Table 5.1 Sternberg's Thinking and Learning Styles

Thinking and Learning Style	Description	Example
Legislative	creates, formulates, imagines, plans	enjoys creating original artwork
Executive	implements and engages	prefers problem solving over problem formulation
Judicial	judges, evaluates, compares	prefers commenting and critiquing
Monarchic	addresses one goal at a time	engages in one project to completion before initiating another
Hierarchic	addresses multiple goals with different priorities concurrently	devotes more time to more difficult assignments
Oligarchic	addresses equally important multiple goals	has several simultaneous projects, but is unable to set priorities
Anarchic	shuns rules, procedures, and formal systems	chooses activities randomly
Global	deals with large picture and abstractions	global messages; "meaning" of art
Local	prefers details and concrete issues	describes details of experiences
Liberal	enjoys change and defying conventions	enjoys figuring out new equipment
Conservative	likes traditions and stability	desires precise instructions for performing tasks

appropriate route to the goal. Gardner (1993) utilizes seven intelligences, which he argues present only a preliminary list:

- Linguistic intelligence, related to language and communication
- Logical-mathematical intelligence
- Spatial intelligence, the ability to form a model of the spatial world and to maneuver and operate using that model
- Musical intelligence
- Bodily kinesthetic intelligence, the ability to solve problems or fashion products using the body or parts of the body
- Interpersonal intelligence, the ability to understand people, motivation, and cooperation
- Intrapersonal intelligence, which is the capacity to form an accurate model of oneself and use that model to operate effectively in life.

In contrast to Gardner's multiple intelligences, is Sternberg's (1988) "triarchic model." Sternberg proposes three different kinds of intellectual abilities: analytic, creative, and practical. Learners who are gifted in each of these different intelligences excel in different activities. Those with strengths in analytic intelligence are strong in analyzing, evaluating, and critiquing. Those who are strong in creativity are good at discovering, creating, and inventing. Learners whose strength is practical are strong in implementing, utilizing, and applying. In addition, Grigorenko and Sternberg (1997) describe several styles of thinking and learning. These styles are presented in Table 5.1.

◊◊ What Interpersonal Interactions and Social Skills Do Learners Identified as Emotionally/Behaviorally Disordered Demonstrate?

Perhaps the most obvious interpersonal interaction and social skills that discriminate learners identified as emotionally/behaviorally disordered from their nonidentified peers are "externalizing" problems, such as overactivity, aggression, and impulsivity. These learners are often referred to as "hard to manage" (Campbell & Ewing, 1990). Although overactivity and defiance among two- and three-year-old children may be age-appropriate signs of a developmental transition, higher levels of overactivity and failing to follow directions may be an indicator of more significant challenges and the potential to be identified as emotionally/behaviorally disordered (Campbell & Ewing, 1990; Campbell, Pierce, March,

Ewing, & Szumowski, 1994). Observations in a clinical laboratory of family stress and overactivity and inattention of a three-year-old child were found to predict teacher ratings of hyperactivity and impulse control at age nine (Campbell & Ewing, 1990). Adults' reports of hard-to-manage behavior in preschool-age boys often reflect actual interaction patterns of activity, impulsivity, noncompliance, and aggression that are likely to lead to identification as emotionally/behaviorally disordered (Campbell et al., 1994).

Another perspective on the longitudinal stability of interaction styles thought to be problematic for school success is the "ill-tempered" temperament. Caspi, Bem, and Elder (1989), explored the *"ill-tempered" temperament,* which they described as the inability to delay gratification, control impulses, and modulate emotional expression. They found that ill-tempered boys and girls become both ill-tempered adults, and ill-tempered parents. In their study population, men identified as ill-tempered as boys were described as undercontrolled, irritable, and moody. These men experienced downward occupational mobility, erratic work lives, and were more likely to divorce. Ill-tempered girls became women who married men with lower occupational status, were more likely to divorce, and were described by their husbands and children as ill-tempered mothers.

"ill-tempered" temperament a temperament recognized by the inability to delay gratification, control impulses, and modulate emotional responses

Many learning styles.

Aggression

aggression behavior
exhibited with the
intent to dominate
others

Using a direct observation procedure, Wehby, Symons, and Shores
(1995) found low overall rates of positive social interactions in the
daily classroom ecology of aggressive learners, or those who exhibit *aggression*—behavior exhibited with the intent to dominate
others. Although there were no significant differences in the rates
of teacher instructions toward somewhat aggressive and highly aggressive learners, the highly aggressive learners received almost 3
times as many statements regarding the consequences of their behavior than did the somewhat aggressive learners. This may be because highly aggressive learners engaged in significantly higher
rates of teacher-directed yelling, noncompliance, and other physical behaviors than the less aggressive students. In peer interactions, highly aggressive learners engaged in negative verbal behavior and physical aggression approximately 10 times more often
than did their low aggressive peers; they also received more threats
from others. Rates of teacher praise toward highly aggressive students were found to be very low and accounted for only a small
proportion of antecedents and consequences of the students' aggression.

The peers of boys identified with emotional/behavioral disorders
characterized them as demonstrating significantly more aggression, disruption, and poor cooperation. Within their social networks, boys identified as emotionally/behaviorally disordered in
third through sixth grades formed social affiliations with groups
that were made up of both identified and nonidentified learners
with emotional/behavioral disorders, but exhibited higher levels of
peer-assessed aggression and disruption and lower levels of peer-
assessed cooperation, leadership, and appropriate academic performance than did the members of other social groups in the same
classes (Farmer & Hollowell, 1995).

In his review of the literature, Safran (1995) concluded that
peers hold negative views of externalizing behavior problems
among fellow students. Younger students can identify aggression
as early as the first grade and social withdrawal is recognized soon
thereafter.

Among learners identified as emotionally/behaviorally disordered who have Attention Deficit Hyperactivity Disorder, social interaction patterns have been described as having high rates of intrusive behaviors, problems in conversation and reciprocity, and
poor emotional regulation. These learners may be in a catch-22
circumstance. Positive peer relations play a prominent role in the
development of self-control of aggressive impulses, feelings of ac-
ceptance and belonging, value, self-esteem, and communication

skills. Learners identified as emotionally/behaviorally disordered may, as a consequence of their own behavior, be challenged in having the positive peer relationships that in turn would help them learn to better manage their social behavior (Guevremont & Dumas, 1994).

Passive Aggression

Although aggression is perceived by teachers to be threatening, many indicate that the most difficult learners with whom they work are those who are passive-aggressive. Passive-aggressive students resist control by others to the extent that they simply cannot allow themselves to be cooperative (Fisher, Osterhaus, Clothier, & Edwards, 1994). *Passive-aggressive* learners are those who, when confronted by directions or indicators of appropriate behavior, simply do not respond cooperatively. One of the most difficult challenges related to these learners is that, even if cooperation is in their best interest, they will not be able to cooperate. Learners who are passive-aggressive tend to sabotage reward systems and negative contingencies. Natural consequences are among the most effective strategies for managing their behavior. Students who are passive-aggressive respond best to sincere, spontaneous encouragement of small steps, to choices, and to strong teacher-student relationships.

passive-aggressive responding to direction or indicators of behavior with a lack of response or cooperation

Young children who appear passive-aggressive are often referred to by the diagnosis of "oppositional/defiant disorder" (American Psychiatric Association, 1994). Some research efforts have been aimed at drawing a link between oppositional/defiant disorder and development of conduct disorders in adolescents (Knowlton, 1995). As with learners demonstrating passive-aggression, learners with *oppositional/defiant behaviors* respond to direction or indicators of behavior by refusal or response opposite to that requested; they have disruptive and short-lived peer relationships, are unwilling to assume responsibility for their personal behavior, and sabotage positive feedback to their behavior. As treatment, in addition to consistent and clear consequences, Knowlton (1994) suggests deferring control through the use of written schedules, relying on "the clock" or the class to be in control, and offering choices.

oppositional/defiant behaviors responding to direction or indicators of behavior by refusal or response opposite to that requested

Social Skills

Although often reported to have deficits in social skills, young children identified as emotionally/behaviorally disordered, Brown and Bauer (1994) found, are at times engaged in social interactions to

Learning is doing.

the extent that their teacher perceives them as disruptive. They suggest that the efforts of young children identified as emotionally/behaviorally disordered to connect socially with others often take precedence for them over their teacher's efforts to conduct an activity.

An important facet of social interaction is empathy. Schonert-Reichi (1993) compared empathy among young adult males who were identified as emotionally/behaviorally disordered and those who were not. She reported that teenage males identified as emotionally/behaviorally disordered demonstrated lower levels of empathy, had less frequent contact with friends, and poorer quality relationships than their nonidentified peers. The amount of empathy in individuals identified as emotionally/behaviorally disordered consistently predicted the quality of their relationships.

Effect of Behavior

The behavior of learners has an effect on their teachers. The teacher's response, positive or negative, has an impact on the learner's future responses. Wood (1981) presented a six-step model that traces the progression of the learner's "disturbing" behavior from the point of teacher's awareness of the behavior through the process of identifying the learner as emotionally/behaviorally disordered. This model is presented below:

Step 1:   The teacher's attention is attracted by the behavior of a student.

Step 2:   The teacher decides whether the behavior is pleasing or disturbing. If the behavior is pleasing the teacher either positively reinforces or ignores it. If the teacher finds the behavior disturbing, continue to Step 3.

Step 3:   Is the teacher disturbed sufficiently to take some action to change or stop the disturbing behavior? The teacher's being sufficiently disturbed can be the result of accumulated instances of being disturbed. If the teacher is not sufficiently disturbed to take action, his or her awareness of the disturbing behavior usually begins to lessen. If the teacher is sufficiently disturbed, continue to Step 4.

Step 4:   Teacher wishes to take some action to bring an end to the disturbing behavior. What alternatives are available? An important factor to be considered is the interpersonal power characteristics of the situation. Based on appraisal of social and political factors, the teacher may decide to do nothing, to act immediately, to seek alliances with others who will support taking action to stop or change the student's behavior, or to escape from the situation through transfer or resignation. Continue to Step 5 if the teacher's decision is to take action either alone or in alliance with others.

Step 5:   The teacher's first action is to have the student's behavior labeled publicly as disordered, disruptive, or problematic. Often, at the same time, an additional label suggesting the perceived severity of the problem is attached by those labeling the behavior. This additional label may be "mild," "moderate," or "severe." Continue to Step 6 if those concerned wish to make or can make inferences about the cause of the disordered behavior.

Step 6:   The teacher, usually acting in alliance with the social worker, psychiatrist, psychologist, or others who lend political authority to the labeling process, infers that the student's disturbing behavior is a function of past learning and present environmental factors. The preferred label is behaviorally disordered and the preferred intervention is behavioral.

and/or

The teacher infers that the student's disturbing behavior is a function of past experiences and a present inner emotional state. The preferred label is emotionally disturbed and the preferred intervention is psychodynamic or psychoeducational.

◊◊ What Is the Relationship Between Communicative Competence and Emotional/Behavioral Disorders?

The number of studies focusing on the language disorders of learners identified as emotionally/behaviorally disordered is growing. In studies of the expressive language characteristics in the conversations of learners identified as emotionally/behaviorally disordered and their nonidentified peers, learners identified as emotionally/behaviorally disordered made more errors in relations, demonstrated poor topic maintenance, made inappropriate responses, and used situationally inappropriate language (McDonough, 1989). Among learners identified as demonstrating mild to moderate emotional/behavioral disorders, Camarata, Hughes, and Ruhl (1988) found that 97% of the children were a minimum of one standard deviation below the mean on language ability. Adolescents in psychiatric placement were significantly less effective in their communication than their nonidentified peers (Rosenthal & Simeonsson, 1991). Learners identified as emotionally/behaviorally disordered in residential treatment had significant language disabilities (Warr-Leeper, Wright, & Mack, 1994).

Learners identified as emotionally/behaviorally disordered were found to have difficulties with nonverbal communication as well. In their study of the facial affect cues of adolescents, Walker and Leister (1994) reported that adolescents identified as emotionally/behaviorally disordered are generally less accurate than their nonidentified peers in recognizing facial affect cues of happiness, sadness, fear, anger, surprise, and disgust.

communicative competence knowledge that individual members of a cultural group need to be able to interact with one another in both socially appropriate and strategically effective ways

Communicative competence is comprised of the communicative knowledge that individual members of a cultural group need to be able to interact with one another in both socially appropriate and strategically effective ways (Schultz, Florio, & Erickson, 1982). Carr and Durand (1985) suggest that challenges in communicative competence may indeed be the basis of many behavioral problems. The literature on normal development suggests that as communicative competence increases, behavior problems decrease. Carr and Durand suggest that working with students on communicative strategies could have the effect of decreasing behavior problems.

◊◊ Summary Points

- Learning styles are neutral; no one learning style is better than another.
- Learners identified as emotionally/behaviorally disordered are not free within themselves to choose different learning or interactional styles.
- Learners identified as emotionally/behaviorally disordered may present externalizing or internalizing behaviors.
- The interactions of learners identified as emotionally/behaviorally disordered are marked by greater aggression than those of their nonidentified peers.
- Students' behavior has an effect on the teacher.
- Problems in communicative competence may be the basis of behavioral problems.

◊ **Self-Evaluation**

Select the most appropriate response.
1. Particular learning styles
   a. have been related to identification of learners as emotionally/behaviorally disordered.
   b. may be modified through social skills training.
   c. are only one set of factors among many that determine identification of learners as emotionally/behaviorally disordered.
2. Emotional/behavioral disorders suggest
   a. a lack of choice on the part of the individual regarding his or her behavior.
   b. aggressive interactions.
   c. disagreement with normative values.
3. Overactivity is
   a. an oppositional/defiant behavior.
   b. an externalizing behavior.
   c. an internalizing behavior.

4. Ill-tempered preschoolers often
   a. outgrow these patterns as they mature.
   b. decrease these behaviors with social skills training.
   c. become ill-tempered adults.
5. Students who are aggressive often
   a. are overtly affectionate.
   b. have low overall rates of positive behavior.
   c. have high overall rates of positive behavior as well as aggressive behavior.
6. Learners who are passive-aggressive
   a. respond well to consistent rewards.
   b. respond well to self-identified rewards.
   c. may sabotage reward systems.
7. The social interactions of young children with disabilities
   a. often take precedence for them over their teacher's efforts to conduct an activity.
   b. are marked by passive-aggression.
   c. are more frequently externalizing than internalizing.
8. One factor that may predict the quality of relationships of individuals identified as emotionally/behaviorally disordered is
   a. withdrawal.
   b. passive-aggression.
   c. empathy.
9. A teacher's response to the learner's behavior
   a. has less impact among learners identified as emotionally/behaviorally disordered.
   b. has an impact on the learner's future.
   c. is often negative to learners identified as emotionally/behaviorally disordered.
10. Learners identified as emotionally/behaviorally disordered have difficulties in
    a. expressive language.
    b. receptive language.
    c. expressive, receptive, and nonverbal language.

Making the Language Your Own

Match each key word or phrase to its definition.

_____ 1. behavior exhibited with the intent to dominate others

_____ 2. knowledge that individuals need to be able to interact with one another in both socially appropriate and strategically effective ways

_____ 3. characterized by the inability to delay gratification, control impulses, and modulate emotional responses

_____ 4. responding to direction or indicators of behavior by refusal or response opposite to that requested

_____ 5. responding to direction or indicators of behavior with a lack of response or cooperation

a. ill-tempered temperament
b. aggression
c. oppositional/defiant
d. communicative competence
e. passive-aggressive

Theory into Practice

Observe a classroom in which learners identified as emotionally/behaviorally disordered are included. Are any of these children trapped in a catch-22 situation, for example, lacking experiences in positive social interaction, yet having their efforts in social interaction thwarted? Describe the situation. How could this cycle be broken?

◊◊ **References**

American Psychiatric Association (1994). *Diagnostic and statistical manual of mental disorders* (4th ed.). Washington, DC: Author.

Brazelton, B. (1983). *Infants and mothers: Differences in development.* New York: Delacorte.

Brown, M. S., & Bauer, A. M. (1994). Acting out or acting together? Social community formation and behavior management. *Beyond Behavior, 5*(3), 15–18.

Camarata, S. M., Hughes, C. A., & Ruhl, K. L. (1988). Mild/moderately behaviorally disordered students: A population at risk for language disorders. *Language, Speech, and Hearing Services in the Schools, 19*(2), 191–200.

Campbell, S. B., & Ewing, L. J. (1990). Follow-up of hard-to-manage preschoolers: Adjustment at age 9 and predictors of continuing symptoms. *Journal of Child Psychology and Psychiatry, 31*(6), 871–889.

Campbell, S. B., Pierce, E. W., March, C. L., Ewing, L. J., & Szumowski, E. K. (1994). Hard-to-manage preschool boys: Symptomatic behavior across contexts and time. *Child Development, 65,* 836–851.

Carr, E. G., & Durand, V. M. (1985). The social-communicative basis of severe behavior problems in children. In S. Reiss & R. R. Boutzin (Eds.), *Theoretical issues in behavioral therapy* (pp. 219–254). New York: Academic Press.

Caspi, A., Bem, D. J., & Elder, G. H. (1989). Continuities and consequences of interactional styles across the life course. *Journal of Personality, 57*(2), 375–406.

Farmer, T. W., & Hollowell, J. H. (1995). Social networks in mainstream classrooms: Social affiliations and behavioral characteristics of students with EBD. *Journal of Emotional and Behavioral Disorders, 2*(3), 143–155, 163.

Fisher, D., Osterhaus, N., Clothier, P., & Edwards, L. (1994). Passive-aggressive children in the classroom: The child who won't do anything. *Beyond Behavior, 5*(2), 9–12.

Gardner, H. (1993). In a nutshell. In H. Gardner, (Ed.), *Multiple intelligences: The theory in practice* (pp. 5–12). New York: Basic Books.

Gardner, H., & Walters, J. (1993). A rounded version. In H. Gardner (Ed)., *Multiple intelligences: The theory in practice* (pp. 13–33). New York: Basic Books.

Greenspan, S. I. (1995). *The challenging child: Understanding, raising, and enjoying the five "difficult" types of children.* Reading, MA: Addison Wesley.

Grigorenko, E. L., & Sternberg, R. J. (1997). Styles of thinking, abilities, and academic performance. *Exceptional Children, 63*(3), 295–312.

Guevremont, D. C., & Dumas, M. C. (1994). Peer relationship problems and disruptive behavior disorders. *Journal of Emotional and Behavioral Disorders, 2*(3), 164–172.

Guild, P. (1994, May). The culture/learning style connection. *Educational Leadership 51*(6), 16–21.

Knowlton, D. (1995). Managing children with oppositional behavior. *Beyond Behavior, 6*(3), 5–10.

McDonough, K. M. (1989). Analysis of the expressive language characteristics of emotionally handicapped students in social interactions. *Behavioral Disorders, 14,* 127–139.

Rosenthal, S. L., & Simeonsson, R. J. (1991). Communication skills in emotionally disturbed and nondisturbed adolescents. *Behavioral Disorders, 16,* 192–199.

Safran, S. P. (1995). Peers' perceptions of emotional and behavioral disorders: What are students thinking? *Journal of Emotional and Behavioral Disorders, 3*(2), 66–75.

Sameroff, A. J., Selfer, R., Barocas, R., Zax, M., & Greenspan, S. (1987). Intelligence quotient scores of 4-year-old children: Social environmental risk factors. *Pediatrics, 79*(3), 343–350.

Schonert-Reichi, K. A. (1993). Empathy and social relationships in adolescents with behavioral disorders. *Behavioral Disorders, 18*(3), 189–204.

Shultz, J. J., Florio, S., & Erickson, R. (1982). Where's the floor? Aspects of the cultural organization of social relationships in communication at home and in the school. In P. Gilmore & A. A. Glatthorn (Eds.), *Children in and out of school: Ethnography and education* (pp. 88–123). Washington, DC: Center for Applied Linguistics.

Sternberg, R. (1988). *The triarchic mind: A new theory of human intelligence:* New York: Viking.

Walker, D. W. & Leister, C. (1994). Recognition of facial affect cues by adolescents with emotional and behavioral disorders. *Behavioral Disorders, 19*(4), 269–276.

Warr-Leeper, G., Wright, N. A., & Mack, A. (1994). Language disabilities of antisocial boys in residential treatment. *Behavioral Disorders, 19*(3), 67–78.

Wehby, J. H., Symons, F. J., & Shores, R. E. (1995). A descriptive analysis of aggressive behaviors in classrooms for children with emotional and behavioral disorders. *Behavioral Disorders, 20*(2), 87–105.

Weinberg, L. A. (1992). The relevance of choice in distinguishing seriously emotionally disturbed from socially maladjusted students. *Behavioral Disorders, 20*(2), 87–105.

Wood, F. H. (1981). The influence of personal, social, and political factors on the labeling of students. In F. H. Wood (Ed.), *Perspectives for a New Decade: Education's Responsibility for Seriously Disturbed and Behaviorally Disordered Children and Youth.* Reston, VA: Council for Exceptional Children.

6 Family Factors

TO GUIDE YOUR READING

After you read this chapter, you will be able to answer these questions:

- What family factors are related to identification of learners as emotionally/behaviorally disordered?
- What are the needs identified by parents of learners identified as emotionally/behaviorally disordered?
- What issues are related to family engagement in the education of learners identified as emotionally/behaviorally disordered?
- What social services are available to families of children identified as emotionally/behaviorally disordered?

◊ "In order to develop, a child needs the enduring, irrational involvement of one or more adults in care and joint activity with the child. By irrational, I mean 'Somebody has got to be crazy about that kid.'" (Bronfenbrenner, 1978).

◊ I still remember going shopping with one of our foster children who was identified as emotionally/behaviorally disordered. He was 3 years old, yet had few words, and couldn't express his anger or frustration with words. I had to stop by the grocery store with him after preschool, even though he was tired and cranky. As we were waiting in the check-out line, which in his mind just wasn't moving fast enough, he began banging on my hands and biting them. He'd grab a candy bar, and I'd take it away. He'd grab a handful of my hair, and I'd have to pry his fingers out of it. The woman in front of me said, "Can't you control him?" I replied, "No." Audibly, yet to herself, she said, "Some parents just shouldn't be parents." What did she know about living with this 35-pound tornado? Who was she to judge that the both of us weren't doing the best we could?

◊ As Jessie's teacher began to get frustrated with her behavior, she began to send me daily notes. These notes weren't efforts at problem solving, but were essentially "shopping lists" of Jessie's behaviors. The notes would say something like: "Today, Jessie scratched herself and two other students, threw her books when she came back from math, and refused to return to her seat after I made several requests." I responded two or three times with questions, such as "When do these problems seem to occur most frequently?" "Has Jessie been getting her medication on time?" "Has there been a change in the schedule?" I was trying to prod the teacher into problem solving. These efforts received no response. After 2 weeks of these notes, I sent the teacher a note that read, "Last night Jessie spit green beans at her brother, squirted toothpaste all over the sink, and refused to go to bed until I made several requests." What makes her think that Jessie only pulls stunts like this at school? And why isn't she trying to figure out what's going on rather than just "tattling" on her?

Gardner (1983) contends that family factors help determine which of our "multiple intelligences" are valued and amplified and which are allowed to remain dormant. In addition, family factors such as socioeconomic status have a powerful influence on the identification of school problems. For example, children with learning disabilities from higher socioeconomic classes are significantly more successful in the long-term than those from lower socioeconomic classes (O'Connor & Spreen, 1988). Green (1992) suggests that improvement, deterioration, or stability of each child's vulnerabilities are partly a function of the child's family context.

In this chapter we explore family factors and interaction styles related to emotional/behavioral disorders. Engaging families is also discussed. The chapter concludes with an examination of social services and learners identified as emotionally/behaviorally disordered.

◊◊ What Family Factors Are Related to Identification of Learners as Emotionally/Behaviorally Disordered?

In his description of the contexts of human development, Bronfenbrenner (1979) emphasizes the potential impact of the family on each learner. In a family in which there is responsiveness, reciprocity, and a mutual positive feeling, the learner is more likely to have a positive impact. Bronfenbrenner stresses the need for the developing individual to have a strong and enduring emotional attachment to another individual in order to facilitate learning and development. Several family factors may, then, have an impact on the individual to the extent that he or she may be identified as emotionally/behaviorally disordered.

Family Composition

Historically, a substantial number of children have spent all or part of their childhood in a one-parent household because of the death of a parent, divorce, or having an unmarried parent. Hernandez (1994) reports that 28% to 34% of Euro-American children born between 1920 and 1960 lived with one or no biological parents during their childhood. Based on projections of children born since 1980, he contends that 50% of Euro-American children may be living with one parent. Among African American children this figure may reach 80%. These projections are linked to an increase in the percentage of parents who divorce in Euro-American families, and an increase in the percentage of parents who divorce or never marry in African American families.

According to Bronfenbrenner (1970), the absence of a father in the family contributes to low motivation for achievement, inability to defer rewards, low self-esteem, susceptibility to group influence, and juvenile delinquency among children. These characteristics are more marked in boys than girls.

Bronfenbrenner (1970) describes the social changes that have occurred in families since World War II as "the unmaking of the

American child." He argues that, for the most part, children are no longer brought up by their parents. For several reasons, actual responsibility for the upbringing of children has shifted away from the family to other settings in society. In past generations, families were larger, allowing for more natural child care practices and greater parent/child support. In addition, children were acquainted with a substantially greater number of adults in different walks of life and were more likely to be active participants in adult settings when they did enter them. Currently, children have a small circle of friends and often friendships are limited to child care settings, school bus or car, telephone contacts, and prearranged activities. Finally, parents simply do not spend as much time with their children as in previous generations. Bronfenbrenner suggests that if institutions in our society continue to remove parents, other adults, and older youth from active participation in the lives of children, and if the resulting vacuum is filled by the age-segregated peer group, we can anticipate increased alienation, indifference, antagonism, and violence on the part of the younger

An evening at home.

generation in all segments of our society, including middle-class and affluent children. If children have contact with only their own age-mates, there is a reduced possibility for learning culturally established patterns of cooperation and mutual concern.

Very young single mothers experience additional stressors. Prater (1992) contends that keeping single mothers in school and successful is essential to the welfare of their children. In her study of 10 African American adolescent mothers at risk of dropping out of school, Prater reports that several structures and strategies supported these mothers in their efforts to remain in school and be supportive of their babies. School-based clinics, with family-planning services, were essential. In addition, peer counseling and a network of positive role models were recommended. The mothers reported a high level of insensitivity from their teachers, who gave them little recognition for their unique roles as parenting students. Affordable day-care or baby-sitting services were essential, in that the intergenerational pattern of early pregnancy produced very young grandmothers who did not have the time, desire, or money to stay home and baby-sit their grandchildren.

Child Maltreatment

Child maltreatment is an ongoing pattern of behavior in which individuals involved influence one another and cause disturbances in the caretaking process (Cicchetti, Toth, & Hennessy, 1989). Asen, George, Piper, and Stevens (1989) found that the identification of the typical pattern of abuse was a helpful first step in planning the management and treatment of families engaged in child abuse. Although educators are not the primary help-giving professionals in cases of maltreatment, they should be aware of the various kinds of maltreatment. Asen et al. identified eight patterns of abuse: helpless and help-recruiting, professional, transgenerational, stand-in, distance-regulating, transferred, cultural, and denied.

In the helpless and help-recruiting pattern, families appear to have a limited range of skills for dealing with everyday issues and thus resort to abuse. In professional abuse, the professional becomes overinvolved in the family's problem and assumes parents' duties and responsibilities. Transgenerational abuse occurs when the grandparents become involved in rearing their grandchildren by accepting the caretaking role or as a consequence of sharing a residence with their child's family. In some cases, this results in a repetition of the cycle of poor parenting and abuse that occurred when the grandparents were rearing their children. In other cases, the fact that the child's biological parents remain dependent on the

child maltreatment
child abuse and neglect

grandparents gives the grandparents a second opportunity to parent. In this situation, unresolved problems related to the parent's own childhood may be reactivated.

The fourth pattern of abuse discussed by Asen et al. (1989) is stand-in abuse. If one parent has a close relationship with the child and the relationship between the parents is distant, then abuse of the child may represent a means of punishing the partner without undermining the marriage. In times of crisis, the child is singled out and punished or the child learns to behave in a manner that elicits abuse. In distance-regulating abuse, the child learns that the only way to achieve close physical contact with the mother or father is to behave in such a way as to evoke punishment. The child appears to seek the positive contact that follows the parent's anger and punishment.

Transferred abuse is a complex and difficult pattern to understand. Intense experiences from the parent's past are transferred to the present, and the child becomes the target of the feeling associated with the parent's past experiences. The parent apparently superimposes the past on the present. Cultural abuse is evident when families state that their behavior toward their children is appropriate from the perspective of their cultural origins, even though their behavior is not accepted in the culture in which they presently live or by authorities within that culture. The final pattern discussed by Asen et al. (1989) is denied abuse, in which the child is injured but the cause of the injury is denied by the abusing parent.

Maltreatment rarely occurs in isolation; the vast majority of maltreated children are submitted to a combination of physical neglect, physical abuse, and verbal abuse (Ney, Fund, & Wickett, 1994). *The Child Abuse Prevention and Treatment Act* (Public Law 93-247), uses the terms *child abuse* and *child neglect* to refer to physical or mental injury, sexual abuse, or neglect of an individual less the 18 years of age by a person responsible for the child's welfare under circumstances that indicate that the child's health or welfare is harmed or threatened. Reported incidents of child abuse and neglect increased 225% from 1978 to 1987 (Alsop, 1990).

Children who have experienced maltreatment demonstrate differences from nonmaltreated peers in behavior and achievement. Crittenden (1989) reported that maltreated children are often disruptive, defiant bullies who have frequent interpersonal confrontations with peers and teachers. Some of these children may be defiant, spending more time fighting than learning. Others may become so compliant and concerned over meeting others' standards that they rarely experience joy or satisfaction. Overcompli-

---

Child Abuse Prevention and Treatment Act of 1974 provided mechanisms for reporting and preventing child abuse and neglect, including legal definitions of *child abuse* and *neglect*

child abuse physical or mental injury or sexual abuse of a child under the age of 18 years by a person responsible for the child's welfare under circumstances that indicate that the child's health or welfare is harmed or threatened

child neglect failing to provide for the physical, medical, emotional, or educational needs of a child by an individual responsible for the child's welfare

ant abused children are so concerned with finding the right answer that they are frequently unable to attend to and manipulate
ideas and concepts.

In a study of the long-term impact of three kinds of abuse—
physical, emotional, and sexual—on children, Mullen, Martin, Anderson, Romans, and Herbison (1996) reported that a history of
any form of abuse was associated with increased rates of psychopathology, sexual difficulties, decreased self-esteem, and interpersonal problems. Mullen et al. found a similarity among the
three kinds of abuse and adult outcomes, although there was a
trend for sexual abuse to be associated with sexual problems,
emotional abuse with low self-esteem, and physical abuse with
marital breakdown. Some of the associations between abuse and
adult problems were accounted for by childhood disadvantages
from which the abuse often emerged.

Child and parent characteristics, alone, are not sufficient to explain child maltreatment (Janko, 1994). The environment may add
elements of stress or support to the child-caregiver relationship,
such as having enough money, food, housing, health care, and the
availability of adults to share caregiving responsibilities. Stressors
occur within the family, through community resources, and in responses to social policies. As Janko suggests, a young mother who
is learning to parent her challenging baby in the context of brief
weekly visits with the child protection worker, while lacking psychological and emotional support that comes from reliable family
and friends, consistent meals, a place to sleep, and the knowledge
that her belongings are accessible and safe, is under significant
stress.

◊◊ What Family Interaction Patterns May Be Related to Emotional/Behavioral Disorders?

Families of individuals with members identified as emotionally/be-
haviorally disordered must be recognized for their strengths. Seligman and Darling (1989) suggest that these strengths are demonstrated by the fact that, despite the challenges of parenting a child
with a disability, most are able to achieve a nearly normal lifestyle,
and that most families adapt. They describe this "normalization"
as a normal-appearing lifestyle. In some families, however, normalization appears elusive, and other adaptations may emerge.
Additional family adaptation patterns may include (a) crusader-
ship, in which the family engages actively in efforts to support social change, ranging from campaigns to increase public awareness
to active participation in advocacy groups; (b) altruism, in which

families remain active with parents of younger children to help them meet their family's needs; and (c) resignation, in which families become resigned to their "problematic existence" and become isolated from their extended family and other families.

Mlawler (1993) further explores the difficulty of families in adapting as "families with a member with a disability." He argues that in the attempt to help parents become better educational advocates for their children with disabilities, parents and professionals have created an advocacy expectation that runs counter to the philosophy of normalization. He suggests that to truly empower parents, programs that are capable of engaging in advocacy along with and on behalf of parents must be developed. These programs should be free, easy to access, and have an available group of independent, uncompromised special educators who serve as experts on behalf of students.

Social systems theory prevents us from making any specific cause-and-effect statements regarding family interaction styles and emotional/behavioral disorders. However, there are family interactions styles that seem to increase the likelihood that a learner will be identified as emotionally/behaviorally disordered.

Green (1992) summarized research on an "underorganized" family structure, which is often related to learners identified as emotionally/behaviorally disordered. In the underorganized family:

- Parents use global and erratic controls with their children to the extent that consistent behavioral contingencies are not present.
- Disciplinary responses are based on the parents' needs rather than their children's needs.
- Conflicts are resolved by threats and counterthreats rather than discussions that lead to closure.
- Verbal and logical communication is replaced by intense physical action and sound.
- Family members do not expect to be listened to and thus resort to yelling.
- Compliance is insured by the use of force, rather than long-term solutions or negotiated responses.
- Communication is marked by disconnected interruptions and abrupt topic changes.

In school, the children of underorganized families have difficulty focusing their attention. Their communication style is disruptive and precludes the integration of new information. Their behavior is focused on eliciting authoritarian or proximal control from the teacher rather than from achievement or from engaging in the tasks at hand. The families of many learners identified as emotionally/behaviorally disordered follow this underorganized pattern, and are chaotic, disorganized, and less cohesive than the families of their nonidentified peers.

A second family structure that Green suggests is the "overorganized" family, characterized by parent intrusiveness, overinvolvement, and protective restrictions. Parents' attempts to control their child result in the child's obsessive worry, performance anxiety, procrastination, passive-aggression, or oppositional behavior. In this pattern, parents take too much responsibility for the child's performance, and the child rebels or takes too little responsibility for achievement.

Green (1992) presents four factors in family interaction patterns that impact on the child's school-related behavior. First, the child may have information-processing problems that are maintained by unusual family communication patterns. Second, the child's problems in attention may be maintained or amplified by an underorganized family structure with disruptive communication patterns. The third factor involves the child's passive-aggression or performance anxiety that is maintained or amplified by an overorganized, rigid family structure. Finally, a child's lack of effort in school may be maintained or amplified by the family's (a) negative attributions about the child's ability and motivation, (b) blaming the child's success or failure on factors outside of the child's control, (c) casting the identified child into an inferior or problem identity when compared to siblings, and (d) parents' modeling of values that minimize the importance of education and undermine school authority.

Whereas some family structures appear to be putting many learners at risk for emotional/behavioral disorders, some family interaction styles may promote the healthy integration of young persons into society. Using a sample of 1,000 eighth graders, Epstein (1983) studied the joint impact of family and classroom processes on change in learners' attitudes and academic achievement during the transition between middle school and high school. She found that children from homes that provided greater opportunities for communication and decision making exhibited greater independence after entering high school and received higher grades. As she contrasted family and classroom processes, family processes were considerably more powerful in producing change than classroom procedures.

With regard to task orientation, Denham, Renwick and Holt (1991) found that in preschool children, a mother who showed affection but set limits allowed the child to be more confident and emotionally positive. Maternal *scaffolding,* or the initial provision of supports with gradual reduction as the child is successful, may influence social/emotional as well as cognitive aspects of development. Denham et al. found that a balance of support and allowance of autonomy enabled children to be more positive. Socially positive girls modeled their mothers' patterns of keeping a social agenda in a friendly way. Boys, however, exhibited less positive social behavior than girls overall. Positive interactions between mother and child, in fact, predicted appropriate emotional and behavioral competence among peers.

In their work with learners identified as having serious problems with social interactions, Ramsey and Walker (1988) studied family management practices related to male fourth graders. Although they found no differences between these learners and their nonidentified peers in the area of involvement, they found significant differences in discipline, monitoring, positive reinforcement, and problem solving. They concluded that learners identified as having serious social interaction problems were exposed to far more negative and less competent family management practices than their peers.

The brothers and sisters of learners identified as emotionally/behaviorally disordered may not be as seriously affected by the behavior of their identified sibling as one may assume. Gargiulo, O'Sullivan, and Wesley (1992) found that differences among families may be related to family resources and characteristics that might foster positive patterns of sibling adjustment, rather than the presence of the individual identified as having emotional/behavioral disorders or another disability.

◊◊ What Are Needs of Parents of Learners Identified as Emotionally/Behaviorally Disordered?

Using the National Education Longitudinal Study of 1988, Masino and Hodapp (1996) chose students with disabilities and their matched peers with no identified disabilities and contrasted parent expectations. Despite lower college participation rates among students with disabilities, parent expectations were found to be slightly higher for these students. Masino and Hodapp concluded that parents of children with disabilities and parents of children without disabilities have similar expectations for their children's educational attainment.

Student outcomes may not be the greatest concern of parents, however. Green and Shinn (1995) reported that parent satisfaction with special education programs was not related to children's academic performance. Rather, parents were most satisfied when their children received individual attention, when teachers were responsive and friendly, and when their child's self-esteem increased.

Professionals must be careful not to make assumptions regarding the needs of parents of learners identified as emotionally/behaviorally disordered. Simpson (1988) found a significant difference between teachers' perceptions of parents' needs and the parents' expressed needs. He reported that the most widely used and/or requested service by parents is information exchange. Parents wanted to receive information through informal feedback, progress reports, conferences, and program information. Parents also requested parent-coordinated service programs, counseling, therapy, consultation, consumer and advocacy training, and home program training.

As children grow older, parents' needs with regard to their children tend to change. In their comparison of parents of children with disabilities and parents of children without disabilities, Whitney-Thomas and Hanley-Maxwell (1996) reported significantly greater discomfort and pessimism among parents of children with disabilities regarding their child's transition to adulthood. Both groups felt that school personnel were important contributors in their child's transition to adulthood.

◊◊ What Are Issues Related to Family Engagement in the Education of Their Child Identified as Emotionally/Behaviorally Disordered?

Family engagement or involvement in the education of children identified as emotionally/behaviorally disordered must be viewed from the perspective of the family, who is the client or consumer. DeChillo and Koren (1995) identified several distinct elements of collaboration from the perspective of family members. First, parents reported the need for support and understanding from professionals in their relationships with family members. Families also needed assistance in the practical aspects of getting services for their child. The clear and open exchange of information between families and professionals was perceived as essential by parents, as well as flexibility and willingness on the part of professionals to modify or change services based on parent feedback. More than half of the families noted the following barriers to engagement in their child's education: (a) professionals' beliefs that families cause children's disorders, (b) insufficient administrative support for staff, (c) child welfare policies that require giving up custody of a

Mom lends a helping hand.

child to get service, (d) the inherent power imbalance between professionals and family members, (e) professionals' lack of knowledge about children's disorders, and (f) professionals' high expectations of families.

Koren and DeChillo (1995) suggest that it is not sufficient to merely provide parents with resources; rather, it is important to foster a process in which parents have both control over current resources and a capability to obtain future resources. Empowering families can occur in three distinct ways: (a) the empowerment of individuals with respect to their circumstances, (b) the empowerment of individuals with respect to others, and (c) the empowerment of groups in relationship to the larger society. By looking at empowerment from this broad perspective, professionals need to help families handle problems within the family at home, deal with service systems on behalf of their child, and influence the service system for all children identified as emotionally/behaviorally disordered.

Voeltz (1994) identified several practices that are counterproductive to engaging parents in the education of their children. One such practice is the use of a menu approach that forces parents into predetermined roles, the shape of which they have little or no control over. Another counterproductive, but common, practice is the way in which school officials "track" or group parents as "concerned parents" who want to be involved in the education of their children and "unconcerned parents" who do not care to be involved in the education of their children. Finally, a lack of sensitivity to cultural differences alienates rather than engages parents.

The successful engagement of parents can have significant impact on children identified as emotionally/behaviorally disordered. Arndorfer, Miltenberger, Woster, Rortvedt, and Gaffney (1994) describe efforts to engage parents, using descriptive and experimental analysis of problem behaviors, in the homes of five young children. The parents were actively involved in the descriptive assessment of their children and manipulated potential control variables during the experimental analysis. The information obtained from different tools, including behavioral interview, direct observation, and experimental analysis, was consistent in indicating the function, or effect, of the behavior for the child. Based on the results of the descriptive analysis, experimental analysis conditions were designed to test specific hypotheses regarding the function of the challenging behavior of the children. The function of the children's behavior was verified in four to six sessions. Intervention involving functional communication training was implemented, based on assessment results, for two of the children. The functional assessment results were validated for the children. The study, which employed parents in the natural environment of the home, indicated that functional assessment procedures may be useful and practical in natural settings.

Using the home and natural conditions to engage parents in the education of their children identified as emotionally/behaviorally disordered may also have an impact on parents' willingness to participate. Reimers and Wacker (1988) found that the amount of disruption an intervention causes, in relationship to the willingness of parents to participate, is initially of greatest importance to parents working with their children's behavior in the home. However, once interventions were in place, the more effective parents believed the treatment to be, the more likely they were to accept and continue the interventions.

Cultural Diversity and Parent Engagement

Cultural, linguistic, and ethnic minority parents often confront stereotypes regarding their engagement in their children's education. Allen, Harry, and McLaughlin (1995) suggest that school systems may not encourage proactive parent involvement, and the we-they stance assumed by many professionals may be the factor that breaks down communication. In their study, Allen et al. found that African American parents not only participated in homework and behavioral issues regarding their children, but also expressed faith in the value of education for success. However, when there was no active communication with teachers, the parents expressed confusion and distress with the special education assessment and placement process. McIntyre and Silva (1992) contend that most educators' lack of knowledge regarding both child abuse and culturally different child-rearing practices creates fertile ground for misjudging the appropriateness of parents' practices. Teachers who adhere to the disciplinary practices of the majority culture may find themselves viewing culturally different practices as being abusive. This would mean that the use of culturally diverse child-rearing practices places parents at greater risk for being reported to agencies responsible for abuse and neglect reports.

In their study relating culture and socioeconomic status and professional collaboration, DeGangi, Wietlisbach, Poisson, Stein, and Royeen (1994) found that professionals reported that they spend more time with families from different cultural backgrounds in (a) identifying family concerns, (b) attempting to understand family needs and customs, and (c) explaining the Individualized Family Service Plan. These professionals also reported that families from lower socioeconomic groups and with limited educational backgrounds were often concerned with basic survival needs, such as housing, food, and clothing, and consequently, tended to defer to the professional when discussing the Individualized Family Service Plan. Finally, it was found that the families had difficulty identifying the child's needs and were cautious in sharing information.

◊◊ What Social Services Are Available to Families of Children Identified as Emotionally/Behaviorally Disordered?

Cohen (1980) argues that services for families occur within a system of interrelated and interacting parts. The client and professional are in the foreground whenever service is provided. However, equally critical background components that impact on the provision of social services also exist. These components include (a) the technology underlying the service, (b) administrative and management personnel, (c) existing pattern of human services into which the new system is introduced, (d) political and economic conditions, and (e) the feedback among components within the system and the consequences of that feedback on system change. In addition, Cohen asserts that human services have an independent life cycle during which these five components change over time.

As a result of his analysis of the outcomes of early intervention practices, Bronfenbrenner (1975) coined the term "family-centered services" and recommended increased parent engagement in their children's early education. Dunst, Johanson, Trivette, and Hamby

(1991) describe several different models for family-oriented programs:

- Professionally centered models, in which professionals are experts who determine child and family needs.
- Family-allied models, in which families are viewed as the agents of professionals and implement interventions that professionals design and determine.
- Family-focused models, in which families are seen as consumers of professional services.
- Family-centered models, in which professionals are instruments of families and professionals intervene in individualized, flexible, and responsive ways.

In their study of parents' assessment of the help-giving practices of professionals, Trivette, Dunst, Boyd, and Hamby (1995) reported that differences were found to be related to the program models and not parent or family characteristics. Parents' perceptions of the amount of control they felt they had over services were also related to the models and not to any parent or family characteristics.

In his discussion of families, Garbarino (1992) suggests that to be successful in raising healthy children families need at least seven things:

- Stable environment: when the environment is not stable children are likely to be neglected or abandoned.
- Security: when parents are threatened by violence, their capacity to nurture and protect children is weakened.
- Positive and involved time together.
- Active, caring community: isolation threatens the welfare of both parents and children.
- Justice: the greater the justice, the more likely it is that the family will receive the support it needs.
- Access to basic resources: the lack of food, housing, and health care places children in jeopardy.

Poverty

With regard to learners identified as emotionally/behaviorally disordered, there is a greater need for comprehensive community services in communities that are poor (Soderland, Epstein, Quinn, Cumblad, & Petersen, 1995). Garbarino (1992) contends that most children experience poverty not as an isolated event but as an on-

going condition of their lives. Poverty persists throughout childhood for at least 1 in 5 children, with the rate for young children
being higher. Currently in our society, there is an increase in need
for social services with a decrease in funding. Among the inner-city
poor, marginal and submarginal economic resources are combined
with personal resources that are diminished as a result of violence,
academic failure, exploitation, despair, fear, and deteriorated community infrastructure. Violence is pervasive in some impoverished
communities. In a recent study of the life of preschoolers in an inner-city public housing project, all the mothers cited "shooting" as
their greatest fear for their children (Dubrow & Garbarino, 1988).

Substitute Care

substitute care the placement of children for rearing with other than their biological parents

When families are no longer able to meet the needs of their children, the children may enter **substitute care,** or the placement of
children for rearing with other than their biological parents. As
larger numbers of children enter foster care, the population of foster children has grown in size and the complexity of the children's
problems has increased (Schor, 1988). Foster children today have
more serious physical and emotional problems than in the past.

foster care substitute-care placement that is typically licensed and regulated by state human service agencies

Foster care is substitute-care placement that is typically licensed and regulated be state human services agencies. Foster
care placement is intended to be a planned, temporary service implemented to strengthen families so that they can again care for
their children (Schor, 1988). Ideally, if after studying the family
and providing appropriate services, uniting the child and the family is impossible or not in the best interest of the child, parents'
rights are terminated and the child is placed with an adoptive family. There are, however, some children for whom neither reunion
with their family nor adoption is feasible. Frequently, these children remain with foster care families, in various settings and on a
temporary basis, until they reach maturity.

The current foster care population is composed of approximately
equal numbers of males and females. Forty percent of the population is children from minority cultures. Twenty-five percent of the
population is disabled. Approximately three quarters of the children are in foster placements because of maltreatment; most of
these children return to their biological families within one year.
Twenty percent of the children re-enter foster care within a year of
discharge. Twenty-five percent of children are likely to remain in
foster care after a two-year placement. The number of children entering foster care and the severity of their physical, emotional, and
social problems are increasing. Social service agencies are having
increasing difficulties recruiting and retaining foster care parents.

Children in foster care may have more frequent and serious health problems than children living with their biological families. Schor (1988) reports that these children tend to be physically smaller than their peers, have more frequent developmental delays, and more serious emotional problems. Learners in foster care have significantly greater delays and major deficits in adaptive behavior (Hochstadt, Jaudes, Zimo, and Schachter, 1987). Many of these children are identified as emotionally/behaviorally disordered.

Substitute care is a challenge to both child and family. Normal developmental family processes are disrupted by foster care (Elbow, 1986). Biological families begin with dependent relationships and progress toward individuation, as the children assume more and more responsibility for their personal lives. The members of the substitute family begin as independent individuals and progress toward attachments. This process is further limited by the temporary nature of the placement.

The *Adoption Assistance and Child Welfare Act of 1980* (Public Law 96-272) was a consequence of national concern for children who were "adrift in foster care" (Seltzer & Blocksberg, 1987). The law emphasized the need to develop plans for the permanent placement of children in need of out-of-home placement for either a short or extended period of time. The idea of permanency planning was described by Maluccio and Fein (1983) as a process of designing and implementing a set of goal-directed activities aimed to help children live in families that offer ongoing relationships with nurturing individuals and the opportunity to establish lifetime relationships. The process of permanency planning is intended to (a) protect the child, (b) support stable relationships between child and caregivers, (c) preserve the biological family, and (d) enhance the psychosocial and behavioral adjustment of the child. Selzer and Blocksberg (1987) report a higher rate of adoption from foster care when social service workers and agencies accept the philosophy of permanency planning.

Adoption Assistance and Child Welfare Act of 1980 provided subsidies for families adopting special needs children; mandated state procedures for promptly terminating parents' rights when appropriate to facilitate permanency for children

Head Start

Head Start, from its inception, included parent engagement in several forms: participating on policy councils and boards, working as classroom volunteers, and assuming paid staff positions. As it developed, Head Start implemented additional demonstration programs to broaden parent engagement, including Home Start and Project Developmental Continuity (PDC). Through work with parents, Head Start is a "two generation program," recognizing parents, as well as their children, as participants (Collins, 1993).

Collins (1993) suggests that Head Start is one of the few institutions trusted by individuals who are poor or from diverse ethnic, cultural, or linguistic groups, as well as local community leaders and service providers. Since 1972, Head Start has collaborated with state and local education agencies to identify children with special needs. In addition, Head Start provides child health screening, and connects families to programs such as the Special Supplemental Food Program for Women, Infants, and Children (WIC). Head Start is placing more emphasis on creating greater family support through the use of family services coordinators grounded in a "family strengths" model (Gage & Workman, 1994).

The Legal-Correctional System

There are four stages in the legal-correctional system for children (Apter & Conoley, 1984). The first stage is stationhouse adjudication, which refers to informal warnings given by police to minors, usually at the police station. Parents are generally called to pick up the children, and no further action is taken against the child. Petition and authorization, the second stage, is the beginning of the formal court referral process. Court intake staff contact the police, parents, and others to develop information about a specific complaint or violation. Unofficial interventions begin at this step, usually involving a juvenile referee or social worker. At the third phase, which may include detention, hearings, and preliminary examinations, the court engages in a series of evaluations and hearings regarding the case. The juvenile referee may make any number of judgments, ranging from confinement in a juvenile detention facility to day treatment, counseling, and community service. During the final stage, the adjudication phase, the child's case goes to court. The child may be "warned and admonished," placed in any number of settings ranging from group home to foster care, or be placed on detention. Probation is frequently used as an alternative.

◊◊ Summary Points

- Family composition and structure may put children at risk for emotional/behavioral disorders.
- Child maltreatment is not a single event; rather, it is an ongoing pattern of behavior.
- Children who experience maltreatment demonstrate differences from their peers in behavior and achievement.
- Although social systems theory eschews any cause-effect relationships between parent behavior and identification of learners

as emotionally/behaviorally disordered, underorganized families are often related to learners identified as emotionally/behaviorally disordered.

- Successfully engaging parents may have a positive impact on the education of learners identified as emotionally/behaviorally disordered.
- Families of learners identified as emotionally/behaviorally disordered may be engaged in community services substitute care, Head Start, or the legal-correctional system.

◊   **Self-Evaluation**

Select the most appropriate response.
1. One-parent households
   a. are a new phenomenon.
   b. are typically dysfunctional.
   c. have historically been home to a substantial number of children.
2. The absence of a father
   a. has little relationship to achievement or behavior.
   b. has less impact when the mother is self-sufficient.
   c. has a greater impact on boys than girls.
3. When children have contact only with their age-mates,
   a. they tend to mature more slowly.
   b. they have less opportunity to learn culturally established patterns of behavior.
   c. they have a greater opportunity to model appropriate behavior.
4. Child maltreatment
   a. is often an isolated event related to parent stress.
   b. often occurs in homes in which the father is absent.
   c. rarely occurs in isolation.
5. Most maltreatment may be explained by
   a. parent characteristics.
   b. child and parent characteristics.
   c. environment, resources, stressors, and individual characteristics.
6. Learners identified as emotionally/behaviorally disordered
   a. have a significant negative effect on their siblings.
   b. frequently force family disruption.
   c. are exposed to more negative and less competent family practices.
7. Professionals
   a. are accurate judges of parents' needs.
   b. should conduct accurate needs assessments.
   c. often perceive parents' needs differently from the parents themselves.

8. Families from diverse cultural backgrounds
   a. are more frequently engaged in child abuse than majority culture families.
   b. frequently use more services than other families.
   c. may be cautious in sharing information.
9. Differences in the engagement of parents in services has been related to
   a. parent characteristics.
   b. program models.
   c. child characteristics.
10. Poverty is experienced by most children as
    a. a transitional event.
    b. an ongoing event.
    c. a short-term problem.

Making the Language Your Own

Match each key word or phrase to its definition.

_____ 1. child neglect

_____ 2. child abuse

_____ 3. substitute care

_____ 4. foster care

_____ 5. child maltreatment

_____ 6. child Abuse Prevention and Treatment Act

_____ 7. adoption Assistance and Child Welfare Act

_____ 8. scaffolding

a. mandated state procedures for promptly terminating parents' rights when appropriate to facilitate permanency for children
b. provided mechanisms for reporting and prevention of child abuse and neglect
c. physical or mental injury or sexual abuse of a child under the age of 18 years by a person responsible for the child's welfare under circumstances that indicate that the child's health or welfare is harmed or threatened
d. failing to provide for the physical, medical, emotional, or educational needs of a child by an individual responsible for the child's welfare
e. child abuse and neglect
f. placement that is typically licensed and regulated by state human service agencies
g. initial provision of supports with gradual reduction as the child is successful
h. the placement of children for rearing with other than their biological parents

Theory into Practice

1. Contact your local child welfare office. Request the licensure requirements for foster care. Are these requirements adequate to prepare foster parents of learners identified as emotionally/behaviorally disordered?
2. Attend a parent support group. What topics were addressed? What were the parents' perceptions of professionals?

◊◊ References

Allen, N., Harry, B., & McLaughlin, M. (1995). Communication versus compliance: African-American parents' involvement in special education. *Exceptional Children, 61*(4), 364–377.

Alsop, R. (1990). *News release: Data on child abuse and neglect.* Denver, CO: American Humane Association.

Amerikaner, M. J., & Omizo, M. M. (1984). Family interaction and learning disabilities. *Journal of Learning Disabilities, 17,* 540–543.

Apter, S. J., & Conoley, J. C. (1984). *Childhood behavior disorders and emotional disturbance.* Upper Saddle River, NJ: Prentice Hall.

Arndorfer, R. E., Miltenberger, R. G., Woster, S. H., Rortvedt, A. K., & Gaffney, T. (1994). Home-based descriptive and experimental analysis of problem behaviors in children. *Topics in Early Childhood Special Education, 14*(1), 64–87.

Asen, K., George, E., Piper, R., & Stevens, A. (1989). A systems approach to child abuse: Management and treatment issues. *Child Abuse and Neglect, 13,* 45–57.

Bronfenbrenner, U. (1975). Is early intervention effective? In M. Guttentag & E. Struening (Eds.), *Handbook of evaluation research* (Vol. 2, pp. 519–603). Newbury Park, CA: Sage.

Bronfenbrenner, U. (1970). *Two worlds of childhood.* New York: Russell Sage Foundation.

Bronfenbrenner, U. (1978). Who needs parent education? *Teachers College Record, 79,* 773–774.

Bronfenbrenner, U. (1979). *The ecology of human development.* Cambridge, MA: Harvard University Press.

Cicchetti, D., Toth, S., & Hennessy, K. (1989). Research on the consequences of child maltreatment and its application to educational settings. *Topics in Early Childhood Special Education, 9*(2), 33–55.

Cohen, S. (1980). Multiple impacts and determinants in human service delivery systems. In R. Turner & H. Reese (Eds.), *Life span developmental psychology: Intervention* (pp. 125–248). New York: Academic Press.

Collins, R. C. (1993). Head Start: Steps toward a two-generation program strategy. *Young Children, 48*(2), 25–73.

Crittenden, P. M. (1989). Teaching maltreated children in the preschool. *Topics in Early Childhood Special Education, 9*(2), 16–32.

DeChillo, N., & Koren, P. E. (1995). Just what is "collaboration"? *Focal Point, 9*(1), 1, 5–6.

De Gangi, G. A., Wietlisbach, S., Poisson, S., Stein, E., & Royeen, C. (1994). The impact of culture and socioeconomic status on family-professional collaboration: Challenges and solutions. *Topics in Early Childhood Special Education, 14*(4), 503–520.

Denham, S. A., Renwick, S. M., & Holt, R. W. (1991). Working and playing together: Prediction of preschool social-emotional competence from mother-child interaction. *Child Development, 62,* 242–249.

Dubrow, N., & Garbarino, J. (1988). Living in the war zone: Mothers and children in a public housing project. *Child Welfare, 68,* 3–20.

Dunst, C. J., Johanson, C., Trivette, C. M., & Hamby, D. (1991). Family-oriented early intervention policies and practices: Family centered or not? *Exceptional Children, 58,* 115–126.

Elbow, M. (1986). From caregiving to parenting: Family formation with adopted older children. *Social Work, 31,* 366–370.

Epstein, J. L. (1983). Longitudinal effects of family-school-person interactions on student outcomes. *Research in Sociology of Education and Socialization, 4,* 101–127.

Gage, J., & Workman, S. (1994). Creating family support systems: In Head Start and beyond. *Young Children, 50*(1), 74–77.

Garbarino, J. (1992). The meaning of poverty in the world of children. *American Behavioral Scientists, 35,* 220–237.

Gardner, H. (1983). *Frames of mind: The theory of multiple intelligences.* New York: Basic Books.

Gargiulo, R. M., O'Sullivan, P. S., & Wesley, K. (1992). Sibling relationships involving school children with acquired/congenital and visible/invisible disabilities. *Issues in Special Education and Rehabilitation, 7*(2), 7–23.

Green, R. (1992). Learning to learn and the family system: New perspectives on underachievement and learning disorders. In M. J. Fine & C. Carlson (Eds.), *The handbook of family-school interventions: A systems perspective* (pp. 157–174). Boston: Allyn & Bacon.

Green, S. K., & Shinn, M. R. (1995). Parent attitudes about special education and reintegration: What is the role of student outcomes? *Exceptional Children, 61*(3), 269–281.

Hernandez, D. J. (1994). Children's changing access to resources: A historical perspective. *Society for Research in Child Development Social Policy Report, 8*(1), 1–23.

Hochstadt, N. J., Jaudes, P. K., Zimo, D. A., & Schachter, J. (1987). The medical and psychosocial needs of children entering foster care. *Child Abuse and Neglect, 11,*(1), 53–62.

Janko, S. (1994). *Vulnerable children, vulnerable families.* New York: Teachers' College Press.

Koren, P. E., & DeChillo, N. (1995). Empowering families whose children have emotional disorders. *Focal Point, 9*(1), 1–3.

Masino, L. L., & Hodapp, R. M. (1996). Parental educational expectations for adolescents with disabilities. *Exceptional Children, 62*(6), 513–523.

Maluccio, A. N., & Fein, E. (1983). Permanency planning: A redefinition. *Child Welfare, 63,* 197.

McIntyre, T., & Silva, F. (1992). Culturally diverse childrearing practices: Abusive or just different? *Beyond Behavior, 4,*(1), 8–12.

Mlawler, M. A. (1993). Who should fight? Parents and the advocacy expectations. *Journal of Disability Policy Studies, 4*(1), 105–106.

Mullen, P. E., Martin, J. L., Anderson, J. C. Romans, S. E., & Herbison, G. P. (1996). The long-term impact of the physical, emotional, and sexual abuse of children: A community study. *Child Abuse and Neglect, 20*(1), 7–21.

Ney, P. G., Fund, T., & Wickett, A. R. (1994). The worst combinations of child abuse and neglect. *Child Abuse and Neglect, 18*(9), 705–714.

O'Connor, S. C., & Spreen, O. (1988). The relationship between parents' socioeconomic status and education level, and adult occupational and educational achievement of children with learning disabilities. *Journal of Learning Disabilities, 21,* 158–143.

Prater, L. P. (1992). Early pregnancy and academic achievement of African-American youth. *Exceptional Children, 59,* 141–149.

Ramsey, E., & Walker, H. M. (1988). Family management correlates of antisocial behavior among middle school boys. *Behavioral Disorders, 13,* 187–201.

Reimers, T. M., & Wacker, D. P. (1988). Parents' ratings of the acceptability of behavioral treatment made in an outpatient clinic: A preliminary analysis of the influence of treatment effectiveness. *Behavioral Disorders, 14*(1), 7–15.

Schor, E. L. (1988). Foster care. *The Pediatric Clinics of North America, 35*(6), 1241, 1252.

Seligman, M., & Darling, L. B. (1989). *Ordinary Families, special children.* NY: Guildford.

Seltzer, M. M., & Blocksberg, L. M. (1987). Permanency planning and its effects on foster children: A review of the literature. *Social Work, 37,* 65–68.

Soderlund, J., Epstein, M. H., Quinn, K. P., Cumblad, C., & Petersen, S. (1995). Parental perspectives on comprehensive services for children and youth with emotional and behavioral disorders. *Behavior Disorders, 20*(3), 157–170.

Simpson, R. L. (1988). Needs of parents and families whose children have learning behavior problems. *Behavioral Disorders, 14*(1), 40–47.

Trivette, C. M., Dunst, C. J., Boyd, K., & Hamby, D. W. (1995). Family-oriented program models, helpgiving practices, and parental control appraisals. *Exceptional Children, 62*(3), 237–248.

Voeltz, D. L. (1994). Developing collaborative parent-teacher relationships with culturally diverse parents. *Intervention in School and Clinic, 29*(5), 288–291.

Whitney-Thomas, J., & Hanley-Maxwell, C. (1996). Packing the parachute: Parents' experiences as their children prepare to leave high school. *Exceptional Children, 63*(1), 76–87.

7 Classroom Factors

TO GUIDE YOUR READING

After you read this chapter, you will be able to answer these questions:

- What are the classroom issues related to learners with emotional/behavioral disorders?
- What educational services are available for learners with emotional/behavioral disorders?

Ms. Pat had been concerned about Chris for some time. Unlike the other kindergarten students who seemed to live for recess, Chris was the last in line, and seemed almost afraid to leave the room. On the playground he stood by himself watching cars, fingering a small car that he kept in his pocket at all times. One day Ms. Pat asked him what he was doing, and he replied, "Just guessing about cars." The other students stopped approaching him, referring to him as "Chris, the car kid."

Jason had a growth spurt when he was 14, which placed him several inches above the heads of his fellow seventh graders. He was already self-conscious about having been retained in fourth grade because of inattentiveness and poor achievement. His stature made him even more uncomfortable. Jason had always been physical, and used his size to bully his way on the playground. The other students began to avoid him because of the rough way he played. One day during a game of flag football, when he wasn't chosen for a team, Jason became very angry and yanked all of the flags off of his classmates. He forced three of them to the ground, bruising and scraping them in the process.

Whether withdrawn or aggressive, school presents unique challenges for learners identified as emotionally/behaviorally disordered. Relationships with peers and teachers interfere with learning. Routines and subtle cues for behavior, apparent to other students, may be difficult for learners identified as emotionally/behaviorally disordered. Their behavior may appear threatening to teachers, pushing professionals into a pattern of suppressing behavior rather than teaching content.

In this chapter, we will explore the roles of classroom factors with learners identified as emotionally/behaviorally disordered. In addition, educational and related services that address the unique needs of these learners will be discussed.

◊◊ What Are the Classroom Issues Related to Learners Identified as Emotionally/Behaviorally Disordered?

Teacher-Student Relationships

In relationships that are necessarily unequal, such as in teaching, Buber (1965) maintains that teachers must practice "inclusion," which means extending the teacher into the reality in which the student participates. Witherell and Noddings (1991) suggest that

Inclusive teachers take the perspective of the student.

teachers can be inclusive by taking the perspective of the student and allowing students to pursue legitimate projects. Through inclusion, the students and teacher must together construct a caring relationship, in which the student responds by fully engaging in the task. The school then becomes a place in which teachers and students live together, talk to each other, reason together, and enjoy each other's company (Noddings, 1991). As Brendtro and Brokenleg (1993) contend, teachers need to move beyond the deviance and deficit model. They must work to belong, rather than continue to further the alienation that occurs in a "climate of control"—a classroom climate aimed at suppressing behavior rather than teaching skills.

Successful teacher-student relationships depend, to a large degree, on teachers. Yet teachers of learners identified as emotionally/behaviorally disordered have a low retention rate. In a study of 96 teachers of learners identified as emotionally/behaviorally disordered, more than a third indicated that they planned to leave the field during the upcoming year, and 10% were unsure about their future career plans (George, George, Gersten, & Grosenick, 1995). Teachers who were leaving the profession varied from their "staying" peers by the type of service delivery model in which they worked, the adequacy of the support they received, and the time available to them for developing curricula and completing paperwork.

Morse (1994) reported a common thread among exemplary teachers: they knew their students and had a deep empathy for the stress in their students' lives. As teachers, they worked out what they felt was best for the child even when it caused pain and resistance. All of the teachers cared deeply. This relationship is essential for children who are at risk or considered problems. Morse suggests that the "salient etiological condition" (p. 3) most often mentioned in the histories of these children is the lack of adequate adult caring.

The efforts of teachers to maintain relationships with their students is challenged by the "de-skilling" of teachers through programmed, "teacher-proof" materials and the emphasis on success with standardized testing (Schubert, 1991). Schubert found, however, that teachers regarded by their peers and students as particularly good somehow resisted pressures to be "de-skilled" and:

- Maintained a holistic perspective on situational problem solving.
- Enjoyed being with students.
- Drew insights from student experiences outside of school.
- Maintained a sense of mission about the importance of teaching.
- Exhibited love and compassion for students.
- Exhibited a clear sense of meaning and direction.
- Guided their work with a quest for that which is worthwhile and just.
- Considered the issue of developmental appropriateness for each situation.
- Were actively involved in self-education.

Bacon and Bloom (1994) conducted focus groups with learners identified as emotionally/behaviorally disordered regarding what teachers need to know to work successfully with these learners. Many of the responses were related to teacher-student relationships. The learners argued that teachers should demonstrate fairness and respect students. In addition, they should be able to form relationships with learners identified as emotionally/behaviorally disordered and have counseling skills to help the students. Teachers' personal qualities, they suggested, should support interaction with learners identified as emotionally/behaviorally disordered.

In another study that "asked the consumers," Crowley (1993) reported that learners identified as emotionally/behaviorally disordered perceived teachers as helpful when they were flexible in their implementation of academic and behavioral programs. These students perceived teacher rigidity and use of discipline as unhelpful. A theme of anger toward rigid teachers was pervasive throughout Crowley's data.

To be supportive of students, Curwin (1994) argues that it is essential that teachers help students "rediscover hope" (p. 27). To do so, teachers should:

- Help students believe that they are competent.
- Present tasks that are not too easy.
- Make the subject or topic for instruction personally important to the students.
- Actively involve students in the learning process.
- Personally demonstrate in obvious ways a genuine energy and love of their subjects and for teaching.
- Communicate to students that classroom activities and goals are real and not gimmicks.
- Present lessons that are fun and enjoyable.
- Welcome students into school and the classroom, helping students feel that they belong in school.
- Make personal connections with students.
- Pay attention to and plan for motivation.

Peer Relationships

Learners identified as emotionally/behaviorally disordered often have difficulty socially relating with their peers. Lieber and Beckman (1991) report that children with disabilities as a group exhibit appropriate social interactions less frequently than their nonidentified peers. To remediate this problem, they suggest that learners should be placed with more competent partners, and that toys that encourage socialization should be provided. In addition, classroom activities should encourage social exchange, and at times, specific social skills should be taught.

Cross-age tutoring, or tutoring among individuals of different ages, may be an effective strategy to improve the achievement, social behavior, and self-perceptions of learners identified as emotionally/behaviorally disordered. Cockran, Feng, Cartledge, and Hamilton (1993) found that pairing African American learners identified as emotionally/behaviorally disordered with African American tutors improved both their grades and behavior. In another cross-age peer tutoring program, adults with learning disabilities were successful tutors for adolescents identified as emotionally/behaviorally disordered, assisting them in developing problem-solving, assertiveness, and self-management skills (Miller, Miller, Armentrout, & Flannagan, 1995).

cross-age tutoring
tutoring among individuals of different ages

Peers identified as emotionally/behaviorally disordered themselves may be effective behavior change agents. Gable, Arllen, and Hendrickson (1994) reported that learners identified as emotionally/behaviorally disordered as partners in peer mediation were effective. Peer confrontation regarding behaviors has also been demonstrated to be effective in increasing positive student behavior (Salend, Jantzen, & Giek, 1992). In peer confrontation, positive peer culture strategies are used to challenge students to change their own behavior, a strategy that has been effective in decreasing disruptive behavior in classrooms (Gable, Arllen, & Hendrickson, 1995).

Teacher Interaction and Instruction

critical instruction instruction that incorporates students' experiences, background knowledge, and meaningful tasks into the teaching/learning process

The concept of "critical" pedagogy has provided recommendations for effective instruction in the classroom for learners identified as emotionally/behaviorally disordered. *Critical instruction* incorporates students' experiences, background knowledge, and authentic tasks that are meaningful to the students and student interests into the teaching/learning process (Goldstein, 1996). Critical pedagogy is grounded in critical theory, which is an effort to provide the social/cultural context to situations involving change. It emphasizes meaning rather than form, and creativity and divergent thinking rather than correctness. Interactive/dialogical teacher-student interactions are in place rather than teacher-centered instruction. In order to implement critical pedagogy, teachers must be well-informed regarding community history, the history of the cultural groups with whom they are working, and community resources, including people and community centers, that can provide additional information and support to teachers and students.

negative reinforcement the contingent removal of an aversive stimulus that results in increased behavior production to escape or avoid the aversive stimulus

Recently attention has been focused on the possibility that teacher interactions may be aversive to students identified as emotionally/behaviorally disordered, in that students' off-task behavior may be interpreted as a result of negative reinforcement (Cipani, 1995). *Negative reinforcement,* Cipani contends, consists of the contingent removal of an aversive stimulus that results in increased efforts to escape or avoid the aversive stimulus. In the classroom, students' off-task behaviors are most likely reinforced by escape or avoidance of teacher instruction.

Teachers may also demonstrate negative reinforcement within their interactions with their students. Carr, Taylor, and Robinson (1991) reported that teachers of preschool children with disabilities presented fewer and easier task demands to children with higher rates of disruptive behavior than to children with lower rates of disruptive behavior. They indicated that the teachers' behaviors may have been avoidance behaviors for student disruptions.

The nature of the task may have an impact on the student's behavior. When students were presented with tasks that were too difficult for them, their disruptive behavior increased (Center, Deitz, & Kaufman, 1982). DePaepe, Shores, Jack, and Denny (1996) found that when presented with difficult tasks, learners identified as emotionally/behaviorally disordered had poorer time-on-task and higher percentages of time engaged in disruptive behavior. Easier tasks produced greater attention and fewer disruptions. In their review of research related to instructional variables and problem behavior, Munk and Repp (1994) found that student choice of task and task variation may reduce problem behaviors. Partial versus whole-task training and decreasing task difficulty may increase the likelihood of fewer disruptions.

Gunter, Shores, Jack, Denny, and DePaepe (1994) further explored the issue of negative reinforcement. In their study, a student identified as emotionally/behaviorally disordered was asked

The classroom can be a fun place to learn.

to perform tasks without sufficient information, which resulted in higher levels of disruptive behavior and lower probabilities of compliance. The study demonstrated that ineffective instructional strategies may be an aversive stimulus from which the child escapes, or attempts to escape, by engaging in disruptive behavior.

The prevalence of language problems in students identified as emotionally/behaviorally disordered highlights a need for examining teachers' instructions to students in relation to students' disruptive behaviors (Harrison, Gunter, Reed, & Lee, 1996). Harrison et al. argue that students may experience failure during classroom activities when they are given verbal directions that they do not fully comprehend; they may choose to act out so that they will be required to leave the room (disengage from the lesson) rather than risk embarrassment from academic failure. Based on the literature, Harrison et al. identified subtle and unintentional stimuli that occur in the reciprocal exchanges of instructional language that may be aversive for students. Students, then, may use disruptive behaviors to escape and avoid teacher instructional language they do not comprehend, and therefore find aversive. In response to this form of negative reinforcement, Harrison et al. recommend:

- Assessment of both student and teacher language patterns, that is, functional assessments.
- Consistency of instruction and the use of scripted lessons.
- Ongoing teacher self-evaluation of the linguistics of his or her instruction.

Homework is often a point of contention between teachers and students identified as emotionally/behaviorally disordered. Saderlund, Bursuck, Polloway, and Foley (1995) found that these learners have serious problems with homework completion. Teachers identified the difficulties with homework to be distractibility, responding poorly to parents' supervising the homework, and procrastination. Parents identified procrastination and distractibility as the greatest challenges. Epstein, Polloway, Foley, and Patton (1993) found that among learners with disabilities, those identified as emotionally/behaviorally disordered had the most pronounced difficulties in homework completion.

Curriculum

Most classrooms are characterized by low rates of positive consequences for appropriate behavior. In a national study of programs for learners identified as emotionally/behaviorally disordered,

Knitzer, Steinberg, and Fleish (1990) reported the presence of a *curriculum of control,* which was evidenced by an emphasis on behavioral management, maintained through elaborate points and levels systems. In these classrooms, maintaining silence and order was emphasized rather than increasing skills. Students were referred for poor social interaction skills, but there was no group work in which students could learn to interact appropriately.

curriculum of control curriculum with an emphasis on behavioral management, maintained through elaborate points and levels systems

Nichols (1992) reports that not only is the curriculum of control dreary, it is counterproductive. Its emphasis on management tends to generate the behaviors that placement for learners identified as emotionally/behaviorally disordered is designed to ameliorate. A curriculum of control works best for students who need control the least; the less control an individual has over objective events, the more satisfaction he or she draws from destructive acts.

Instead of a curriculum of control, Henley (1994) supports a curriculum of "self-control" designed to help students develop the skills needed to cope with social situations in and out of school and to serve as preventive discipline. Learners identified as emotionally/behaviorally disordered should be supported in learning to:

- Control their impulses when using instructional materials, moving in unstructured space, and making classroom transitions.

- Assess the social reality of a setting through accommodating to rules, organizing materials, accepting feedback, and appreciating feelings.

- Manage group situations through maintaining their composure, appraising peer pressure, cooperating, and evaluating the effect of their behavior.

- Cope with stress through adapting to new situations, managing competition, tolerating frustration, and demonstrating patience.

- Solve social problems through focusing on the present, learning from past experience, recalling personal behavior, and resolving conflicts.

Learning self-regulation is essential if students are to increase their independence, task engagement, and ability to self-evaluate their behavior (Graham, Harris, & Reid, 1992).

Clarke, Dunlap, Foster-Johnson, Childs, Wilson, White, and Vera (1995) reported that students' behavior could be improved if their interests were incorporated into curricular activities. In their study, after identifying curricular assignments associated with high levels of problem behavior, assignments were modified in accordance with the students' interests while maintaining the in-

constructivist ap-
proach an approach
that assumes that stu-
dents' understanding is
developmentally, so-
cially, and culturally
mediated and subjective

tegrity of the instructional objectives. These modifications both reduced problem behavior and increased desirable behavior.

Academic instruction, in addition to traditional social and behavioral interventions, may provide strong support for learners identified as emotionally/behaviorally disordered. According to Swicegood
and Linehan (1995), a **constructivist approach** to academic instruction assumes that students' understanding is developmentally, socially, and culturally mediated and subjective. The constructivist approach also assumes self-regulation, which is a need of learners
identified as emotionally/behaviorally disordered. The implementation of self-regulation strategies, such as self-recording of success in
meeting specific teacher expectations, have been found to increase
the positive behavior of such learners (Clees, 1995).

Relationships found between reading problems and behavior support an emphasis on literacy instruction for learners identified as emo-
tionally/behaviorally disordered. Lamm and Epstein (1992) reported
that individuals with severe reading disabilities frequently had emotional problems. These problems testified to high levels of anxiety and
difficulties in concentration, both conditions that occur in learners
identified as emotionally/behaviorally disordered. Learners identified
as emotionally/behaviorally disordered who have reading disabilities
may demonstrate more aggressive behavior than their peers identified
as emotionally/behaviorally disordered who do not have reading disabilities (Cornwell & Bawden, 1992).

Steinberg and Knitzer (1992) have several suggestions for addressing the problems associated with the curriculum of control.
They propose that special educators, parents, and mental health
professionals within each school community enter into discussions about curriculum, teaching strategies, and classroom interactions in programs serving learners identified as emotionally/be-
haviorally disordered. In addition, state departments of education
should assess the in-service and pre-service training programs for
teachers with regard to the curriculum of control and the management of behavior. Ongoing intensive in-service teacher supports
should be built into every program for children labeled emotion-
ally/behaviorally disordered. Finally, research should be conducted on effective programs for these learners.

In his work on extrinsic reinforcement systems, Kohn (1993)
suggested that rewards are in themselves punishment. He contends that there are "three c's" that provide an alternative to "control": content, collaboration, and choice. In terms of content, Kohn
suggests that we examine the demands of the setting to insure that
we aren't asking students to react in a way that isn't sensible in
view of their development, such as demanding that students recognize long-range consequences of behavior before they are able to

do so. Regarding collaboration, he suggests mutual problem solving, and argues that teacher and student should come to a mutual understanding of what constitutes inappropriate behavior. In terms of choice, Kohn suggests that the more the child feels part of the process, the more his point of view is solicited and taken seriously. If students are provided a choice, there are fewer behavior problems, and students have the opportunity to make real decisions about what is happening to them.

◊◊ What Educational Services Are Available for Learners Identified as Emotionally/Behaviorally Disordered?

Placement Decisions for Learners Identified as Emotionally/Behaviorally Disordered

Reinforcing the findings of Kauffman, Cullinan, and Epstein (1987), Glassberg (1994) found that cognitive, academic, and behavioral factors did not appear to have a dominant role in placement decisions. Rather, age at the time of diagnosis is most often related to the placement decision. She found that younger, brighter students tended to be mainstreamed and older students with more externalizing behaviors tended to be placed in more restrictive settings. Two sets of children emerged with regard to placement decisions. The first group included those children who were educated in public school settings, who had disrupted or reduced peer and social relationships with or without problem behavior at home, and whose academic achievement was one standard deviation below school district age-mates. The second group included those children who were not educated in public school settings, who avoided peer and social relationships, and who had behavior problems across all settings.

Inclusive Education

In his review of case law, Yell (1995) reports that the inclusion of learners identified as emotionally/behaviorally disordered may be evaluated differently by the courts from other cases of learners with disabilities. Yell suggests several principles of case law derived from the following cases: *Daniel R. v. State Board of Education* (1989). *Greer v. Rome City School District* (1991), *Oberti v. Board of Education of the Borough of Clementon School District* (1993), and *Sacramento City Unified School District v. Rachel H.* (1994). First, the courts support the concept that students with disabilities have a presumptive right to be educated in inclusive settings. The key to insuring good faith efforts on the part of the school district to maintain a child with disabilities in the inclusive setting lies in the provision of supplementary aids and services. One supplementary service, the Individualized Education Plan, remains the proper forum for placement decision making. Although school districts must have, by case law, a complete continuum of alternative placements available, the needs of classroom peers must be considered in cases of the least restrictive alternative. Schools must bear the burden of proof in defending their decisions regarding the educational benefit of a student's placement.

Idol (1994) reported that much of the resistance experienced from general education teachers regarding the inclusion of learners identified as emotionally/behaviorally disordered was founded in fear. Webber, Anderson, and Toey (1991) address this fear in their description of the "mindsets" for teacher's working with learners identified as emotionally/behaviorally disordered. They suggest that these teachers should develop mindsets that include: (a) problems have solutions, (b) small successes should be celebrated, (c) give without expecting thanks or something in return, (d) don't be afraid of students, (e) find humor in your day, and (f) be realistic.

Differences have been reported between the academic performance and social competence of learners in inclusive placements and learners in restrictive placements (Meadows, Neel, Scott, & Parker, 1994). Overall, compared to students in restrictive placements, students in inclusive settings had higher reading and written language scores, better work habits, and a higher grade point average. Their teachers reported that they were more attentive, worked harder, and were better adjusted. Students who remained in self-contained classrooms demonstrated more aggression and less self-control, or were introverted and withdrawn. The majority of teachers reported that they used the same curricula with all students and used the same criteria to evaluate all students. Teachers participating in the study of Meadows et al. reported that they made minimal classroom modifications for students identified as emotionally/behaviorally disordered, and that placement in inclusive settings meant a major reduction or complete cessation of individualized programming.

In his investigation of teachers' perceptions of program options, Harvey (1996) reported that staff perceived self-contained programs to be superior to inclusive programs in both resources and teaching strategies. In addition, well-established self-contained programs were perceived as superior to newly implemented inclusion programs in resources, teaching strategies, program components, and parent/school relationships. Regardless of the program, students identified as emotionally/behaviorally disordered were perceived as making moderate progress and as being moderately aggressive. Staff did not perceive significant differences between student progress in self-contained and mainstreamed programs.

Teachers appear to have diverse opinions about placement alternatives (Martin, Lloyd, Kauffman, & Coyne, 1995). In their interviews with teachers, Martin and associates found that teachers felt that schools are faced with problems they are unable to handle, and administrative procedures often impede appropriate services. There was also a reported lack of collaboration and support among those making placement decisions and those providing services. Teacher indicated that they felt they had little influence in placement decisions.

Cascade of Services

The *cascade of services* (Reynolds, 1962) is a continuum of services that provides a framework for meeting the individual needs of learners identified as emotionally/behaviorally disordered as well as other learners with disabilities. These services range from the least restrictive, or the most like general education, to the most restrictive, which includes noneducational and "inpatient" services. The range of services provided in this continuum includes:

cascade of services a continuum of services that provides a framework for meeting the individual needs of learners identified as emotionally/behaviorally disordered as well as other learners with disabilities

- General education classes, in which the student is served with or without supportive services outside of the school day.

- General education classrooms with supplementary services. In this setting, the special educator serves as a "support facilitator" (Stainback, Stainback, & Harris, 1989) who, in consultation with the general education teacher, identifies the assistance and supports needed, determines possible interventions, and facilitates implementation. Students may also be served through a resource room program. However, Jenkins and Heinen (1989) found that students overwhelmingly prefer to receive services in the general education classroom rather than in a resource program.

- Part-time general education/part-time special education placement. In this placement, students attend both programs depending on student needs and content areas.

- Special-class placement. In special classes, the student typically remains with a single teacher for the entire school day. These programs were those studied and reported as demonstrating the "curriculum of control" by Knitzer et al. (1990).

- Special schools. In the past decade, the number of students served in special schools has significantly decreased with the trend toward inclusion. Special schools are used to serve the most disabled students.
- Homebound services. Usually short-term interventions, homebound services are the most restrictive "outpatient" services, in that students have no interaction with other students, and the number of hours of instruction is severely limited, usually one hour daily or a few hours weekly.
- Instruction in hospital or residential settings. Students in these programs are usually a danger to themselves and others.

related services supportive services required to assist the learner to benefit from special education

Public Law 94-142 insures that students receive *related services,* which include "transportation and such developmental, corrective, and other supportive services as are required to assist the handicapped child to benefit from special education (Federal Register, 1977, 121.550). In addition to transportation, students identified as emotionally/behaviorally disordered are required to receive the following services if the services are necessary to profit from special education: speech pathology, audiology, psychological services, physical and occupational therapy, recreation, early identification, medical and school health services, counseling and social work services, and parent counseling and training. Public Law 101-476 added rehabilitation counseling to the list of related services. Psychotherapy as a related service has remained controversial; Osborne (1984) suggests that if a state requires that psychotherapy be provided by a licensed psychiatrist, then it is an exempt medical service.

Learners from Diverse Ethnic, Cultural, or Linguistic Groups

McIntyre (1996) suggests that issues of race, class, culture, language, gender, and sexual orientation often impact on programming for students identified as emotionally/behaviorally disordered. The Council for Children with Behavioral Disorders Task Force for Cultural Issues urged the adoption of the following goals related to providing appropriate services for culturally diverse learners identified as emotionally/behaviorally disordered (1996):

- Insure that students from diverse cultures are truly exhibiting emotional/behavioral disorders rather than culturally based behavior.
- Provide respectful, culturally appropriate services.
- Implement culturally and linguistically competent assessment procedures.

- Recruit professionals who represent various cultural, ethnic, and linguistic groups.
- Provide preservice and in-service training to professionals in modifications of practice to better address the characteristics of learners identified as emotionally/behaviorally disordered who are from various cultural, ethnic, or linguistic groups.
- Create a welcoming climate in which learners from various cultural, linguistic, or ethnic groups feel valued, respected, and physically and psychologically safe.
- Enhance the cultural knowledge base of professionals, clients/students, and the public at large.

◊◊ Summary Points

- Successful programs for learners identified as emotionally/behaviorally disordered depend on teachers who form strong relationships with their students.
- Learners identified as emotionally/behaviorally disordered often have difficulty socially relating to their peers.
- Peers identified as emotionally/behaviorally disordered themselves may be effective change agents and work as tutors and peer counselors.
- Teacher interactions may contribute to the disruptive behavior of their students.
- Students identified as emotionally/behaviorally disordered often have language disorders that may affect their classroom interactions.
- Traditionally, programming in classrooms for students identified as emotionally/behaviorally disordered has been a curriculum of control.
- A constructivist approach to academic instruction may support learners identified as emotionally/behaviorally disordered.
- A cascade of services must be available to learners identified as emotionally/behaviorally disordered.
- Issues of race, class, culture, language, gender, and sexual orientation often impact on programming for learners identified as emotionally/behaviorally disordered.

Self-Evaluation ◇

Select the most appropriate response.

1. Teachers of learners identified as emotionally/behaviorally disordered demonstrate
   a. retention rates similar to general education teachers.
   b. retention rates greater than general education teachers.
   c. retention rates lower than general education teachers.
2. Exemplary teachers
   a. are consistently firm.
   b. maintain their objectivity.
   c. care deeply.
3. Learners identified as emotionally/behaviorally disordered are disruptive, and they
   a. demonstrate similar levels of appropriate social interactions as their peers.
   b. initiate social interactions more frequently than their peers.
   c. demonstrate lower levels of appropriate social interactions than their peers.
4. Peer confrontation
   a. remediates aggression.
   b. increases positive behavior.
   c. decreases positive behavior.
5. Teacher interactions with their students
   a. may control the behavior of students identified as emotionally/behaviorally disordered.
   b. may be aversive to students identified as emotionally/behaviorally disordered.
   c. are formed by their students' behavior.
6. The disruptive behaviors of learners identified as emotionally/behaviorally disordered
   a. increase when difficult tasks are presented.
   b. are consistent across tasks.
   c. decrease when challenging, more difficult tasks are presented.
7. The language difficulties of learners identified as emotionally/behaviorally disordered
   a. are similar to those of learners with learning disabilities.
   b. may contribute to an aversive reaction to a teacher's instruction.
   c. may contribute to inattention.
8. One of the greatest challenges identified by parents regarding homework completion by learners identified as emotionally/behaviorally disordered is
   a. aggression.
   b. defiance.
   c. passive-aggression.

9. The constructivist approach assumes
   a. carefully constructed goals and objectives.
   b. self-regulation.
   c. high management needs to construct appropriate schema.
10. Court cases regarding inclusion of learners identified as emotionally be-
    haviorally disordered
    a. have decided on behalf of the parents.
    b. are evaluated differently by the courts from those involving other dis-
       abilities.
    c. are evaluated on the basis of school information.

Making the Language Your Own

Match each key word or phrase to its definition.

_____ 1. emphasizes behavioral management over academic learning

_____ 2. a continuum of special education services

_____ 3. supportive services required to assist the learner to benefit from special education

_____ 4. contingent removal of an aversive stimulus

_____ 5. instruction that incorporates the students' developmental contexts into the teaching/learning process

_____ 6. employs students of different ages

_____ 7. assumes that students' learning is developmentally, socially, and culturally mediated

a. cascade of services
b. constructivist approach
c. critical instruction
d. cross-age tutoring
e. curriculum of control
f. negative reinforcement
g. related services

Theory into Practice

Observe a classroom of learners identified as emotionally/behaviorally disordered. Is there indeed a curriculum of control? Are the students provided options and opportunities to interact? Is there an emphasis on academic learning, or controlling behavior? What behaviors does the teacher demonstrate to support or counteract a curriculum of control?

◊◊ **References**

Bacon, E. H., & Bloom, L. A. (1994). "Don't ratl the kids." *Journal of Emotional and Behavioral Problems, 3*(1), 8–10.

Brendtro, L. K., & Brokenleg, M. (1993). Beyond the curriculum of control. *The Journal of Emotional and Behavioral Problems, 1*(4), 2–12.

Buber, M. (1965). *Between man and man.* New York: Macmillan.

Carr, E. G., Taylor, J. C., & Robinson, S. (1991). The effects of severe behavior problems in children on the teaching behavior of adults. *Journal of Applied Behavior Analysis, 24,* 325–535.

Center, D. B., Deitz, S. M., & Kaufman, M. E. (1982). Student ability, task difficulty, and inappropriate classroom behavior: A study of children with behavior disorders. *Behavior Modification, 6,* 355–374.

Cipani, E. C. (1995). Be aware of negative reinforcement. *Teaching Exceptional Children, 27,* 36–40.

Clarke, S., Dunlap, G., Foster-Johnson, L., Childs, K. E., Wilson, D., White, R., & Vera, A. (1995). Improving the conduct of students with behavioral disorders by incorporating student interests into curricular activities. *Behavioral Disorders, 20*(4), 221–237.

Clees, T. J. (1995). Self-recording of students' daily schedules of teachers' expectancies: Perspectives on reactivity, stimulus control, and generalization. *Exceptionality, 5*(3), 113–129.

Cockran, L., Feng, H., Cartledge, G., & Hamilton, S. (1993). The effects of cross-age tutoring on the academic achievement, social behavior, and self-perceptions of low achieving African-American males with behavioral disorders. *Behavioral Disorders, 18*(4), 292–302.

Cornwell, A., & Bawden, N. H. (1992). Reading disabilities and aggression: A critical review. *Journal of Learning Disabilities, 25*(5), 281–288.

Crowley, E. P. (1993). A qualitative analysis of mainstreamed behaviorally disordered aggressive adolescents' perceptions of helpful and unhelpful teacher attitudes and behaviors. *Exceptionality, 4*(3), 131–151.

Curwin, R. (1994). Helping students rediscover hope. *Journal of Emotional and Behavioral Problems, 3*(1), 27–30.

Daniel R. v. State Board of Education, 874 F.2d 1036 (5th Cir. 1989).

DePaepe, P. A., Shores, R. E., Jack, S. L., & Denny, R. K. (1996). Effects of task difficulty on the disruptive and on-task behavior of students with severe behavior disorders. *Behavioral Disorders, 21*(3), 216–225.

Epstein, M. H., Polloway, E. A., Foley, R. M., & Patton, J. R. (1993). Homework: A comparison of teachers' and parents' perceptions of the problems experienced by students identified as having behavioral disorders, learning disabilities, or no disabilities. *Remedial and Special Education, 14*(5), 40–50.

Federal Register, (1977). Public Law 94-142, Sec. 11-550.

Gable, A. R., Arllen, N., & Hendrickson, J. (1994). Use of students with emotional/behavioral disorders as behavior change agents. *Education and Treatment of Children, 17,* 267–276.

Gable, A. R., Arllen, L. N., & Hendrickson, M. J. (1995). Use of peer confrontation to modify disruptive behavior in inclusion classrooms. *Preventing School Failure, 40*(1), 25–28.

George, N. L., George, M. P., Gersten, R., & Grosenick, J. K. (1995). To leave or to stay? *Remedial and Special Education, 16*(4), 227–236.

Glassberg, L. A. (1994). Students with behavioral disorders: Determinants of placement outcomes. *Behavioral Disorders, 19*(3), 181–191.

Goldstein, B. S. C. (1996). Critical pedagogy in a bilingual special education classroom. In M. S. Poplin & P. T. Cousins, (Eds.), *Alternative views of learning disabilities: Issues for the 21st century* (pp. 145–167). Austin: Pro-Ed.

Graham, S., Harris, K. R., & Reid, R. (1992). Developing self-regulated learners. *Focus on Exceptional Children, 24*(6), 1–16.

Greer v. Rome City School District, 950 F.2d 688 (11th Cir. 1991).

Gunter, P. L., Shores, R. E., Jack, S. L., Denny, R. K., & DePaepe, P. (1994). A case study of the effects of altering instructional interactions on the disruptive behavior of a child with severe behavior disorders. *Education and Treatment of Children, 17,* 435–444.

Harrison, J. S., Gunter, P. L., Reed, T. M., & Lee, J. M. (1996). Teacher instructional language and negative reinforcement: A conceptual framework for working with students with emotional and behavioral disorders. *Education and Treatment of Children, 19*(2), 183–196.

Harvey, V. S. (1996). Educators' perceptions of effectiveness of programs for students with emotional and behavioral disorders. *Behavioral Disorders, 21*(3), 205–215.

Henley, M. (1994). A self-control curriculum for troubled youngsters. *Journal of Emotional and Behavioral Problems, 3*(1), 40–46.

Idol, L. (1994). Don't forget the teacher. *Journal of Emotional and Behavioral Problems, 3,* 28–33.

Jenkins, J. R., & Heinen, A. (1989). Students' preference for service delivery: Pull-out, in-class, or integrated models. *Exceptional Children, 55,* 515–523.

Kauffman, J. M., Cullinan, D., & Epstein, M. H. (1987). Characteristics of students placed in special programs for the seriously emotionally disturbed. *Behavioral Disorders, 12*, 175–184.

Knitzer, J., Steinberg, Z., & Fleisch, F. (1990). *At the schoolhouse door. An examination of the programs and policies for children with behavioral and emotional problems.* New York: Bank Street College of Education.

Kohn, A. (1993). *Punished by rewards: The trouble with gold stars, incentive plans, A's, praise, and other bribes.* New York: Houghton Mifflin.

Lamm, O., & Epstein, R. (1992). Specific reading impairments: Are they to be associated with emotional difficulties? *Journal of Learning Disabilities, 25*(9), 605–614.

Lieber, J., & Beckman, P. J. (1991). Social coordination as a component of social competence in young children with disabilities. *Focus on Exceptional Children, 24*(4), 1–10.

Martin, K. F., Lloyd, J. W., Kauffman, J. M., & Coyne, M. (1995). Teachers' perceptions of educational, placement decisions for pupils with emotional or behavioral disorders. *Behavioral Disorders, 20*(2), 106–117.

McIntrye, T. (1996). Guidelines for providing appropriate services to culturally diverse students. *Behavioral Disorders, 21*(2), 137–144.

Meadows, N. B., Neel, R. S., Scott, C. M., & Parker, G. (1994). Academic performance, social competence, and mainstream accommodations: A look at mainstreamed and nonmainstreamed students with serious behavioral disorders. *Behavioral Disorders, 19*(3), 170–180.

Miller, R. S., Miller, F. P., Armentrout, A. J., & Flannagan, W. J. M. (1995). Cross-age peer tutoring strategy for promoting self-determination in students with severe emotional disabilities/behavior disorders. *Preventing School Failure, 39*(4), 32–37.

Morse, W. C. (1994). The role of caring in teaching children with behavior problems. *Contemporary Education, 65,* 3.

Munk, D. D., & Repp, A. C. (1994). The relationship between instructional variables and problem behavior: A review. *Exceptional Children, 60*(5), 390–401.

Nichols, P. (1992). The Curriculum of Control: Twelve reasons for it, some arguments against it. *Beyond Behavior, 3*(2), 3–5.

Noddings, N. (1991). Stories in dialogue: Caring and interpersonal reasoning. In C. Witherell & N. Noddings (Eds.), *Stories lives tell: Narrative and dialogue in education* (pp. 157–170). New York: Teachers College Press.

Oberti v. Board of Education of the Borough of Clementon School District, 995 F.2d 1204 (3rd Cir. 1993).

Osborne, A. (1984). How the courts have interpreted the related services mandate. *Exceptional Children, 51,* 249–252.

Reynolds, M. (1962). A framework for considering some issues in special education. *Exceptional Children, 28,* 367–370.

Rhodes, W. C. (1996). Liberatory pedagogy and special education. In M. S. Poplin & P. T. Cousin, (Eds.), *Alternative views of learning disabilities: Issues for the 21st century* (pp. 135–144). Austin: Pro-Ed.

Sacramento City Unified School District v. Rachel H. 14 F.3d 1398 (9th Cir. 1994).

Salend, S. J., Jantzen, N. R., & Giek, K. (1992). Using a peer confrontation system in a group setting. *Behavioral Disorders, 17*(3), 211–218.

Schubert, W. H. (1991). Teacher lore: A basis for understanding praxis. In C. Witherell & N. Noddings (Eds.), *Stories lives tell: Narrative and dialogue in education* (pp. 207–233). New York: Teachers College Press.

Shores, R. E., Jack, S. L., Gunter, P. L., Ellis, D. N., DeBriere, T. J., & Wehby, J. H. (1993). Classroom interactions of children with behavior disorders. *Journal of Emotional and Behavioral Disorders, 1,* 27–39.

Soderlund, J., Bursuck, B., Polloway, E. A., & Foley, R. A. (1995). A comparison of homework problems of secondary school students with behavior disorders and nondisabled peers. *Journal of Emotional and Behavioral Disorders, 3*(3), 150–155.

Stainback, S. B., Stainback, W. C., & Harris, K. C. (1989). Support facilitation: An emerging role for special educators. *Teacher Education and Special Education, 12,* 148–153.

Steinberg, Z., & Knitzer, J. (1992). Classrooms for emotionally and behaviorally disturbed students: Facing the challenge. *Behavioral Disorders, 17* (2), 145–156.

Swicegood, P. R., & Linehan, S. L. (1995). Literacy and academic learning for students with behavioral disorders: A constructivist view. *Education and Treatment of Children, 18*(3), 335–347.

Webber, J., Anderson, T., & Toey, L. (1991). Teacher mindsets for surviving in the BD classrooms. *Intervention in School and Clinic, 26,* 288–291.

Witherell, C., & Noddings, N. (1991). Prologue: An invitation to our readers. In C. Witherell & N. Noddings (Eds.), *Stories lives tell: Narrative and dialogue in education* (pp. 1–12). New York: Teachers College Press.

Yell, M. L. (1995). Clyde K and Sheila, D v. Puyallup School District: The courts, inclusion, and students with behavioral disorders. *Behavioral Disorders, 20*(3), 179–189.

8 Cultural Diversity and Gender

TO GUIDE YOUR READING

After you read this chapter, you will be able to answer these questions:

- What are the issues related to cultural diversity and identification of learners as emotionally/behaviorally disordered?

- What are the issues related to gender and the identification of learners as emotionally/behaviorally disordered?

Daming's first-grade teacher was delighted. After 3 months in her classroom, the young Chinese girl was finally warming up. At the parent-teacher's conference, she and her teaching assistant discussed her new relaxed manner with Mrs. Lu, Daming's mother. The teaching assistant mentioned that Daming finally calls her by her first name. Mrs. Lu, shocked, apologized profusely, and offered to keep Daming home until she learned respect.

Albert is a congenial, smiling, African American in fourth grade. His teacher was at the point of initiating a referral on his behavior. Whenever presented with a task, Albert spent more than 5 minutes getting out pencils, arranging the paper, and straightening his desk before he began. He frequently made comments following her statements, such as "uh-huh," and "that's right." His teacher found it most infuriating that he seemed to need the affirmation of his classmates following his responses in class, and would look at them, encouraging their "uh-huh's" and "that's rights".

In 1990, Euro-American students comprised approximately 70% of school enrollment in kindergarten through the 12th grades. The remaining 30% of the students were from diverse ethnic, cultural, and linguistic groups. Garcia (1995) predicts that in the year 2026, we will have the inverse of this student representation, and that 25% of the students in our schools will be residing in homes in which English is not the primary language.

In the classroom, each student and teacher reflects his or her personal culture. Individual students and teachers tend to react as if the norms he or she follows represents the natural way human beings do things. Those who behave otherwise may be judged wrong. This behavior is based on *ethnocentricity,* which is the belief that an individual's own culture represents the best, or at least the most appropriate, way for human beings to live (Spradley & McCurdy, 1984).

ethnocentricity the belief that an individual's personal culture reflects the most appropriate behavior

In this chapter, we will explore issues related to cultural diversity and gender as these factors relate to emotional/behavioral disorders. Both cultural diversity and gender appear to have an impact on who is referred to, determined eligible for, and placed in special education services for learners identified as emotionally/behaviorally disordered.

◊◊ What Are the Issues Related to Cultural Diversity and Identification of Learners as Emotionally/Behaviorally Disordered?

In the literature on emotional/behavioral disorders, cultural diversity is often discussed in the context of teacher-student interactions and school. Branch, Goodwin, and Gualtieri (1993) facilitate this discussion by providing definitions of several key terms related to the issue of cultural diversity. They describe *culture* as a patterned way of thinking, feeling, and reacting that has been acquired over time. These patterns are transmitted by symbols, actions, and artifacts that constitute the distinctive achievements of a human group.

Diversity is described by Branch et al. as the quality or condition of being different. Diversity is used primarily for labeling and identifying someone as different, rather than attempting to understand those individuals who are labeled as diverse or different. Identifying a person as belonging to a particular group does not provide information about what things are important to him or her, nor the customs he or she practices.

Pluralism (Branch et al., 1993) is the relative lack of assimilation into society. Groups of people may live separately from the mainstream culture and have maintained their own customs, values, and ways of life or may migrate to mainstream cultures, becoming assimilated. In a pluralistic society, cultural groups are able to maintain their collective identify as well as memberships in the mainstream culture.

When a population to be served by special education is culturally diverse, all activities and services provided to that population must take into consideration its major cultural characteristics: language, culture, and disability (Garcia & Yates, 1994). There is both overrepresentation and underrepresentation of various cultural groups in programs for students identified as emotionally/behaviorally disordered. Underidentification occurs among Asian Americans (3% of the general population, 1% of those served), Hispanic Americans (12% of the general population, 6% of those served), and Euro-Americans (68% of the general population, 21% of those served). Overidentification exists among African American students (12% of the general population, 22% of those served).

Although each cultural group has distinctive learning style patterns, the great variation among individuals within each group means that educators must use diverse teaching strategies with all students. Guild (1994) contends that "generalizations about a group of people have often led to naive inferences about individu-

culture a patterned way of acting, thinking, and feeling that is acquired over time and transmitted through and to members of a group

diversity the quality or condition of being different

pluralism the relative lack of assimilation into society

als within that group" (p. 16). He suggests that there are five components on which researchers in cultural diversity and education concur:

1. Students of any particular age will differ in the ways in which they learn.
2. Learning styles are a function of both nature and nurture.
3. Learning styles, in themselves, are neither good nor bad.
4. Within any group, the variations among individuals are as great as their commonalities.
5. There is cultural conflict between some students and the typical learning experience in school.

Adaptive behavior in one culture may be considered maladaptive behavior when exhibited in another culture (Dunn & Tucker, 1993). Both adaptive and maladaptive functioning are vital indicators of the life success of children from various cultural groups. The conflicts generated from the mismatch between various perceptions of behavior may be, in fact, significant predictors of minority children's behavior problems (Dunn & Tucker, 1993).

Learners of four minority cultural groups with which teachers most frequently interact in the schools are African American learners, Hispanic American learners, Native American learners, and Asian American learners.

African American Learners

African Americans individuals whose ancestry can be traced to Africa

Since 1900, the *African American* population, or individuals whose ancestry can be traced to Africa, of the United States has remained between 10% and 12% of the total population. By the year 2000, there will be approximately 35 million African Americans in the United States (Allen & Majidi-Ahi, 1989). According to McAdoo (1978), the lifestyles, values, and experiences of African Americans vary, but as a group, they share the common experience of economic isolation, prejudice, and legally reinforced racism. Long-established cultural patterns and a high level of maternal employment have led to shared decision-making processes in many African American families.

An important socialization issue for African American learners is coping with racism. African American parents, in efforts to combat racism, emphasize the development of achievement motivation, self-confidence, and high self-esteem (Peters, 1981). In addition, there may be cultural differences in attitudes towards time, which may be perceived as resistance or apathy by Euro-American individuals.

There are several aspects of African American culture that may lead to inappropriate identification of these learners as emotionally/behaviorally disordered. The differences in cohesiveness between the African American and Euro-American cultures may be viewed as problems by Euro-American teachers (Hanna, 1980). Cooperation among African American learners when confronted with a task or problem, for example, may be interpreted by some teachers as cheating.

New children in the classroom negotiate interpersonal relationships and participants probe for common experiences with their peers. They seek cues in how to act or what to expect from the teacher. African American learners may benefit from cooperative learning strategies because of their cultural heritage, family background, and socialization processes (Haynes & Gebreyesus, 1992).

Communication patterns among some African American students may be perceived as inappropriate, resistant, or apathetic by Euro-American teachers. Among African American learners, it is possible to converse without constant eye contact (Allen & Majidi-Ahi, 1989), which may be interpreted as inattention by a Euro-American teacher. African American students may be less likely to verbally reinforce one another in conversation (Smith, 1981). African American children may be operating in a dual system of standard English dialect and Black English Vernacular, and, as a consequence, carrying a more demanding cognitive burden than

We can be what we want to be.

individuals operating in a single language system in which there are fewer translations necessary. Communication skills valued among peers, such as verbal dueling and arguments, may be viewed as aggressive and disruptive by teachers (Lynch, 1993).

Cultural differences in parental discipline may also cause a mismatch between students and their teachers. Nweke (1994) reported that although both parents of Euro-American and African American students would punish misbehavior occurring outside the home, the place and time of punishment differed. Whereas 87.54% of the mothers were responsible for discipline in African American families, only 51% of the mothers in Euro-American families had that responsibility.

Hispanic American Learners

Hispanic Americans
individuals of all races whose cultural heritage is tied to the use of the Spanish language and Latino culture including Mexican American, Chicano, Puerto Rican, Cuban, and Central and South American

Hispanic Americans are those persons of all races whose cultural heritage is tied to the use of the Spanish language and Latino culture (Fradd, Figueroa, & Correa, 1989). Hispanic American students may belong to any of a large number of ethnic subgroups: Mexican, Chicano, Puerto Rican, Cuban, or Central and South American.

The Hispanic American population has entered a significant growth period that may result in an American demographic picture composed of 47 million Hispanics out of 265 million Americans by the year 2000 (Hodgkinson, 1985). The poverty rate among Hispanic American families in 1986 was about 2.5 times greater than among non-Hispanic families (Buenning, Tollefson, & Rodriguez, 1992).

Hyland (1989) describes the Hispanic American population as highly concentrated in urban areas and highly isolated in housing and schooling. This isolation is reputedly related to linguistic skills, in that Hispanic children are usually placed in classrooms or schools where children of limited English proficiency are in the majority.

Hispanic American learners may enter school with a significantly different social, economic, and cultural background than do their peers who understand Euro-American culture (Hyland, 1989). For example, "copying" may be viewed as a legitimate activity among Hispanic American students. Copying work may be based on home socialization patterns that stress collectivity and social cohesiveness. Rather than representing low ability and lack of motivation, copying may be considered a constructive approach to intellectual exchanges and the acquisition of new knowledge in a social unit composed of peers (Delgado-Gaitan & Trueba, 1985). In addition, the organization of classroom instruction may limit the abilities of Hispanic American students to demonstrate their full range of competence in two languages. As a consequence, a lack of English language structural proficiency and a lack of vocabulary in Spanish may be interpreted by teachers as a lack of conceptual ability (Commins & Miramontes, 1989).

Native American Learners

Native Americans, or members of the indigenous peoples of North and South America, share a history of cultural, psychological, and physical genocide. Once estimated at 10 million, the Native American population has been reduced through cultural genocide to fewer than 2 million. Rather than accepting tribally defined membership or community consensus, federal programs require one-quarter genealogically derived Native American ancestry to be legally recognized as Native American and therefore eligible for many federal, state, and Indian nation benefits. In the United States, there are 517 federally recognized Native American entities (196 of which are in Alaska) and 36 state-recognized Native American tribes. Each of these entities maintains unique customs, traditions, social organizations, and ecological relationships (Leap, 1981).

Native Americans are economically and educationally challenged. The median income of Native Americans living on reservations is approximately one third of the median income of Euro-American households and approximately one half of the median income of African Americans (U.S. Bureau of Census, 1986). About one third of adult Native Americans are illiterate and only 20% have attained a high school education (Brod & McQuiston, 1983). An extreme problem for Native American youth is alcohol and substance abuse. The use of alcohol among Native American youth is 3 times that of youth in the population at large (Bobo, 1985).

As a consequence of efforts first to eliminate them, and, then to assimilate them, many Native Americans experience a sense of alienation from Euro-Americans (LaFramboise & Low, 1989). Through their work with the Menominee tribe, Spindler and Spindler (1994) describe the responses of Native Americans to this sense of alienation. These responses include reaffirmation, withdrawal, constructive marginality, biculturalism, and assimilation. Among the Menominee, reaffirmation was represented by a group of cultural "survivors" from the past and a larger number of younger people who had interacted with Euro-American culture in school and the workplace. This group was trying to recreate and sustain a recognizable Native American way of life. Another group of Native Americans was so torn by cultural conflict that they

Native Americans members of the indigenous peoples of North and South America

could identify with neither traditional Native American nor Euro-American cultural symbols or groups. This group withdrew either into self-destruction through substance abuse or by simply doing nothing about their conflict.

Some Native Americans exhibited "constructive marginality," described by Spindler and Spindler (1994) as the forming of a personal culture that was instrumentally productive but composed of several different segments, some of which were Euro-American. Among those who assimilated into the Euro-American culture, two groups emerged: (a) those who were more "respectable" than most Euro-Americans and denigrated Native Americans who did not conform, and (b) those who were undifferentiated culturally from Euro-Americans but were interested in Native American traditions in a distant way. Bicultural Native Americans were equally at home in both their traditional culture and the Euro-American culture. Spindler and Spindler describe these cultural strategies as defensive, because the self-esteem of the people is threatened.

Grimm (1992) reports that several issues challenge the identity of learners who are Native Americans, such as removal from the family for boarding schools and foster placements, high dropout rates (60% among children attending boarding school), overidentification as special education students, high incidence of alcohol and drug abuse, high suicide rates, chronic health problems, and low income.

Perhaps of greatest difficulty to Native American learners is the conflict between their traditional cooperative learning styles and the competitive setting of the school. Native American children often learn by observation rather than by displays of curiosity and verbal questioning. They tend to prefer cooperation and harmony. In school, these behaviors are perceived to be a general lack of individual competition and a reliance on peer structure (Brod & McQuiston, 1983).

Several values among Native Americans may potentially put learners in contrast to conventional school behavior. For example, expectations to comply with authority and an uncomplaining attitude may be perceived as complacency or lack of motivation. Subordinancy to the group may be inconsistent with a competitive classroom style. Silence and esteem for "the middle position" may be out of place in a classroom in which the student must request help or materials.

Asian Americans Learners

Asian Americans have roots in Asia, including China, Japan, and the Southeast Asian nations.

Chinese family structure, according to Huang and Ying (1989), is based on Confucian ethics. Sons are more highly valued than

Asian Americans individuals whose ancestry can be traced to Asia, including China, Japan, and the Southeast Asian nations

daughters, with the first born son perceived as the most valued child. Fathers, removed from the everyday tasks of the family, are often figurative heads of the family, while mothers may in fact be the driving force in the family. The expression of emotion is highly frowned upon in Chinese American families, and the ability to suppress undesirable thoughts or emotions is highly valued. There is an essential need to avoid shame and to save face among Chinese Americans (Shon & Ja, 1982). Placing group and family wishes above individual desires is highly valued (Huang & Ying, 1989).

Yamamoto and Kubota (1989) describe the Japanese American family structure as one that emphasizes the family over the individual, hierarchical relationships, conformity, and social control based on shame, guilt, and duty. Japanese culture values being "reserved," that is, not expressing one's wishes or preferences, deferring to those in authority, and repressing or internalizing emotions.

Southeast Asian refugee children and youth have spent a significant part of their lives amid violence, experiencing great personal loss, anxiety, and discontinuation of education and health care. The extended family, so vital in the Asian culture, is not accessible to these children and youth. These families have undergone sociocultural changes, in which children viewed their parents as changing from previous competent, independent individuals into persons who acculturate more slowly than they do. Yet, self-control and repression of emotions remain highly valued (Huang, 1989).

Unlike other cultural, ethnic, and linguistic groups, Asian Americans have a positive stereotype as related to school achievement. Dao (1991) contends, however, that changes have occurred in the Asian American population that put many of these children at risk for school failure. Today, many Asian American children are from families whose life and educational experiences vastly differ from children from established Asian American families. Recent immigrant or refugee children face the triple burden of learning English and a new school curriculum, adjusting to a new culture, and surviving in an impoverished environment. In addition, many recent refugees may have had traumatic experiences, including death, piracy, and extreme violence in their recent past, and may not be emotionally ready to benefit from instruction.

Assessment

Learners from most cultural minorities have higher rates at which they enter the special education referral to placement process, which increases the likelihood of their identification as emotionally/

behaviorally disordered (Executive Committee of the Council for Children with Behavioral Disorders, 1989).

Gonzalez and Yawkey (1993) suggest that there are three approaches in the assessment of children who are culturally and linguistically different: (a) the traditional psychometric model, (b) the "missionary" model of acculturation, and (c) the developmental model. The traditional psychometric model assumes the presence of innate abilities and traits inherited genetically and related to maturational and neurological factors that can be quantitatively measured. The "missionary" model uses standardized tests to demonstrate internal or racial causes for the low scores of culturally and linguistically different learners compared with mainstream students. In this model, learners who are different are viewed as "exotic aliens" who need acculturation. The developmental assessment model, used by ethnic researchers, assumes that individual potential can be actualized or expressed differently in various sociocultural environments that can only be appreciated in the uniqueness of each individual through qualitative descriptors. From this perspective potential is not fixed and cannot be quantitatively valued. Potential is influenced by both internal and external factors.

Skiba (1989) reviewed 89 correlations between classroom observations and behavioral ratings drawn from 16 studies. He found very low correlations between what was actually observed and what was rated by teachers using formal rating scales. He suggests that there are serious problems with the validity of assessments that look for the problems within the students themselves. He maintains that the recognition of the "problem situation" should be used to identify and describe behavior problems in schools.

The lack of consensus regarding the designation and description of learners identified as emotionally/behaviorally disordered extends to researchers in the field. Kavale, Forness, and Alper (1986) found in their survey of 323 studies in behavioral/emotional disorders that the research literature presents a divergent picture in regard to the nature and prevalence of behavioral/emotional disorders, and reflects a lack of consensus regarding standard identification criteria. The Executive Committee of the Council for Children with Behavioral Disorders (1989) argues that until definition, classification, and measurement criteria for learners identified as behaviorally/emotionally disordered are made more objective and verifiable, assessment of emotional/behavioral disorders will continue to be highly subjective and open to multiple sources of bias. The Executive Committee offers the following recommendations for the conduct of a nonbiased, functional assessment of learners from diverse ethnic, cultural, and linguistic groups:

1. Attention should be focused on classroom and school learning environments rather than on medical or mental health–based models.

2. The culture, expectations, tolerance, learning, and reinforcement of the history learner, teacher, and administrator, as well as the family situation, should all be considered.

3. Attention should be focused on student and teacher behaviors and the contexts in which they occur.

4. The conditions under which behaviors are observed, taught, and required should be studied.

5. Specific, measurable, instructionally based standards for academic and social behaviors should be established.

6. An assessment of the student's current learning environment, with documentation of prereferral interventions, should be implemented prior to referral.

7. Effective and efficient instructional procedures should be applied.

8. Teaching behaviors, instructional organization, and instructional supports should be assessed.

9. The responsibility for learning or performance failure should not be placed on the student.

10. Teachers should be prepared in a functional assessment perspective that focuses on children at risk for academic and/or behavioral difficulties.

11. Professionals should be realigned toward a functional assessment perspective.

Interactions in the Classroom

In a study of student teachers, Valli (1995) records several experiences that have an impact on teacher-student classroom interaction. Teachers reported a "disappearance of color," and claimed that they no longer noticed what color the students were (actually, color no longer functioned as a barrier and ceased to signify hostility or otherness). In addition, the student teachers confronted a challenge to white privilege, where for the first time that their whiteness was not a privileged skin color. In fact, being white, they may be actively accused of racism. As white teachers, they did not view themselves as racialized individuals, that is, they did not regard their whiteness as a racial identity or define themselves by

Attention should focus on the learning environment.

color. However, eventually these teachers admitted to themselves
that they, too, were people with a racial identity. They found that
by adding a multicultural emphasis to their teaching, they appeared more legitimate. The teachers realized that their education
was Eurocentric and that they needed to see the color of the children in order to design a multicultural curriculum and then had
to move beyond that color to value multicultural curriculum for
everyone. In addition, the teachers needed to establish a diverse
environment, and move from the perspective of adapting the child
to the classroom to the perspective of adapting the classroom to
the child.

Canning (1995) offers three general strategies for working with
learners from diverse cultures. First, the teacher should have an enabling attitude (being open-minded, questioning, and being willing
to listen). Next, teachers should be emotionally available, which may
require risk taking and a willingness to be vulnerable. Finally, teach-

ers need to observe from the inside, as a member of one culture trying to enter another.

The Council for Children with Behavior Disorders presented several guidelines for providing appropriate services to learners from
diverse cultures identified as emotionally/behaviorally disordered
(McIntyre, 1996). These guidelines took the form of goals for programs. These goals included:

- Identifying learners of diverse cultures being served in special
  programs who are actually demonstrating culturally based behaviors rather than emotional/behavioral disorders.
- Providing educational and treatment services to learners identified as emotionally/behaviorally disordered that are appropriate
  and respectful of culture.
- Implementing culturally and linguistically appropriate assessment.
- Recruiting professionals from diverse cultural groups.
- Providing pre-service and in-service training that is more appropriate for meeting the needs of individuals from various cultures.
- Creating welcoming atmospheres in schools.
- Enhancing the cultural knowledge base of professionals,
  clients/students, and the public at large.

◊◊ What Are Issues Related to Gender and Emotional/Behavioral Disorders?

In special education, although boys significantly outnumber girls,
research has rarely focused on gender issues. The more "subjective" the diagnosis, such as "emotionally disturbed" or "learning
disabled," the higher the representation of boys (American Association of University Women [AAUW], 1992). In *How Schools Shortchange Girls* (AAUW, 1992), the traditional explanation for the disproportionate number of boys in special education programs—that
boys are born with more disabilities—is challenged by a thorough
review of the literature. Medical reports on learning disabilities
and attention-deficit disorders indicate that they occur almost
equally in boys and girls. However, schools continue to identify
many more boys than girls in these disability areas. In addition,
girls who are identified as having learning disabilities have lower
tested intelligence quotients that do boys referred to these classes
(Vogel, 1990). The AAUW report suggests that girls who sit quietly
are ignored, and boys who act out are placed in special education
programs.

In their study of prevalence and incidence, Caseau, Luckasson, & Koth (1994) found that boys far outnumbered girls among students identified and served in public schools and students identified as emotionally/behaviorally disordered in public schools but receiving other mental health services. However, girls outnumbered boys among students who were not identified by the public schools but received mental health services. In addition, girls were more likely to have serious problems of depression, family conflict, suicidal ideation, and suicide attempts. Girls had behavioral and mental health problems serious enough to warrant identification, but not of the type that would lead to identification in the public schools. The small number of girls who did receive services in the public schools exhibited externalizing behaviors (aggression, hyperactivity, delinquency) similar to those of boys. Caseau et al. suggest that services for learners identified as emotionally/behaviorally disordered in the public schools may actually serve the purpose of containment rather than treatment.

Miller (1994) found that female adolescents identified as behaviorally/emotionally disordered report a higher frequency of suicidal ideation and attempts than do male adolescents with or without behavioral/emotional disorders. His survey results, which may be generalized, indicated that females identified as emotionally/behaviorally disordered may be particularly vulnerable in terms of both suicide ideation and suicide attempts. He recommends the teaching of alternative problem-solving strategies and facilitating the belief that adolescents can construct their futures (versus choosing suicide). Miller offers this charge to all adults who interact with adolescents, but especially teachers of students identified as emotionally/behaviorally disordered.

In reviewing issues related to gender, it appears that just as learners from diverse cultures may be overidentified because of culturally specific behaviors, female learners may be underidentified because of their gender-related behaviors.

Brown, Bauer, and Elgas (1996) reported that among kindergarten children identified as behaviorally disordered, boys who followed the male communication pattern of listing facts and sequences during "sharing time" received positive teacher interactions. Girls' comments, which were more social in nature and described personal interactions around the objects they brought during "sharing time" were judged as "off-topic" and tangential by the teacher.

◊◊ **Summary Points**

- Because of ethnocentricity, teachers may identify individuals from diverse cultures as emotionally/behaviorally disordered.
- When a population to be served by special education is culturally diverse, all activities and services provided to that population must take into account its major cultural characteristics.
- There is both overrepresentation and underrepresentation of various cultural groups in programs for students identified as emotionally/behaviorally disordered.
- Behavior seen as adaptive by one culture may be seen as maladaptive in another.
- Girls are far less frequently served in programs for learners identified as emotionally/behaviorally disordered.
- Girls tend to demonstrate internalizing behaviors; boys tend to externalize.

Select the most appropriate response.

1. A teacher who strives to have her students assume her behaviors and style of interaction represents
   a. diversity
   b. pluralism
   c. ethnocentricity
2. When serving a special population, special education services should
   a. account for the disability.
   b. consider additional classroom support.
   c. take into consideration cultural characteristics.
3. The members of each cultural group
   a. interact in the same ways.
   b. have the same adaptive behaviors.
   c. vary in both learning and interactions.
4. An African American student interacting cohesively may
   a. be viewed by his teacher as cheating.
   b. be more aggressive than Hispanic learners.
   c. cooperate less than Euro-American learners.
5. In African American families
   a. mothers may discipline more than in Euro-American families.
   b. fathers discipline most frequently.
   c. fathers discipline as often as fathers in Euro-American families.
6. Classroom instruction may limit Hispanic American students' ability to
   a. interact in Spanish.
   b. interact in English.
   c. demonstrate their language competence.
7. The use of alcohol is
   a. 3 times more common among Native American youth than the population at large.
   b. more common among minority culture youth than Euro-American youth.
   c. 3 times more common among Hispanic American youth than the population at large.
8. Although they are challenged by adversity, Southeast Asian refugee families
   a. connect often with extended families.
   b. value self-control and repression.
   c. value assimilation into American culture.
9. In a study by Valli (1995), student teachers
   a. did not consider themselves as "racialized" individuals.
   b. remained conscious of racial differences of their students.
   c. quickly adapted to the cultures of their students.

10. Girls are more likely to
    a. be found in public school programs serving learners identified as emotionally/behaviorally disordered.
    b. violently act out than boys.
    c. demonstrate depression and suicidal ideation than boys.

Making the Language Your Own

Match each key word or phrase to its definition.

_____ 1. belief that an individual's personal culture reflects the appropriate behavior

_____ 2. a patterned way of acting, thinking, and feeling

_____ 3. the quality or condition of being different

_____ 4. relative lack of assimilation into society

_____ 5. individuals whose ancestry can be traced to Africa

_____ 6. individuals whose ancestry can be traced to Asia, including China, Japan, and the Southeast Asian nations

_____ 7. indigenous peoples of North and South America

_____ 8. individuals of all races whose cultural heritage is tied to the use of the Spanish language and Latino culture

a. African Americans
b. Asian Americans
c. culture
d. diversity

e. ethnocentricity
f. Hispanic Americans
g. Native Americans
h. pluralism

Theory into Practice

1. Observe an educational program that includes learners identified as emotionally/behaviorally disordered from diverse cultures. Is there evidence in the classroom, in the instructional methods, or in the subject matter content that the diversity among the learners is given consideration?
2. Observe an educational program that includes learners identified as emotionally/behaviorally disordered who are female. Are there any observable differences in the behavior of the male and female members of the class? Does the teacher respond differently to the behavior of the female and male members of the class?

◊◊ **References**

Allen, L., & Majidi-Ahi, S. (1989). Black American children. In J. Gibbs & L. Huang, (Eds.), *Children of color* (pp. 148–178). San Francisco: Jossey Bass.

American Association of University Women (AAUW) (1992). *How schools shortchange girls.* Washington, DC: Author.

Bobo, J. K. (1985). Preventing drug abuse among American Indian adolescents. In L. D. Gilchrist & S. P. Schinke (Eds.), *Preventing social and health problems through life skills training* (pp. 97–105). Seattle: University of Washington School of Social Work.

Bowman, B. T. (1994, November). The challenge of diversity. *Phi Delta Kappan, 218–224.*

Branch, R. C., Goodwin, Y., & Gualtieri, J. (1993). Making classroom instruction culturally pluralistic. *The Educational Forum, 58*(1), 58–70.

Brod, R. L., & McQuiston, J. M. (1983). American Indian adult education and literacy: The first national survey. *Journal of American Indian Education, 1,* 1–16.

Brown, M. S., Bauer, A. M., & Elgas, P. M. (1996). Dual agenda and social participation of young children with disabilities. *International Journal of Qualitative Research, 30,* 49–72.

Buenning, M., Tollefson, N., & Rodriguez, F. (1992). Hispanic culture and the schools. In M. J. Fine & C. Carlson (Eds.), *The handbook of family-school interventions: A systems perspective* (pp. 86–101). Boston: Allyn & Bacon.

Canning, C. (1995). Getting from the outside in: Teaching Mexican Americans when you are an "Anglo." *The High School Journal, 78*(4), 195–205.

Caseau, D. L., Luckasson, R., & Kroth, R. L. (1994). Special education services for girls with serious emotional disturbance: A case of gender bias? *Behavioral Disorders, 20,* 51–60.

Commins, N. L., & Miramontes, O. B. (1989). Perceived and actual linguistic competence: A descriptive study of four low-achieving Hispanic bilingual students. *American Educational Research Journal, 26,* 443–472.

Dao, M. (1991). Designing assessment procedures for educationally at-risk southeast Asian-American students. *Journal of Learning Disabilities, 24,* 594–601; 629.

Delgado-Gaitan, C., & Trueba, H. T. (1985). Ethnographic study of participant structures in task completion: Reinterpretation of "handicaps" in Mexican children. *Learning Disability Quarterly, 8,* 67–75.

Dunn, C. W., & Tucker, C. M. (1993). Black children's adaptive functioning and maladaptive behavior associated with the quality of family support. *Journal of Multicultural Counseling and Development, 21,* 79–87.

Executive Committee of the Council for Children with Behavioral Disorders (1989). White paper on best assessment practices for students with behavioral disorders: Accommodations to cultural and individual differences. *Behavioral Disorders, 14,* 263–278.

Fradd, S., Figueroa, R. A., & Correa, V. I. (1989). Meeting the multicultural needs of Hispanic students in special education. *Exceptional Children, 56,* 102–104.

Garcia, E. E. (1995). The impact of linguistic and cultural diversity on America's schools. In M. C. Wang & M. C. Reynolds (Eds.), *Making a difference for students at risk: Trends and alternatives* (pp. 156–181). Thousand Oaks, CA: Sage.

Garcia, S., & Yates, J. (1994). Diversity: Teaching a special population. *CEC Today, 1*(6), 1, 10.

Gonzalez, V., & Yawkey, T. (1993). The assessment of culturally and linguistically different students: Celebrating change. *Educational Horizons, 72*(1), 41–49.

Grimm, L. L. (1992). The Native American child in school: An ecological perspective. In M. J. Fine & C. Carlson (Eds.), *The handbook of family-school intervention: A systems perspective* (pp. 102–118). Boston: Allyn & Bacon.

Guild, P. (1994, May). The culture/learning style connection. *Educational Leadership,* 16–21.

Hanna, J. (1988). *Disruptive school behavior: Class, race, and culture.* New York: Holmes & Meyer.

Haynes, N. M., & Gebreyesus, S. (1992). Cooperative learning: A case for African-American students. *School Psychology Review, 21*(4), 577–585.

Hodgkinson, H. (1985). *All one system.* Washington, DC: Institute for Educational Leadership.

Huang, L. N. (1989). Southeast Asian refuge children and adolescents. In J. T. Gibbs & L. N. Huang (Eds.), *Children of color: Psychological interventions with minority youth* (pp. 278–321). San Francisco: Jossey Bass.

Huang, L. N., & Ying, Y. (1989). Chinese American children and adolescents. In J. T. Gibbs & L. N. Huang (Eds.), *Children of color: Psychological interventions with minority youth.* (pp. 30–66). San Francisco: Jossey Bass.

Hyland, C. R. (1989). What we know about the fastest growing minority population: Hispanic Americans. *Educational Horizons, 67*(4), 124–130.

Kavale, K. A., Forness, S. R., & Alper, A. E. (1986). Research in behavioral disorders/emotional disturbance: A survey of subject identification criteria. *Behavioral Disorders, 11,* 159–167.

Klein, H. A. (1995). Urban Appalachian children in northern schools: A study in diversity. *Young Children, 50*(3), 10–16.

LaFramboise, T. D. & Low, K. G. (1989). American Indian children and adolescents. In J. Gibbs & L. Huang (Eds.), *Children of color* (pp. 114–147). San Francisco: Jossey Bass.

Leap, W. L. (1981). American Indian Language maintenance. *Annual Review of Anthropology, 10,* 271–280.

Lynch, E. M. (1993). Negotiating status and role: An ethnographic examination of verbal dueling among students with behavior disorders. In A. M. Bauer (Ed.), *Children who challenge the system* (pp. 29–44). Norwood, NJ: Ablex.

McAdoo, H. P. (1978). Minority families. In J. H. Stevens & M. Matthers (Eds.), *Mother-child, father-child relationships.* Washington, DC: The National Association for the Education of Young Children.

McIntyre, T. (1996). Guidelines for providing appropriate services to culturally diverse students with emotional and/or behavioral disorders. *Behavioral Disorders, 21*(2), 137–144.

Miller, D. (1994). Suicidal behavior of adolescents with behavior disorders and their peers without disabilities. *Behavioral Disorders, 20*(1), 61–68.

Nweke, W. (1994). *Racial differences in parental discipline practices.* (ERIC Document Reproduction Service No. ED 388 741)

Peters, M. (1981). Parenting in Black families with young children. In H. McAdoo (Ed.), *Black Families.* Newbury Park, CA: Sage.

Shon, S., & Ja, D. (1982). Asian families. In M. McGodrick, J. K. Pearce, & J. Giordano (Eds.), *Ethnicity and family therapy.* New York: Guilford Press.

Skiba, R. J. (1989). The importance of constructive validity: Alternative models for the assessment of behavioral disorders. *Behavioral Disorders, 14,* 175–185.

Smith, E. (1981). Cultural and historical perspectives in counseling blacks. In D. W. Sue (Ed.), *Counseling the culturally different: Theory and practice.* New York: Wiley.

Spradley, B. A., & McCurdy, D. W. (1984). Culture and the contemporary world. In J. P. Spradley & D. W. McCurdy (Eds.), *Conformity and conflict: Readings in cultural anthropology* (5th ed; pp. 1–13). Boston: Little Brown.

Spindler, G., & Spindler, L. (1994). What is cultural therapy? In G. Spindler & L. Spindler (Eds.), *Pathways to cultural awareness: Cultural therapy with teachers and students* (pp. 1–35). Thousand Oaks, CA: Sage.

U.S. Bureau of Census (1986). *Money income and poverty status of families and persons in the United States, 1985.* Washington, DC: U.S. Government Printing Office.

Valli, L. (1995). The dilemma of race: Learning to be color blind and color conscious. *Journal of Teacher Education, 46*(2), 120–129.

Vogel, S. A. (1990). Gender differences in intelligence, language, visual-motor abilities, and academic achievement in students with learning disabilities: A review of the literature. *Journal of Learning Disabilities, 23,* 44–52.

Yamamoto, J., & Kubota, M. (1989). The Japanese American family. In G. Powell, J. Yamamoto, & A. Morales (Eds.), *The psychosocial development of minority group children* (pp. 135–201). New York: Brunner-Mazel.

Screening to Placement

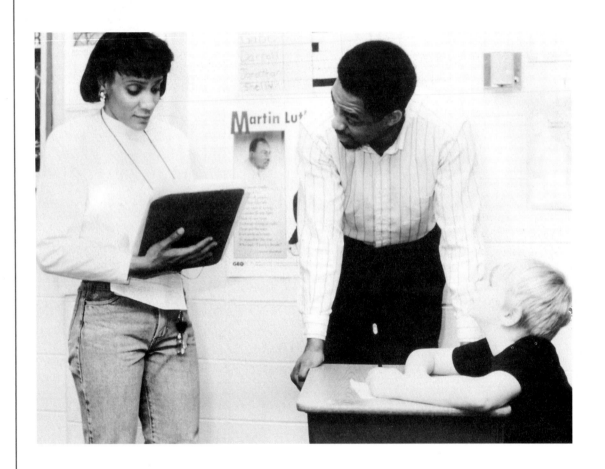

TO GUIDE YOUR READING

After you read this chapter, you will be able to answer these questions:

- What is the role of screening in identifying learners as emotionally/behaviorally disordered?

- What are prereferral activities for learners at risk for emotional/behavioral disorders?

- What are the referral processes used with learners identified as emotionally/behaviorally disordered?

- What are the assessment processes used with learners identified as emotionally/behaviorally disordered?

- What is the special education eligibility and placement process applied with learners identified as emotionally/behaviorally disordered?

- What are the Individualized Education Plan, the Individualized Family Service Plan, and the Individualized Transition Plan and how are these applied in services for learners identified as emotionally/behaviorally disordered?

Louis had been disrupting his fourth-grade mathematics class since school began in August. Ms. Taylor, his teacher, requested help from Drake Middle School's Student Assistance Team. Ms. Farrell, the assistant principal and chair of the team, called Louis's teachers together to discuss the behaviors that Ms. Taylor had been observing. In the meeting, it became apparent that Louis's disruptive behaviors—which included taking other students' homework and putting his name on it, challenging the teachers verbally in class, punching and taunting students who completed their work, and playing wastebasket basketball during class—occurred not only during mathematics, but during the other classes as well. Ms. Farrell suggested that she observe Louis in class, and that the teachers keep daily notes on Louis's activities during each class for two weeks. At the end of that time, the team would reconvene, and discuss potential interventions to attempt to help Louis be more successful in class.

This chapter presents several processes and procedures essential to the provision of services to learners identified as emotionally/behaviorally disordered, beginning from the point at which a learner is first viewed as potentially at risk for emotional/behavioral disorders to the placement of the learner identified as emotionally/behaviorally disordered in an Individualized Education Program responsive to his or her needs. The procedures are screening, prereferral, referral, assessment, eligibility determination, and placement. Many of the processes and procedures presented in this chapter are mandated in federal and state laws. Procedures vary somewhat from state to state and from school district to school district.

◊◊ What Is the Role of Screening in the Identification of Learners as Emotionally/Behaviorally Disordered?

The Individuals with Disabilities Education Act requires that all individuals with disabilities be identified by their school districts. However, few school districts actively carry out screening programs for emotional behavioral disorders, possibly because the identification of large numbers of students as emotionally/behaviorally disordered would have a significant financial impact on the school districts (Kauffman, 1996). Most school districts rely on teachers and parents for referrals in place of screening programs.

Screening is the process of identifying students who, at least on the basis of a first look, are at risk for emotional/behavioral disorders and require further study. In screening, an entire population of students is evaluated to determine whether any may need additional assessment (Witt, Elliott, Kramer, & Gresham, 1994). Learners who do not perform to a specified level on screening instruments are considered "at risk" and are referred to a more detailed, individualized assessment process.

As a result of screening, the learner may be classified as (a) having no problem, (b) having a transitory problem, (c) having a problem that is a response to social and academic stressors in the school or classroom that could be altered, or (d) having a problem that is evident in school, home, and neighborhood (Long, Morse, & Newman, 1980). The result of screening is not to classify a learner as emotionally/behaviorally disordered but to identify for further study the learner who is at risk for such a problem.

Screening is based on the assumption that the early identification of learners with emotional/behavioral disorders can prevent behavioral and school-related problems (Walker, Colvin, & Ramsey, 1995). Screening young children for emotional/behavioral disorders is a challenge because of the great variability in behavior among young children. In addition, the remediation of behavior problems becomes more difficult as children grow older and behavior patterns become more established (Bower, 1981). Three fourths of all children who show early signs of behavior problems, such as disobedience, tantrums, fighting, and stealing, move to more serious acting-out behaviors as they age (Reid, 1993). However, young children with mild to moderate behavior problems are the most likely to be overlooked by traditional developmental screening (Beare & Lynch, 1986).

Several strategies are available for screening learners for emotional/behavioral disorders. Walker, Colvin, and Ramsey (1995) suggest that screening procedures should be proactive, seeking out students who may be at risk for emotional/behavioral disorders rather than responding when students are demonstrating serious behavior problems. In addition, the learner should be evaluated by a variety of people in a variety of settings. To serve the intended function of prevention, screening efforts should take place at the preschool and kindergarten levels. Finally, although teacher nominations and rankings of behavior are helpful to initiate a screening process, additional information, such as observation data, school records checks, and peer or parent ratings should be used.

screening the process of identifying learners who, at least on the basis of first-level study, deserve further assessment

Rating Scales

Rating scales have been traditionally used as a part of the screening process for learners referred for possible special education services (Elliot, Busse, & Gresham, 1993). Elliot et al. present five issues that influence the use and interpretation of these scales:

1. Ratings are summaries of observations of the perceived relative frequency of a behavior. For example, a teacher may rate a student as "sometimes" demonstrating a behavior if it occurs between two and five times a day, although there may be a real difference between a student who demonstrates a behavior two times and one who demonstrates a behavior five times.

2. Ratings are judgments affected by the environment and the rater's standards. An individual's behavior may change depending on the situation, and depending on the rater's judgment of how the learner is functioning.

social validity the importance attributed to behavior by significant others in the environment

3. The *social validity,* that is, the importance attributed to the behavior by significant individuals in the environment, should be recognized. Ratings may be distorted when the focus becomes the tolerance of the rater for a behavior rather than the importance of the behavior to the student's functioning.

4. Several assessors of the same student's behaviors may only moderately agree. Rating scales use rather simple frequency counts for quantifying behaviors that, in context, vary a great deal in frequency, intensity, and duration.

5. Ratings may be related to a student's gender. Interpretations of rating scales must be done with norms that are sensitive to gender differences.

Elliot et al. (1993) also suggest several guidelines for the evaluation of rating scales. These guidelines are summarized in Figure 9.1.

One example of a screening system for children identified as emotionally/behaviorally disordered is the Systematic Screening for Behavior Disorders (SSBD) procedure (Walker and Severson, 1990). Based on the assumption that teacher judgment is valid for the identification of learners with emotional/behavioral disorders, the SSBD includes three steps or gates for identification of emotional/behavioral disorders: (a) a teacher ranking, (b) a teacher rating, and (c) direct observation in formal and informal environments by a professional, usually the teacher. The SSBD identifies students in the elementary grades who are at risk for externalizing or internalizing behavioral disorders.

Another instrument used for screening is the Child Behavior Checklist (Achenbach & Edelbrock, 1991), which includes several

Is the rating scale practically useful?

- Is training necessary for raters?
- Does the interpretive framework match the purpose of the raters?

Is the rating scale reliable?

- Is there test-retest reliability?
- Is there interrater reliability?

Is the rating scale internally valid?

- Is the content valid?
- Are the items meaningful and useful?

Is the rating scale externally valid?

- Can the scale be used for the purpose for which it was intended?

Figure 9.1   Guidelines for the Evaluations of Behavior Rating Scales (Elliot, Busse, & Gresham, 1993)

forms: parent's report, teacher's report, and self-report. In schools, the most frequently used form is the teacher's report, in which the teacher rates 112 behavior problems on a 3-point scale: (1) Not true, (2) somewhat or sometimes true, or (3) very or often true. The teacher's report, which can be used with learners from 5 through 18 years of age, generates a profile relating specific items to problem factors. Some of the items rated by teachers are (a) cries a lot; (b) complains of loneliness; (c) physically attacks people; (d) seems preoccupied with sex; and (e) dislikes school.

◊◊ What Are Prereferral Activities for Learners at Risk for Emotional/Behavioral Disorders?

Prereferral activities are strategies implemented in the general education classroom by the general education teacher to address the individual needs of learners prior to referral for assessment for special education services. The goal of prereferral activities is to provide learners with behavior problems assistance in the general education classroom and thus make referral to special education unnecessary (Shea & Bauer, 1997). Such activities are not considered to be an initial step in the special education assessment and

prereferral activities
strategies implemented in the general education classroom by the general education teacher to address the individual needs of learners prior to referral for assessment for special education services

The purpose of intervention is to avoid classification.

placement process, but are developed by general education personnel through collaborative consultation and problem-solving activities. Prereferral activities are recommended or required in at least 34 states (Carter & Sugai, 1989).

Nelson, Smith, Taylor, Dodd, and Reavis (1991) contend that prereferral interventions are systematic and collaborative efforts, designed to reduce the need for special education services by providing assistance to students in the general education classroom, decrease the overidentification of students as having disabilities, facilitate inclusion, and improve the general classroom teachers' attitudes towards students with learning and behavioral problems through improving their abilities to work with those students.

Several assumptions underlie prereferral interventions (Pugach & Johnson, 1989):

- The purpose of these interventions is to avoid the classification of students as disabled.

- All educational professionals in a school, at one time or another, serve as consultants to each other; that is, consultation is multidirectional.

- Classroom teachers, given time and support, are able to solve many of their students' classroom problems without the direct intervention of specialists.
- The process for supporting students varies with the student's problem and personnel involved.

An example of a prereferral intervention with a learner who is potentially at risk for classification as emotionally/behaviorally disordered is presented in Figure 9.2 (Shea & Bauer, 1997).

The behaviors that prompt prereferral interventions may vary by nature or degree for children by ethnicity or gender. MacMillan, Gresham, Lopez, and Bocian (1996) reported differences among Euro-American, African American, and Hispanic American students. Euro-American children demonstrated higher tested verbal intelligence quotients and reading achievement scores. Referred African American children were more likely to have more behavior problems than were Hispanic American children. Severe academic problems characterized children across all ethnic groups. Differences by gender were related to the acting-out behaviors typically exhibited by males; differences were not reported, however, on cognitive and achievement measures. Overall, teachers rated referred girls higher on overall academic competence than referred boys.

Noll, Kamps, and Seaborin (1993) studied the three-year implementation of a prereferral intervention model for learners with emotional/behavioral disorders. Each year, between 43% and 64% of referred students remained in the general education classroom, between 14% and 22% were identified as having other disabilities, and between 23% and 39% were identified as having behavioral disorders, with half of the last group of students being able to continue in the general education classroom with support. Noll et al. prereferral process included "best practice" for behavioral consultations, including (a) a collaborative agreement with teacher, pupil, and parents; (b) a contractual agreement with goals and set criteria for progress evaluation; (c) built-in consequences with systematic reinforcement and loss of privileges for noncompliance; (d) self-monitoring, which encouraged self-management and intrinsic control as an end result; (e) easily implemented interventions across settings and teachers/staff; and (f) a design or plan to reduce the need for external procedures through fading and delayed reinforcement strategies. In addition, an itinerant teacher was used to support the prereferral interventions.

The use of school-based prereferral intervention teams has been related to an increase in referrals that, after case studies, qualify for special education services, while providing ongoing support to classroom teachers with students not eligible for special education

Louise was doing well in Mr. Raphael's fourth-grade classroom until December, when her behavior changed. Louise no longer completed her homework, did not participate in games during recess, and on two occasions, had pinched children who were swinging in "her" swing on the playground. After receiving no responses to notes to Louise's mother regarding concerns about these behaviors, Mr. Raphael telephoned Louise's home. Louise's 19-year-old aunt, who was "helping out with the kids," reported that Louise's mother had entered a hospice program for terminal cancer patients. Louise's father was spending a great deal of time at the hospice, but "just couldn't bring himself to take the kids to visit."

Mr. Raphael approached Ms. Turner, the principal, to discuss Louise's behavior. They agreed that an Intervention Assistance Team should be formed. Mr. Raphael recommended that Ms. Holt, the art teacher, with whom Louise had particular rapport, be included in the team. Ms. Turner suggested that Ms. Michael, the school counselor, and Ms. Wang, who had recently worked her classroom through the death of a student's mother in an automobile accident, also be included.

The Intervention Assistance Team met and discussed Louise's behavior. The plan that was formulated included the following:

- Hold weekly meetings for Louise with the school counselor.

- Increase efforts to encourage Louise to participate appropriately during recess, while recognizing her feelings. Louise was to receive a cue such as the following: "I know it's hard to have fun when you're worried about someone. Would you like to talk about how you're feeling before you go join the game?" or "I know you're feeling worried right now, but the rule is to keep your hands to yourself on the playground. How could you ask (child's name) to move to another swing? Could you swing on another one?

- Review materials Ms. Wang had received from the local children's hospital regarding dealing with death, separation, and loss in the classroom.

- Continue communication attempts with the home, recognizing that the family was in crisis and all contacts should be supportive rather than report negative behavior.

- Hold meeting again in four weeks to evaluate the plan and Louise's behavior.

Figure 9.2 An example of prereferral intervention

(Ivarie & Russell, 1992). Ivarie and Russell found that following implementation of the team on behalf of a child, teachers expressed concern for time for consultation. Teachers described the most significant advantage to the prereferral intervention team as receiving immediate help when it was needed.

Two types of prereferral interventions have emerged (Noll, et al., 1993): behavioral interventions and social skills programs. Behavioral interventions are systematic and data-based. To design behavioral interventions, formal and informal observation must be conducted across settings. In addition, the teacher should perform an anecdotal record review, documenting his or her prior attempts to modify the student's educational program and environment. Social skills programs may include skills such as self-awareness, self-control, peer interactions, problem solving, and communication. Social skills groups may be conducted by consulting teachers or in the general education classrooms by the teachers themselves.

Some learners may not respond to prereferral interventions, and, as a consequence, are referred for special education assessment and services.

◊◊ What Are the Referral Processes Used with Learners Identified as Emotionally/Behaviorally Disordered?

In addition to screening, discussed in a previous section of this chapter, learners may be identified for assessment for special education services through the referral process. *Referral* is the process of soliciting and accepting nominations for assessment from others. A referral may be accepted from school personnel, parents, physicians, community human service agency personnel, or other persons responsible for the learner's welfare (Shea & Bauer, 1997).

referral the process of soliciting and accepting nominations for assessment for special education services from others

Teachers' judgments about learners' social behavior is the primary basis for referral in schools (Hoge, 1983). Gresham and Reschly (1988) describe a "model behavioral profile" applied by teachers when judging learners to be behavior problems. This profile is comprised of behaviors that (a) facilitate academic performance and (b) are marked by the absence of disruptive behaviors that disturb the teacher and the classroom. In their study of teachers as judges of social competence, Gresham, Noell, and Elliott (1996) reported that teacher ratings of social skills were much more accurate in ruling out low social competence rather than identifying the presence of social incompetence. Teachers appear to base their judgments of low social competence for both boys and girls on the absence of teacher-preferred skills.

School referral is a two-step process. First, information is collected from all individuals who currently interact with the learner in the school. The general education classroom teacher, for example, may be requested to assist in completing rating scales or checklists, or to complete information sheets. In addition, teachers present documentation of the interventions, accommodations, and resources that they have used to address the referral issue. These materials are presented to the team or individual responsible for determining the appropriateness of the referral. When a Student Support Team has been in place, assisting the teachers in designing, implementing, and evaluating prereferral interventions, the team is usually engaged in making the decision that current efforts are not adequate and the student should be referred for evaluation. In other settings, a principal or special educator may be responsible for reviewing the referral information and determining the appropriateness of the referral.

If the referral is deemed appropriate, the next step is taken: parents are invited to a conference, at which the concerns of school personnel are explained and parents are asked for permission to assess the child for special education services. A parent must sign a "consent for evaluation" form for the evaluation process to continue. If the parent does not agree to the evaluation, the school district has the right to follow due process procedures to appeal the parent's decision. When the consent is granted, the multifactored evaluation proceeds.

◊◊ What Are the Assessment Processes Used with Learners Identified as Emotionally/Behaviorally Disordered?

assessment the process of studying a learner to determine the nature of the problem, if, in fact, there is a problem

The *assessment* process, often referred to as "diagnostic evaluation," or simply "evaluation," is the process of studying a learner to determine the nature of the problem, if, in fact, there is a problem. The basic purpose of assessment for intervention is to identify changes that are needed in the learner's behaviors or environments and deciding how to accomplish the goals of the needed changes (Barnett, Bauer, Barnhouse, Ehrhardt, Lentz, Macmann, & Stollar, in press).

Assessment for intervention has been greatly neglected in the education of learners identified as emotionally/behaviorally disordered. Dunlap and Childs (1996), in a review of 13 years of intervention research, reported that interventions were rarely individualized and rarely based on assessment data. They concluded that interventions were designed independent of assessment information on the children.

Assessment processes are controversial.

The Nature of Assessment

The process used for the assessment of all learners has been questioned in the past 20 years. The National Association of Early Childhood Teacher Educators, for example, urged a replacement of current questionable testing practices with those more in line with the knowledge base on how young children demonstrate what they know (1989). The National Center for Fair and Open Testing (1989) indicated that more than 100 million standardized tests were administered annually to public school students.

The overriding purpose of all assessments is to gather information to facilitate decision making (Witt et al., 1994). These decisions may be related to screening, classification and placement, student progress, programming or instruction, or program effectiveness (Salvia & Ysseldyke, 1991).

There are two general models of assessment: the medical model and the behavioral-ecological model (Witt et al., 1994). The medical model assumes that behavior that deviates negatively from some standard is a reflection of personal disease, disturbance, disorder, or dysfunction, and that treatment must bring about changes within the individual. The behavioral-ecological model, on the other hand, acknowledges the impact of other people and environmental factors in shaping a child's behavior. Unusual behavior is viewed as inappropriate or maladaptive rather than caused by an internal problem.

Witt et al. (1994) describe four general approaches to assessment: norm-referenced, criterion-referenced, informal, and ecological. The general assumptions, advantages, disadvantages, and questions answered by each of these general approaches is presented in Table 9.1.

Appropriate assessment is grounded in the following assumptions (Witt et al., 1994):

- Differences among learners derive their meaning from the situation in which they occur.
- Tests are only samples of behavior and should only provide support to making decisions.
- Assessments are conducted to improve instructional or intervention activities.
- Individuals who are conducting assessments should be properly trained.
- No assessments are free from errors.

The Individuals with Disabilities Education Act mandates that an multidisciplinary team, including professionals and parents, conduct a diagnostic evaluation that concludes in (a) a child study report and (b) a written Individualized Education Plan. The team must include at least one teacher or specialist in the area of disability in question—in this case, a teacher or specialist in emotional/behavioral disorders. All assessment instruments must be administered in the learner's native language or other mode of communication, be valid for the purpose for which they are administered, and be administered by a qualified person who follows the protocol of the instrument. No single instrument may be used to determine a learner's eligibility for services. Assessment instruments should provide specific as well as general measures and should be selected and administered so that the learner's real aptitude or achievement is measured. Learners also must be assessed in all areas related to the suspected disability, including, as appropriate, health,

Table 9.1 General Approaches to Assessment

	Norm-Referenced	Criterion-Referenced	Informal	Ecological
Description	Individuals are compared to the performance of a large, collectively representative sample referred to as the "norm."	Individuals' performance is compared to some pre-established standard.	Process is adapted to the individual child and situation.	Assesses child, teacher, expectations environment, and task.
Advantages	Present information that is easily communicated; compares to group.	Identifies specific skills.	Is relevant to the instructional process.	Expands the focus of assessment, recognizes complexity of behavior
Disadvantages	Information is too general to be useful; discrepancy exists between what is taught and what is tested; tends to promote belief that locus of problem is within the child.	Difficult to establish a criterion; teachers may "teach to the test."	Depends on examiner to select appropriate tests, problem-solve, and interpret; values may affect recommendations.	Process is complex; lack adequate instruments.
Question answered	How does this student compare with others his or her age?	How well does this individual perform this skill?	What seems to be contributing to the problem?	What is happening here when this behavior occurs?

vision, hearing, social and emotional status, general intelligence, achievement, communication skills, and motor skills (Turnbull, 1993).

◊◊ What Are the Special Education Eligibility and Placement Processes Applied with Learners Identified as Emotionally/Behaviorally Disordered?

eligibility the process of determining if a learner meets specific criteria for classification as a learner with emotional/behavioral disorders

placement assignment of a learner classified as emotionally/behaviorally disordered to a specific special education and related services program

Eligibility is the process of determining if a learner meets state criteria for classification as a learner with emotional/behavioral disorders. *Placement* is the assignment of a learner classified as emotional/behaviorally disordered to a specific special education and related services program.

After the learner is assessed, as discussed in the previous section, the multidisciplinary team is responsible for determining if the learner meets specific criteria for classification as emotional/behaviorally disordered. The criteria for classification vary somewhat from state to state. In making this decision, the members of the team are required to take into consideration all of the available information on the learner. If adequate information is not available to the team to make a prudent decision, then additional information must be obtained.

Placement is also a responsibility of the multidisciplinary team. During the placement process, the team:

- Reviews all information available on the learner and the environments in which the learner is functioning.

- Seeks parent evaluation of the information and determines if additional information is needed before placement can be recommended.

- Analyzes the learner's academic and behavioral strengths, weaknesses, and learning style to use as a basis for educational goals and objectives.

- Considers the placement alternatives in view of the learner's educational goals, objectives, and learning style.

- Reviews the placement selected with regard to its restriction on the learner's inclusion with typical students and responsiveness to the learner's individual needs.

◊◊ What Are the Individualized Education Plan, the Individualized Family Service Plan, and the Individualized Transition Plan, and How Are These Applied in Services for Learners Identified as Emotionally/Behaviorally Disordered?

Regardless of the specific diagnostic label assigned to a learner with disabilities, the beginning point for special education services is the Individualized Education Plan. The *Individualized Education Plan,* or the IEP, is a year-long plan of the services and activities conducted with a learner with a disability—in this case, a learner identified as emotionally/behaviorally disordered.

The IEP is developed in a multidisciplinary team meeting in which the learner's parents, and, if appropriate, the learner, are important and essential contributors. Team members develop the IEP on the basis of the individual assessment information discussed in the previous section, in response to the learner's individual needs.

The IEP includes (Federal Register, 1977, 121a.346):

- A statement of the learner's present level of performance.

- Annual goals and objectives.

- The specific special education and related services to be provided to the learner, including the amount of time to be spent with peers without identified disabilities.

- Projected dates of the initiation of services and anticipated duration of services.

- Criteria for determining at least annually, progress made toward the goals and objectives.

- If the learner is at least 16 years of age (or as early as 14 years of age) a description of transition services must be included.

The IEP is a sequential process, which answers the following questions (Ohio Department of Education, 1995):

1. What is the long-term vision or goal for this child?

2. What is the child's current functioning?

3. How far can we go toward the vision for this child this year?

4. What services will be provided to move toward that vision?

5. Where will the services be provided?

An example of an IEP for a learner identified as emotionally/behaviorally disordered is provided in Figure 9.3.

Several additional legal questions have recently emerged in the development and implementation of IEPs (Ohio Department of Ed-

Individualized Education Plan a year-long plan of the services and activities to be conducted with learners identified as emotionally/behaviorally disordered

Individualized Transition Plan a plan to facilitate the movement of a learner identified as emotionally/behaviorally disordered from home to preschool, from preschool to kindergarten, from program to program within general and special education, or from an educational program to postsecondary education or training or employment or supported employment

Student's Name: *Lucas Wang*   Birth Date: *7-6-92*   Date of IEP Conference: *9-15-99*

School: *Knox Elementary*   Date of Initial Placement: *5-15-97*

Summary of Present Levels of Functioning:

Strengths:
Can verbalize his feelings regarding interactions with others
Can state his strategy for managing his aggression towards others
Strong reading skills

Weaknesses:
Difficulty completing tasks
Aggressive towards others when asked to correct or repeat tasks
Distractibility during large-group activities

Annual Goals	Description and Amount of Time in General Education	Special Consideration and Comments	Committee Members
1. *Increase tasks completed during the school day.*	*100%*	*Consultation with school counselor regarding participation in social skills groups*	*Mei Wang, Mother; Luis Hernandez, School Counselor; Margaret Carroll, Teacher; Meg Brooks, Special Education Teacher*
2. *Express frustration verbally.*			
3. *Increase attention in large-group activities.*			

Committee Recommendations for Specific Procedures, Techniques, Materials, etc.	Objective Evaluation Criteria for Annual Goal Statements
Daily parent-teacher journal *Personal journal of behavior*	*Weekly conferences with teacher and Lucas* *Anecdotal records and self-recorded data*

Figure 9.3   Example IEP

Placement recommendations: *General education classroom*

Short-Term Objective	Services	Person Responsible	Amount of Time	Beginning Date	Review Date
1a. *Lucas will complete at least three pencil and paper tasks during the school day.*	*Special Ed. Consult.*	*Teacher*	*100%*	*9/1*	*1/1*
1b. *Lucas will complete at least five pencil and paper tasks during the school day.*	*Special Ed. Consult.*	*Teacher*	*100%*	*1/1*	*6/1*
2a. *Lucas will have no more than one aggressive out-burst each week.*	*Special Ed. Consult., School Counselor*	*Teacher*	*100%*	*9/1*	*6/1*
2b. *When provided a model, Lucas will express frustration verbally.*				*9/1*	*1/1*
2c. *Lucas will independently express frustration verbally.*				*1/1*	*6/1*
3a. *Using a "study-buddy," Lucas will physically remain with the group during large-group activities.*	*Teacher*	*Teacher*	*100%*	*9/1*	*1/1*
3b. *While working at his desk, Lucas will self-record no more than one distraction during each ten-minute period.*				*6/1*	*6/1*

ucation, 1995). During the IEP meeting, participation in testing and assessment programs, including statewide proficiency testing, must be discussed. In addition, if the child is between the ages of 3 and 5, the transition from early childhood to school-age special education services must be specifically described. If the student is at least 16, a plan must be included for the transition from school to work and community living. All behaviors that may interfere with the child's learning and the opportunity of his or her peers to learn must be addressed. The physical education needs of the child must be discussed, as well as the possibility for extended school year services, if, as a consequence of the interruption between school years, the child may be unlikely to achieve his or her short-term objectives.

Individualized Family Service Plan a year-long plan of services and outcomes for the family of a child with a disability who is younger than 3 years of age

For infants and toddlers with disabilities, the *Individualized Family Service Plan* (IFSP) replaces the IEP. The IFSP is reviewed semiannually and evaluated annually. It includes:

- A statement of the infant's or toddler's present level of functioning.
- A statement of the family's strengths and needs as related to the development of the infant or toddler with disabilities.
- A statement of the major anticipated outcomes for the infant or toddler and the family, and the criteria, procedures and time lines used to determine the degree to which progress is being made and whether revisions of the anticipated outcomes are necessary.
- A description of the specific early intervention services necessary to meet the unique needs of the infant or toddler and the family.
- The projected dates for initiation of services and the anticipated duration of the services.
- The name of the case manager for the service most relevant to the needs of the infant or toddler and family, who is responsible for the implementation of the plan and coordination with other agencies and persons.
- A plan for the transition of the toddler to preschool.

◊◊ Summary Points

- Screening is based on the assumption that behavioral and school-related problems can be prevented through early identification and intervention.
- Teachers' judgments about learners' behavior is the primary basis for referral in schools.

- Prereferral activities provide learners with behavior problems the assistance required in general education classrooms, thus making referral to special education unnecessary.

- The overriding purpose of assessment is to gather information necessary for decision making.

- Eligibility is determined by a multidisciplinary team.

- The multidisciplinary team writes the IEP, which describes the special education and related services required by the learner and the placement in which those services will be delivered.

Select the most appropriate response.

1. The purpose of screening is to
    a. classify learners as disabled.
    b. identify for further study learners at risk for disabilities.
    c. determine eligibility for special education.
2. Teachers base their judgments of low social competence on
    a. the absence of teacher-preferred skills.
    b. aggression.
    c. the absence of prosocial skills.
3. The goal of prereferral activities is to
    a. provide an initial step in the special education assessment program.
    b. engage general and special educators collaboratively in problem solving activities.
    c. provide documentation of special needs.
4. Prereferral interventions assume that teachers
    a. need additional support to meet students' needs.
    b. have difficulty planning for learners with special needs.
    c. are able to solve many of their student's classroom problems without the direct intervention of specialists.
5. Assessment for intervention has been
    a. well-established for learners identified as emotionally/behaviorally disordered.
    b. seriously neglected in the education of learners identified as emotionally/behaviorally disordered.
    c. documented as effective for learners identified as emotionally/ behaviorally disordered.
6. Behavior is viewed as deviating from a standard and a reflection of personal disease in the
    a. informal assessment model.
    b. ecological model
    c. norm-referenced model.
7. Appropriate assessment assumes
    a. proper training of professionals.
    b. a medical model.
    c. standardization.
8. Placements are identified in
    a. referral forms.
    b. IEPs.
    c. eligibility reports.
9. The responsibility for determining eligibility rests with the
    a. diagnostic evaluation team.
    b. school psychologist.
    c. multidisciplinary team.

10. Differences between learners derive their meaning from
    a. the presence of a disability.
    b. the situation in which they occur.
    c. their perception of the situation.

Making the Language Your Own

Match each key word or phrase to its definition.

_____ 1. the process of determining if a learner meets specific criteria for classification as a learner with emotional/behavioral disorders

_____ 2. a year-long plan of services and activities

_____ 3. included on the IEP to facilitate movement from early childhood to school-age programs or from school to work and community living

_____ 4. the process of soliciting and accepting nominations for assessment

_____ 5. assignment of a learner to a specific special education and related services program

_____ 6. a year-long plan of services and outcomes for the family of an infant or toddler with a disability

_____ 7. strategies implemented in the general education classroom by the general education teacher prior to referral

_____ 8. the importance attributed to the behavior by significant individuals in the environment

_____ 9. the process of identifying learners who deserve further study

_____ 10. the process of studying a learner to determine the nature of the problem, if, in fact, there is a problem

a. assessment
b. eligibility
c. Individualized Education Plan
d. Individual Family Service Plan
e. Transition Plan
f. placement
g. prereferral activities
h. referral
i. screening
j. social validity

Theory into Practice

1. With the permission of all involved, observe an IEP or IFSP meeting. Describe the roles of the individuals present. What process was followed?
2. Interview the administrator of a school regarding the Student Assistance Team in his or her building. Describe the team composition and processes related to supporting students.

◊◊ References

Achenbach, T. M., & Edelbrock, E. (1991). *Manual for the Child Behavior Checklist/4–18 and 1991 Profile*. Burlington, VT: University of Vermont.

Barnett, D. W., Bauer, A. M., Barnhouse, L., Ehrhardt, K. E., Lentz, F. E., Macmann, G., & Stollar, S. (out of press). Ecological foundation of early intervention: Planned activities and strategies sampling. *Journal of Special Education, 30*(4), 471–490.

Beare, P. L., & Lynch, E. C. (1986). Underidentification of pre-school children at risk for behavioral disorders. *Behavioral Disorders, 11,* 77–183.

Bower, E. M. (1981). *Early identification of emotionally handicapped children in school* (3rd ed.). Springfield, IL: C. C. Thomas.

Carter, J., & Sugai, G. (1989). Survey on prereferral practices: Responses from state departments of education. *Exceptional Children, 55,* 298–302.

Dunlap, G., & Childs, K. E. (1996). Intervention research in emotional and behavioral disorders: An analysis of studies from 1980–1983. *Behavioral Disorders, 21*(2), 125–136.

Elliot, S. N., Busse, R. T., & Gresham, F. M. (1993). Behavior rating scales: Issues of use and development. *School Psychology Review, 22*(2), 313–321.

Federal Register (1977), 1219346.

Gerken, K. (1988). Best practice in academic assessment. In A. Thomas & J. Grimes (Eds.), *Best Practice in School Psychology* (pp. 157–170). Washington, DC: National Association of School Psychologists.

Gresham, F. M., Noell, G. H., & Elliott, S. (1996). Teachers as judges of social competence: A conditional probability analysis. *School Psychology Review, 25*(1), 108–117.

Gresham, F. M., & Reschly, D. J. (1988). Issues in the conceptualization and assessment of social skills in the mildly handicapped. In T. R. Kratochwill (Ed.), *Advances in school psychology* (Vol. 6, pp. 203–247). Hillsdale, NJ: Lawrence Erlbaum.

Hoge, R. (1983). Psychometric properties of teacher-judgement measures of pupil aptitudes, classroom behaviors, and achievement levels. *Journal of Special Education, 17,* 401–429.

Ivarie, I. J., & Russell, J. (1992). Prereferral interventions. Paper presented at the Teacher Education Division of the Council for Exceptional Children, Cincinnati, OH.

Kauffman, J. (1996). *Characteristics of children and youth with behavior disorders* (6th ed.). Columbus, OH: Merrill.

Long, N. J., Morse, W. C., & Newman, R. G. (1980). *Conflict in the Classroom* (4th ed.). Belmont, CA: Wadsworth.

MacMillan, D. L., Gresham, F. M., Lopez, M. F., & Bocian, K. M. (1996). Comparison of students nominated for prereferral interventions by ethnicity and gender. *The Journal of Special Education, 30*(2), 133–151.

National Association of Early Childhood Teacher Educators (1989). *Resolution on testing practices.* Washington, DC: Author.

National Center for Fair and Open Testing (1989). *Fallout from the testing operation.* Cambridge, MA: Author.

Nelson, J. R., Smith, D. J., Taylor, L., Dodd, J. M., & Reavis, K. (1991). Prereferral intervention: A review of the research. *Education and Treatment of Children, 14,* 243–253.

Noll, M. B., Kamps, D., & Seaborn, C. F. (1993). Prereferral interventions for students with emotional/behavioral risks: Use of a behaviorial consultation model. *Journal of Emotional and Behavioral Disorders, 1,* 203–214.

Ohio Department of Education (1995). *Whose IDEA is this?* Columbus, OH: Author.

Pugach, M., & Johnson, L. J. (1989). Prereferral interventions: Progress, problems, and challenges. *Exceptional Children, 56,* 217–226.

Reid, J. B. (1993). Prevention of conduct disorder before and after school entry: Relating interventions to developmental findings. *Development and Psychopathology, 5,* 311–319.

Salvia, J., & Ysseldyke, J. E. (1991). *Assessment.* Boston: Houghton Mifflin Co.

Shea, T. M., & Bauer, A. M. (1997). *An introduction to special education: A social systems perspective.* Madison, WI: Brown & Benchmark.

State of Ohio (1995). *Whose IDEA is this?* Columbus, OH: Ohio Department of Education.

Turnbull, H. R. (1993). *Free appropriate public education: The law and children with disabilities* (4th ed). Denver: Love.

Walker, H. M., Colvin, G., & Ramsey, E. (1995). *Antisocial behavior in school: Strategies and best practices.* Pacific Grove, CA: Brooks/Cole.

Walker, H. M., & Severson, H. H. (1990). *Systematic Screening for Behavior Disorders: User's guide and administration manual.* Longmont, CO: Sopris West.

Witt, J. C., Elliott, S. N., Kramer, J. J., & Gresham, F. M. (1994). *Assessment of children.* Madison, WI: Brown & Benchmark.

10 Behavior Change: Individual Interventions

TO GUIDE YOUR READING

After you read this chapter, you will be able to answer these questions:

- What are the components of an intervention plan?

- What are several behavior management strategies that are grounded in the principles of reinforcement and how are these applied with learners identified as emotionally/behaviorally disordered?

- What are several crisis intervention strategies and how are these applied with learners identified as emotionally/behaviorally disordered?

- What are scaffolds, scripts, and self-regulation strategies and how are these applied with learners identified as emotionally/behaviorally disordered?

Joseph was working at his seat on his reading log. He looked out the window, and gazed at the garbage truck backing in position to empty the dumpster. When he glanced back to his paper, he noticed his "attention card" taped to the corner of his desk. He looked at his watch, and put a tally mark next to the time slot 10:00 to 10:15. He continued to work until Ms. Jefferson told the students to transition to writing workshop. He brought his card to Ms. Jefferson, who said, "What do you think, Joseph? I think you're really paying more attention to your work!" At the end of each hour, Joseph showed Ms. Jefferson his attention card. Before he boarded the bus, he recorded the total number of times his mind wandered off task on his graph.

Even the most skillful teacher is, at times, confronted with learners identified as emotionally/behaviorally disordered who require help specific to a behavioral pattern or problem. Individual interventions have frequently been behavioral in nature, emphasizing what happens before the behavior (antecedents) and events that encourage the behavior to recur (reinforcement). In the social systems perspective, however, the developmental context of each learner must be considered. Simple linear models of antecedent-behavior-consequence don't always provide adequate information for what is happening with a learner.

This chapter describes individual interventions that are designed to support behavior change. It begins with a presentation of a five-step intervention plan that is applicable to the intervention strategies presented in the chapter. Also discussed are the principles of reinforcement, the consequences of behavior, and generalization and discrimination. The information in this first section of the chapter is exemplified through its application in the PASSkey strategy (Barnett, Ehrhardt, Stollar, & Bauer, 1993).

Presented next are several behavior management interventions grounded in the principles of reinforcement, which include positive reinforcement, extinction, punishment, differential reinforcement, shaping, contingency contracting, timeout, and token economy.

The third section of the chapter focuses on crisis intervention strategies and their application with learners identified as emotionally/behaviorally disordered. These strategies include life space interview, classroom conferencing, and the behavior influence techniques. The chapter concludes with a discussion of scaffolds, scripts, and self-regulation strategies as these are applied with learners identified as emotionally/behaviorally disordered.

◊◊ What Are the Components of an Intervention Plan?

Often designed from a behaviorist perspective, intervention plans allow teachers and students to specifically determine the target for change, design a way to promote the change, arrange documentation of change, and evaluate the rate and nature of changes. Applying this model of intervention design is not incompatible with the social systems perspective; rather, the systems perspective can well incorporate the problem-solving nature of intervention planning.

The practitioner with a behaviorist perspective sees the emotional/behavioral disorders of learners as problems of learning. Inappropriate behaviors are assumed to be learned from the environment. The individual who is misbehaving is presumed to either not have the learned behaviors required to successfully work in the environment or has learned inappropriate or nonproductive behaviors.

The behavioral practitioner is concerned with *what* the individual does, not *why* the individual exhibits specific behaviors. The cause of the behavior is assumed to exist outside of the individual in the environment. Thus, to change a behavior, referred to as a ***target behavior,*** the practitioner manipulates the consequence the individual's behavior has on the environment (Walker & Shea, 1995).

target behavior the specific behavior to be changed as a result of intervention

To the behavioral practitioner, the learning of both appropriate and inappropriate behavior is primarily dependent on the systematic application of the principles of reinforcement. These principles are inherent in the behavior management strategies presented in this section. The principles are:

Principle 1: Reinforcement depends on the exhibition of the target behavior.

Principle 2: The target behavior is reinforced immediately after it is exhibited.

Principle 3: During the initial stages of the behavior change process, the target behavior is reinforced each time it is exhibited.

Principle 4: When the target behavior reaches a satisfactory rate, it is reinforced intermittently.

Principle 5: Social reinforcers are always applied with tangible reinforcers.

Behavioral consequences are assumed to have a direct influence on the behavior an individual exhibits. Behavior can be changed by the systematic manipulation of its consequences. The four possible consequences of behavior are: positive reinforcement, negative reinforcement, extinction, and punishment. Table 10.1 offers several examples of appropriate and inappropriate behaviors, the consequences of those behaviors, the probable effects of the consequences on the repetition of the behavior in the future, and the classification of the behavior.

In *positive reinforcement,* a reward is presented to the individual after the behavior is exhibited. The consequence is pleasurable to the individual and thus tends to increase the frequency with which the target behavior is exhibited in the future. For example, a student who has difficulty completing his or her assignment is provided a reward after the accurate completion of one activity. At home, the student who cleans his or her room is provided a reward or given an allowance.

Negative reinforcement is the removal of an already-operating aversive stimulus. As a consequence of the removal of the negative reinforcer, the behavior is strengthened. Axelrod (1983) describes negative reinforcement in the classroom setting as an instance in which a student performs a desired behavior and the teacher removes something the student dislikes, or, perceives as unpleasant. To continue the example of the student who has difficulty completing an assignment, the student is permitted to leave the group following the accurate completion of the task. At home, the student is allowed to leave his or her room once it is cleaned.

Extinction is the removal of a reinforcer that sustains or increases a target behavior. The consequence of extinction (ignoring) is that the behavior will decrease. Extinction is difficult to apply when a task should or must be completed. In the classroom, it is often difficult to remove the reinforcer that maintains a behavior.

positive reinforcement presentation of a desirable reinforcer after a behavior has been exhibited; the process of reinforcing a target behavior in order to increase the probability that the behavior will recur

negative reinforcement the strengthening of a behavior as a consequence of the removal of an already-operating aversive stimulus

extinction the discontinuation or withholding of a reinforcer that has previously been reinforcing a behavior

Table 10.1 Behaviors, Consequences, Potential Effects, and Classification

Behavior	Consequences	Potential Effect	Classification
Louise empties dishwasher.	Parents praise.	Louise continues to empty dishwasher.	Positive reinforcement
Chris empties the trash.	Parents ignore, make no comments.	Chris does not empty trash again.	Extinction
Kara sits with her feet on sofa.	Parents tell her she has to sit on the floor.	Kara keeps her feet off sofa.	Punishment
Michael doesn't practice trumpet because it is so hard.	Parents tell him not to practice parts that are hard.	Michael practices trumpet less and less.	Negative reinforcement

For example, the teacher can hardly ignore a student's failure to accurately complete assigned tasks.

Punishment, or the presentation of an aversive stimulus as a consequence of a target behavior, may be accomplished by either adding a punishment or subtracting a pleasurable activity. An *aversive stimulus* is a noxious consequence of a behavior. The student who is having difficulty accurately completing assignments would lose a recess each time he or she has an incomplete or inaccurate assignment. At home the student who fails to clean his or her room may lose the privilege of using videogames for an evening.

Two additional concepts basic to the understanding of behavioral intervention are generalization and discrimination. *Generalization* is the process by which a behavior reinforced in the presence of one stimulus will be exhibited in the presence of another stimulus. If generalization did not occur, each response would have to be learned by the individual in each specific situation in which it is to be applied. For example, students often generalize the behavior of raising hands for recognition. Even at a birthday party or at home, members of a group of children may raise their hands when asked, "Who wants cake?" Students generalize handwriting from large pencils, to smaller pencils, to ink pens without having to relearn the entire task of writing.

Through the process of *discrimination,* the individual learns to act in one way in one situation and another way in a different situation. Without the ability to discriminate, we would generalize behavior to a variety of situations in which they would be inappropriate. We learn to discriminate by means of *differential reinforcement:* a behavior is reinforced in the presence of one stimulus, but the same behavior is not reinforced in the presence of another stimulus. Students learn through discrimination that they may use loud voices on the playground, but must use quiet voices in the school building.

The five steps in the *behavioral intervention plan* are (a) selecting the target behavior, (b) collecting and recording baseline data, (c) identifying reinforcers, (d) implementing interventions and collecting and recording intervention data, and (e) evaluating the effect of the intervention.

The first step is the identification of the target behavior. Usually, it is not difficult to select one or more behaviors exhibited by an individual that appear inappropriate to some other individual under certain circumstances. When selecting target behaviors, the following variables should be considered: the number of behaviors potentially needing change; their frequency, duration, and intensity; and the type of behavior. Potential target behaviors should be

punishment the addition of an aversive stimulus or the substraction of a pleasurable stimulus as a consequence of behavior in order to decrease the probability that the behavior will recur

aversive stimulus noxious and sometimes painful consequence of behavior; undesirable result of behavior the individual would normally wish to avoid

generalization a learned process whereby behavior reinforced in the presence of one stimulus will be exhibited in the presence of another (also known as the "transfer of learning")

discrimination ability to act in one way in one situation and in another way in a different situation

differential reinforcement the process of reinforcing a behavior in the presence of one stimulus not reinforcing the behavior in the presence of another stimulus

behavioral intervention plan a five-step process used in the application of behavior management strategies ranked in order of priority with regard to their significance to the individual in the environment in which the individual is functioning.

The need for and probable effectiveness of an intervention on a target behavior are determined by the behavior's frequency, duration, intensity, and type. These variables bear on (a) whether a behavioral intervention is appropriate or even necessary, (b) the intervention to be applied, (c) the probable course of the behavior change process, and (d) the probable results of the intervention. More specifically, some behaviors respond effectively and efficiently to behavioral intervention; others do not. Some behaviors must be changed for the sake of the individual's well-being; others are relatively innocuous and do not require change. The practitioner must use professional judgment, common sense, and experience when selecting target behaviors.

After selecting the target behavior, the practitioner considers the direction of the change in behavior, which can be either increased or decreased. Finally, if changes in the behavior are to be objectively evaluated, the target behavior must be observable and measurable.

The second step in behavioral intervention is collecting and recording baseline data. Quantitative data collected on the target behavior before any behavior change intervention is implemented is called *baseline data.* Baseline data provide the foundation on which the behavior change process is established. These data are used to determine the effectiveness of the intervention during the implementation and evaluation steps. During intervention, reinforcement is initiated at a level of performance immediately above or below the baseline level, depending on whether the behavior is being increased or decreased.

baseline data quantitative data collected on the target behavior before a behavior change intervention is implemented

To obtain meaningful baseline data, the practitioner engages in two activities: counting the target behavior and charting the target behavior. Counting the behavior means enumerating the times a behavior occurs in a given period of time. Charting the behavior means preparing a visual display of the behavior in a graphic form. When the practitioner knows the rate or average duration of the occurrence of a behavior in a time frame, then he or she can plan a potentially efficient reinforcement schedule before implementing the intervention. Equally important is the application of the baseline data during implementation and evaluation. By comparing baseline data with intervention data, the effectiveness of the intervention can be evaluated. Decisions can be made regarding the responsiveness of the target behavior to intervention; that is, is the number of times the behavior occurs increasing or decreasing as projected?

The third step in the behavioral intervention is identifying reinforcers. A *reinforcer* is the consequence of a behavior that increases the likelihood that it will recur. A behavioral intervention is only as effective as its reinforcers. Regardless of the intervention applied, if the change in the target behavior is not reinforced with a reward that is acceptable to the individual exhibiting the behavior, the probability of the individual's continuing to exhibit that behavior is reduced. The only true test of the effectiveness of a reinforcer is to try it.

The two most effective means of selecting reinforcers for an individual are (a) observing the individual to determine the reinforcers he or she selects when given the opportunity, and (b) asking the individual what is preferred. To help the practitioner select effective reinforcers, the literature discusses a variety of aids, including reinforcement surveys; scales and kits; reinforcement lists; and open-ended, multiple-choice, and rank-order questionnaires (Walker & Shea, 1995).

The next step in behavioral intervention is implementing interventions and collecting and recording intervention data. After selecting a potentially effective intervention, the practitioner selects a reinforcement schedule to be applied during intervention. A *schedule of reinforcement* is the pattern with which the reinforcer is presented or not presented in response to the exhibition of a target behavior.

Concurrent with the implementation of an intervention, the practitioner collects data on its effectiveness by means of counting and charting, as during the baseline step. The practitioner must apply the intervention consistently and persist in its application if it is to be effective.

The final step in behavioral intervention is evaluating its effectiveness. Intervention data, collected during the previous step, provide the practitioner with a yardstick for evaluating changes in the target behavior. By collecting and charting intervention data, the practitioner can evaluate the effectiveness of the intervention throughout the behavior change process by comparing intervention data with baseline data. If the behavior is changing in the desired direction, the practitioner may proceed as planned. However, if the behavior is not changing as projected, the practitioner must reevaluate the behavior change process: that is, the reinforcer, the intervention, and the schedule of reinforcement. Research designs for evaluating the effectiveness of an intervention include withdrawing or otherwise manipulating the consequence or reinforcer of the behavior and then reinstating the reinforcer.

Behavioral intervention can also contribute to self-management. Cognitive behavior modification (CBM) is an application of behav-

reinforcer the consequence of a behavior that increases the likelihood that it will recur

schedule of reinforcement the pattern with which the reinforcer is presented or not presented in response to the exhibition of a target behavior

ioral principles that were merged in response to an interest in helping students learn to manage their own behavior and develop strategies for learning. Harris (1982) defines cognitive behavior modification as "the selective, purposeful combination of principles and procedures from diverse areas into training regiments or interventions, the purpose of which is to instate, modify, or extinguish cognitions, feelings, and/or behaviors" (p. 5).

Lloyd (1980) describes several procedures that are common to those used in cognitive behavior modification, including self-assessment, self-recording, and self-management. The student is highly engaged in these procedures. They often involve a sequence of designated steps, as well as monitoring and evaluating the successful implementation of the strategy or technique (Meichenbaum, 1986). The teacher first models the procedures or technique, supports the student through the learning process, and gradually turns the intervention itself over to the student. Verbalization, a key component, guides the student through the strategy. The student uses verbalization, or "self-talk," which often includes questions such as "What is my problem? What is my plan? Am I using my plan? "How did I do?" (Camp & Bash, 1981).

PASSKey

From a systems perspective, learners and their behavior must be understood in context. "Naturalistic" interventions are interventions that place importance on the natural systems, such as families and classrooms, in which individuals interact rather than on individual behaviors and their contingent variables (Carta & Greenwood, 1985). Naturalistic interventions are emerging as strategies to intervene with individual learners and their families, encouraging generalization to other environments.

Barnett et al. (1993) describe a model for naturalistic assessment and intervention design that incorporates Planned Activities, Strategic Sampling, and Keystone behaviors (PASSKey). The user of this model, identifies problems and plans interventions that are based on natural interactions and activities, and the realities of settings. The model is grounded in collaborative consultation, in which a consultant works directly with the teacher or parent in developing interventions.

The components of PASSKey include:

- Planned activities, which represent the goals and behaviors teachers and parents wish to accomplish. These activities may include classroom routines, group instruction, riding the bus, lunchtime, and recess.

- **_Strategies sampling,_** which involves selecting times to observe the planned activities and target behaviors, as well as times to intervene.

- Keystone behaviors, which are behaviors related to desirable learner and teacher behaviors; keystone behaviors are "pivotal or prerequisite" for other behaviors (Evans & Meyers, 1985). Looking for keystone behaviors is an effective strategy because many learners have multiple problem behaviors for which priorities must be set (Barnett & Carey, 1992).

The steps of PASSKey, discussed below, provide an example of the application of the five-step intervention plan presented above.

The first step of PASSKey involves selecting the planned activities that are important to the teacher, parent, and learner. The teacher and consultant gather information on specific routines and events, and describe the day using a Waking Day Interview (Wahler & Cormier, 1970; Barnett & Carey, 1992), which is presented in Figure 10.1.

As a problem setting is identified, teacher and consultant work through a "problem-solving interview" (Barnett & Carey, 1992) in which they clarify the concerns of the teacher. Questions in the problem-solving interview may include:

- What are some specific examples of what happens in this setting? What happens right before the behavior occurs? Right after?

- How long does this behavior occur? Is it the same in other settings? Are there times when the behavior does not occur?

- What strategies have you tried to manage this behavior? How effective have they been?

sampling selecting times to observe planned activities and target behaviors, as well as times to intervene

---

Describe the child's behavior in the following settings or situations.
On the bus:
Entering the classroom:
"Morning work":
Transitions:
Recess:
Lunch:
Seat work:
Specialized classes (art, music, P.E.):
Cooperative learning activities:
Moving through the building:
End-of-day activities:

Figure 10.1   Waking Day Interview (School Setting)

• What would have to change for this child to benefit during this situation?

Once the target situation or setting has been described, strategic sampling takes place. Several strategies are used to provide more specific information concerning the behaviors and the contexts in which they occur. These include real-time observations, in which the observer records meaningful and complete units of behavior and the clock time for each behavior. For example, an observer might write, "1:10: Teacher says 'Get out your pencils.' Student says, 'What pencils?'" An "ABC" chart may be used to gather more specific information. This "Antecedent-Behavior-Consequence" chart describes events in a detailed "flow of activity" manner. An example is provided in Table 10.2.

Next, the teacher selects the keystone behavior. The basic strategy for selecting the keystone behavior involves the identification of other important behaviors that may be linked to the development of the keystone behavior. The social validity of the behaviors should also be considered. In the "ABC" example in Table 10.2, the keystone behavior that may be identified is "the student comes prepared for class."

scripts personalized and detailed guidelines for intervention; specific action plans that describe intervention steps in natural language

Scripts, or personalized and detailed guidelines for intervention, are then described. A baseline is determined, and step-by-step procedures for each occasion that the intervention will be used is developed. On the script, a check off for the teacher is provided, so that he or she may record the way in which the script is being followed. A script for the example behavior, "the student comes prepared for class," is provided in Table 10.3.

Table 10.2   Antecedent-Behavior-Consequence Chart

Antecedent	Behavior	Consequence
Teacher: Get out a pencil.	Student: What pencil?	Teacher: Your pencil.
Teacher: Your pencil.	Student: Don't have one.	Teacher: You need a pencil.
Teacher: You need a pencil.	Student: Guess you'll have to give me one.	Teacher: Excuse me?
Teacher: Excuse me?	Student: (shouting, mouthing words broadly) Guess—you'll —have—to—give—me—one.	Class laughs.
Class laughs.	Student shrugs and shakes head.	Teacher: I will not continue until this room is quiet.

Table 10.3 Sample Script

Target Behavior: James Will Bring His Materials to Class.	Dates

Steps

1. Teacher meets James at door and asks, "Do you have your materials?"
2. If James says "Yes," teacher puts check mark on his "Earn a night without homework" card.
3. If James says "No," teacher provides James with a pencil, which he must return at the end of class.
4. Teacher intermittently provides check marks on "earn a night without homework" cards for students who have all materials for class.

Scripts may require modifications as they are implemented. A teacher may refine a script by role playing with another teacher or having a peer teacher observe the intervention and provide feedback. As teacher fine-tunes the script, he or she takes data on the student's response. The teacher studies the stability, level, and trend of the target behavior, and modifies the script if needed.

An emerging issue in intervention design is functional analysis. *Functional analysis,* or assessment, is the process of identifying functional relationships between environmental events and the occurrence and nonoccurrence of a target behavior. A functional assessment consists of the methods and procedures used to identify associations between behavior and variables in the environment (Dunlap, Kern, dePerczel, Clarke, Wilson, Childs, White, & Falk, 1993). Dunlap et al. suggest that functional analysis is important in identifying which variables may be directly manipulated in order to clarify the relationship between behavior and environmental variables. In their study, certain classroom variables did exert influence over the behaviors of individual students.

A functional assessment includes identifying the problem behaviors, setting priorities, and delineating operational definitions (Demchak, 1993). Hypotheses are then developed, using strategies such as structured interviews; systematic observations using scatter plots; "ABC" analyses, or focus on communicative intent; and testing. Finally, the results of this assessment are linked to intervention planning.

functional analysis the process of identifying functional relationships between environmental events and the occurrence and nonoccurrence of a target behavior

◊◊ **What Are Several Behavior Management Strategies that Are Grounded in the Principles of Reinforcement and How Are These Applied with Learners Identified as Emotionally/Behaviorally Disordered?**

There are several behavior management strategies grounded in the principles of reinforcement, including positive reinforcement, extinction, punishment, differential reinforcement, shaping, contingency contracting, timeout, token economy, and modeling (Walker & Shea, 1995).

Positive Reinforcement

Positive reinforcement is the process of rewarding an appropriate behavior to increase the probability that it will recur. The advantages of positive reinforcement are that it is responsive to the individual's natural need for attention and approval and, thus, de-

Working one-to-one.

creases the probability the individual will exhibit inappropriate behavior. Three guidelines should be used when applying positive reinforcement. First, reinforce the target behavior only after it occurs. Second, when individuals are initially learning a new behavior, reward them each time the behavior occurs. Finally, once the behavior is established at a satisfactory level, reinforce it intermittently. Public reinforcement may be unwelcome by some learners, so the practitioner should be careful to ascertain if the learner is embarrassed by positive reinforcement in the presence of peers, teachers, and others. The practitioner must be observant to determine if the reinforcers being used are in fact positively reinforcing the learner.

Extinction

Extinction is the discontinuation or withdrawal of the reinforcer of a target behavior that has been previously reinforcing or sustaining it. When consistently and persistently applied, extinction results in the gradual decrease and elimination of the target behavior. Generally, behaviors that are ignored become nonfunctional and consequently stop. Extinction is an effective means of eliminating annoying and nonproductive behaviors. Because it is a benign intervention, extinction avoids the potential for conflict between practitioner and learner. Among the behaviors responsive to the extinction are whining, tattling, mild tantrums, and demands for attention. It may also be applied to decrease inappropriate language, derogatory comments, meaningless questions, and annoying affectations and fads. Extinction is generally not recommended for more complex and severe behaviors that may be damaging to the individual, others, or property.

The key to applying extinction effectively is learning to completely and totally ignore the target behavior and being consistent and persistent in its application. In many cases, when extinction is initially applied, an "extinction burst" occurs, in that the behavior being ignored increases dramatically in frequency for a brief period of time before it decreases.

Punishment

Punishment is imposed on learners to decrease or eliminate inappropriate behavior. Punishment is the presentation of an aversive stimulus as a consequence of an inappropriate behavior. Punishment may be accomplished by adding an aversive stimulus or by taking away a positive reinforcer. Punishment may be physical or psychological.

The short-term effectiveness of punishment is difficult to dispute. It does effectively attain for the punisher his or her immediate objective: to stop the inappropriate behavior. However, there are several reasons for avoiding the use of punishment:

- Inappropriate behavior is suppressed; it is not eliminated.
- An acceptable model is not provided for the learner.
- The punisher's aggression provides an unacceptable model for the learner.
- The results of punishment, such as fear, tension, stress, and withdrawal, may be psychologically damaging to the learner.
- The learner's frustration level may increase and further deviation may result.

The practitioner must recognize that punishment may result in real physical or emotional damage to the learner. Punishment is not recommended by the authors of this text. The number and variety of alternative management strategies make its use unnecessary.

Differential Reinforcement

Differential reinforcement is the process of reinforcing an appropriate behavior in the presence of one stimulus and not reinforcing an inappropriate behavior in the presence of another stimulus. There are several types of differential reinforcement: (a) differential reinforcement of zero rates of behavior (DRO), (b) differential reinforcement of incompatible behaviors (DRI), and (c) differential reinforcement of lower rates of behavior (DRL). When using DRO as an intervention, the learner is reinforced for not exhibiting the target behavior during a specific period of time. Occurrence of the target behavior is ignored. The learner is reinforced for exhibiting appropriate behavior in other circumstances. DRO may be effectively applied for fighting, cursing, name-calling, talking back, and so on.

At times it is necessary or desirable to decrease a behavior by systematically reinforcing a behavior that is in opposition to or incompatible with it. For example, a learner cannot be in his seat and out of his seat at the same time. In the DRI intervention the practitioner will reinforce in-seat behavior and ignore out-of-seat behavior. DRL intervention is frequently appropriate for use with behaviors that are habits, do not need to be reduced rapidly, and do not need to be reduced completely. It is used to gradually reduce the behavior by reinforcing progressively lower rates of the behavior. The DRL intervention may be applied with various behaviors, such as attention seeking, completing assignments, and hand raising.

Shaping

Shaping is reinforcing successive approximations of behavior leading to the appropriate target behavior. Primarily used to establish behavior not previously or infrequently exhibited by the learner, it is accomplished by the consistent, systematic, and immediate reinforcement of approximations of the target behavior. During shaping, the practitioner reinforces only those behavioral manifestations that most closely approximate the target behavior. The practitioner should never reinforce lower level approximations; to do so would be to reinforce a behavior that is the reverse of the proposed direction of change.

Shaping is similar to climbing a ladder; that is, one rung is mounted at a time while one foot is firmly placed on the previous rung. The learner is reinforced for climbing each rung on the ascent to the top of the ladder, or the target behavior. The learner is reinforced only when he or she ascends to the highest rung to which he or she is capable of climbing at a particular point in the shaping process. The learner is never reinforced for climbing to a rung lower than that to which he or she is capable.

> **shaping** the systematic, immediate reinforcement of successive approximations of a target behavior until the behavior is established

Contingency Contracting

A *contingency contract* is a verbal or written agreement between two or more individuals that stipulates the responsibilities of each concerning a specified item or activity. It is based on Premack's (1959) principle: A behavior that has a high rate of occurrence can be used to increase a behavior with a lower rate of occurrence. This concept is exemplified by the statement, "If you do x, then you can do or get y." Some examples of contracts are:

> **contingency contract** a written or verbal agreement between two or more parties that stipulates the responsibilities of the parties concerning a specific item or activity

- If you eat your peas, then you can have some ice cream.
- If you do 90% of your class assignments this week, then you may attend the class party and movie on Friday afternoon.
- If you complete your workbook assignment, then you may have 10 minutes of free time.

An example of a written contract is presented in Figure 10.2.

Timeout

Timeout, or time away from positive reinforcement, is the removal of a learner from an apparently reinforcing setting to a presumably nonreinforcing one for a specified and limited period of time. Such a removal, if applied with persistence and consistence, can decrease some inappropriate behaviors. There are various levels of

March 15, 1988.

I, Sarah, will turn in my homework for all four days on which it is assigned (Monday, Tuesday, Wednesday, and Thursday). If all of my homework is turned in, Ms. Derrick will allow me to go to the first grade and
read a story to a small group on Friday afternoon. If my homework is not
turned in, I will use Friday afternoon freetime to get caught up on missing
assignments.

Ms. Derrick and I will go over this contract after we try it for two weeks.

Signed: *Sarah*
Ms. Derrick

Figure 10.2   Contingency contract.

timeout: ignoring, contingent observation, removal of materials,
reduction of response-maintenance stimuli, exclusion, and seclu-
sion (Walker & Shea, 1995).

Ignoring, or extinction, has been discussed previously in this section. Observational timeout, or contingent observation, is an intervention in which the child is withdrawn from a reinforcing environment and placed on the perimeter of the environment, where she or
she may see and hear the activity but not participate. During observational timeout, the learner can observe the appropriate behavior
as it occurs among the members of the group from which the
learner has been removed. Removal of materials is a form of timeout
during which the materials the learner is using inappropriately are
removed. Reduction of response-maintenance stimuli is a timeout
intervention that involves the reduction or elimination of stimuli in
the environment necessary for a response, such as turning out the
lights when the learner's response is inappropriate.

Exclusionary timeout is an extremely restrictive intervention in
which the learner leaves the reinforcing environment for a presumed nonreinforcing environment yet remains in the classroom.
In this case, there may be a private, out-of-the-way area of the
room to which the learner retires for a period of time. In seclusion-
ary timeout, the child leaves the reinforcing environment and retires to a timeout room or other isolation area generally not in the
classroom. In many states, the parameters for time out are delineated in the education standards or regulations. Timeout removes
the learner from the opportunity to engage in other educational activities.

The effectiveness of timeout depends on several factors: the learner, the teacher's application of the intervention, the learner's understanding of the rules of timeout, the characteristics of the timeout area, the duration of timeout, and the evaluation of the intervention's effectiveness. The practitioner must know the learner's reaction to timeout. It is often effective with aggressive, group-oriented learners who want to be with their peers and involved in activities, but is contraindicated for withdrawn, passive, solitary learners. It would never be applied with fearful learners. To be effective the practitioner must apply the timeout with consistency over a period of time. Special facilities for timeout are generally not necessary. The timeout area, however, must be safe, properly lighted, and ventilated. Timeout is generally more effective if the timeout periods are brief rather than long. A log must be maintained to determine the effectiveness of this intervention.

Because of its restrictive nature, timeout must be carefully implemented and evaluated. The practitioner must include such an intervention on the learner's IEP, and obtain parent permission for it application. All potential side effects of such an intervention (losing instructional time or self-injury, for example) must be carefully explored. Any time the intervention is applied the learners should be carefully observed and the time should be logged.

Token Economy

Token economy is an exchange system that provides the learner whose behavior is being changed with near-immediate feedback cues on the appropriateness of his or her behavior. The cues, or tokens, are at a later time exchanged, or traded, for backup reinforcers, which are items and activities. The token economy intervention is often combined with a cost-response intervention in which the learner may lose tokens for inappropriate behavior. Initially during this intervention, the tokens are valueless to the learner. However, their value becomes apparent when the learner understands that he or she can exchange the tokens for backup reinforcers. When planning a token economy, the practitioner must first select the target behavior or behaviors. These behaviors are discussed and clarified with the learner. After selecting a token, a menu or list of backup reinforcers is developed and posted. Time must be provided for the exchange of tokens. As time progresses, the practitioner must frequently revise the reward menu of backup reinforcers to avoid satiation on the part of the learner.

The properly managed token economy is effective because individuals are only competing with themselves and the reinforcer menu offers a variety of desirable items and activities. In addition, any token economy should include a way of fading the tokens so that students become more self-regulated and generalize productive behaviors to times when the token economy cannot be implemented.

Modeling

modeling the provision of an individual or group behavior to be imitated or not imitated by the individual

Modeling is providing behavior after which the learner is to pattern his or her behavior. During this intervention the learner is systematically reinforced for imitating or not imitating the model. Exposure to a model has three potential effects (Clarizio & Yelon, 1976):

- The learner may acquire a behavior from the model that was not previously part of the learner's behavioral repertoire.
- The learner may inhibit inappropriate target behavior for which the model is punished or otherwise discouraged.
- The learner exhibits approximations of the model's behavior that are not necessarily "new" behaviors but behaviors that were previously learned but not presently exhibited.

Before implementing the modeling intervention, the practitioner should make sure that the learner is developmentally capable or ready to imitate a model and that the model is an acceptable model.

◊◊ What Are Several Crisis Intervention Strategies and How Are These Applied with Learners Identified as Emotionally/Behaviorally Disordered?

crisis intervention strategies techniques applied to respond immediately to behavior problems the student is confronting in the environment in which he or she is functioning

Crisis intervention strategies are techniques applied to respond immediately to behavior problems the student is confronting in the environment in which he or she is functioning.

Teachers working with learners identified as emotionally/behaviorally disordered should be prepared for crisis situations. Gilliam (1993) makes several suggestions for preparation for crisis management. The teacher should stay calm, send for help if necessary, and stay out of striking range. The teacher should tell the student that the behavior needs to stop. To calm the situation, Gilliam urges that the teacher use as little action as possible, and sustain from counteraggression. The student should be removed from the environment to regain self-control. When the student is calmed down, the teacher should rehearse with the student appropriate behaviors and the reasons that the student needed to be removed from the situation.

Among the interventions that are supportive of crisis intervention are the life-space interview, classroom conferencing, and the behavior influence techniques. These interventions are also helpful in the prevention of crisis.

Life-space Interview

Redl (1959) recommended the life-space interview as a here-and-now intervention built around the learner's direct life experience. It is applied by a practitioner who is perceived by the learner to be an important part of the learner's life space. The interview is used to structure an incident in the learner's life so that the problem or crisis confronting the learner can be resolved. The interview is conducted as soon as possible after the occurrence of the behavioral incident and, if possible, in the location in which the incident occurred.

life space interview here-and-now interviewing intervention built around an individual's direct life experience to enable the individual to solve the problem confronting him or her

The life-space interview is used for one of two purposes: clinical exploitation of life events, and emotional first aid on the spot. In clinical exploitation of life events, the practitioner uses a behavioral incident to explore with the learner a habitual behavioral characteristic. The practitioner attempts to use an incident to attain a long-range therapeutic goal that has been previously established for the learner. The practitioner helps the learner to increase conscious awareness of (a) distorted perceptions of existing realities, (b) habitual inappropriate behavioral characteristics, (c) hidden social and moral values and standards, or (d) reactions to the behaviors and pressures of the group. The interview is used to encourage the learner to adopt more personally productive and socially acceptable means of solving conflicts.

The practitioner may apply the life-space interview with students for emotional first aid on the spot in times of stress, to assist the learner over a rough spot in the road of daily functioning in order to continue an ongoing activity. For this purpose, the interview is conducted to (a) reduce learner's frustration level, (b) support the learner in emotionally charged situations, (c) restore strained learner-practitioner communications, (d) reinforce existing behavioral and social limits and realities, and (e) assist the learner in efforts to find solutions to everyday problems of living and to emotionally charged incidents, such as fights and arguments.

Morse (1980) outlined a series of steps that occur during the life-space interview. Generally, the interview commences as a consequence of a specific incident in the learner's life. The practitioner encourages those involved in the incident to state their personal perception of it. At this time, the practitioner must determine if this incident is an isolated event or a significant part of a recurring theme. The practitioner listens to those involved in the incident as

Talking it over.

they reconstruct it. Their feelings and perceptions are accepted without moralizing or attacking. Although these individual perceptions are accepted, the practitioner may suggest alternative perceptions for consideration by the learner.

The interview then moves into a nonjudgmental resolution phase. Many conflicts and confrontations are resolved at this point, and the interview is terminated. However, if the problem is not resolved, the practitioner may offer his or her view of the incident in which the learner or learners find themselves. Finally, the learner and the practitioner develop an acceptable plan to deal with the present problem and similar problems in the future.

Classroom Conference

McIntyre (1987) developed a method of classroom conferencing specifically designed for teachers of learners with behavioral problems. The "long talk" is an easily implemented conferencing procedure and is especially responsive to a variety of interpersonal interaction and counseling styles. The "long talk" is applied to help learners analyze their behavior and develop better self-control.

The steps in the conferencing process are: (a) meet, (b) review, (c) discuss respect, (d) discuss typical behavior, (e) devise another response, and (f) reconvene. The teacher should (a) meet privately with the learner as soon as possible after the behavioral incident. During the conference, the student is requested to (b) review the incident. The teacher should clarify the student's perception to insure that both student and teacher are discussing a common perception. The teacher may make corrections in the student's perception on the basis of first-person knowledge. Next, the teacher and the student (c) discuss respect to clarify what actions and feelings resulting from the incident were right and wrong and whose rights and privileges were violated. Student and teacher (d) discuss typical behavior during the next step in the conference. The teacher helps the student to see the inappropriateness of the behavior and informs the student that it is unacceptable.

Next, the student and the teacher (e) devise another response. The teacher asks the student to suggest alternative ways of responding in like and similar situations in the future. The teacher accepts all suggestions, writes them on paper, and asks the student to select the alternative he or she will use in the future. Teacher and student discuss this alternative's use in various situations, and its pros and cons. If the alternative the student selects is unrealistic, he or she is requested to select another. The teacher may assist students who are unable to generate alternatives.

Finally, student and teacher (f) reconvene to review student progress and performance and engage in further planning, as necessary. A series of conferences is often necessary because behavior change takes time.

Behavior Influence Techniques

The behavior influence techniques were suggested (Redl & Wineman, 1957; Long & Newman, 1965; Shea, Whiteside, Beetner, & Lindsey, 1974) to respond immediately to ongoing behavior problems. These techniques are used to respond to problems that

- Present a real danger.
- Are psychologically harmful to the learner and others.
- Lead to excessive excitement, loss of control, or chaos.
- Prohibit continuation of the program.
- Lead to the destruction of property.
- Encourage the spread of negativism in the group.
- Provide opportunities to clarify individual and group values, standards, and social rules.
- Lead to conflict with others outside of the group.
- Compromise the practitioner's mental health and ability to function.

The behavior influence techniques are: planned ignoring, signal interference, proximity control, interest boosting, tension reduction through humor, hurdle helping, program restructuring, support from routine, direct appeal, removal of seductive objects, antiseptic bouncing, and physical restraint. These techniques are summarized in Table 10.4.

Table 10.4 Behavior Influence Techniques.

Technique	Description	Example
Planned ignoring	Teacher ignores behaviors that, although inappropriate, don't interfere with learning.	Teacher ignores student tapping his pencil while he is working on math problems.
Signal interference	Teacher provides nonverbal gesture to communicate that behavior should stop.	Teacher gives two students whispering to each other a "teacher look."
Proximity control	Teacher physically moves toward students engaging in undesirable behavior.	During spelling test teacher moves to stand near student who may have been peeking in his book.
Interest boosting	Teacher injects personal interest into activity.	Teacher uses learners' names in spelling sentences.
Tension decontamination through humor	Teacher provides humor.	Teacher laughs at personal mistake or tells humorous story about self.
Hurdle helping	Teacher aids learner with difficult task.	Teacher provides one on one help with student struggling with long division problem.
Restructuring program	Teacher changes activities when students are bored or disengaged.	Teacher provides colored paper for students to complete math work. Teacher stops in the middle of a long written test and tells students to stand up and stretch.
Support from routine	Teacher uses daily routines.	Teacher has set "opening" activity each morning.
Direct appeal	Teacher makes direct appeal to stop behavior.	Teacher tells students that teasing younger children about their art in the hall is not fair.
Removal of seductive object	Teacher removes distracting object and returns it at appropriate time.	Teacher takes Polly Pocket pencil case from student during math.
Antiseptic bouncing	Teacher removes learner from situation in which he or she is about to behave.	Teacher sends squirming student out to get a drink.
Physical restraint	Teacher holds student.	Teacher puts her hand over the hand of a student who is pounding the desk in anger.

◊◊ What Are Scaffolds, Scripts, and Self-Regulation Strategies and How Are These Applied with Learners Identified as Emotionally/Behaviorally Disordered?

Scaffolding suggests that teachers initially provide supports, or *scaffolds,* and withdraw them as the student is successful, much as scaffolding is put in place as a building is constructed, and removed as it becomes stable. Scaffolding is used, for the most part, to increase the communicative competence of learners identified as emotionally/behaviorally disordered, and thus increase their socially proactive behaviors.

scaffolds supports provided to enhance student functioning, which are withdrawn as the student learns to function successfully without them

Role-playing techniques assist teachers in scaffolding instruction in safe situations. Anderson (1992) suggests a technique called "Theatre Rehearsal Technique" to assist learners identified as emotionally/behaviorally disordered from diverse cultures to organize and control their conversational behaviors. In these improvisational activities, students can experiment with their perceptions about social interactions, try various responses to determine what works for them and why, and attempt to influence others and achieve their desired social consequences. Anderson contends that through these techniques, students can learn to identify, use, and recognize relationships between thinking and acting. In a similar manner, puppet theatre may be used to help students master non-threatening and rational solutions to issues confronting them (Caputo, 1993).

Communicative competence assumes the ability to coordinate attention to people and objects, imitate, and play (Lieber & Beckman, 1991). To support young children, Lieber and Beckman suggest placing learners with more competent partners, and providing toys that encourage social interaction. In addition, teachers should observe their classroom activities and note those that encourage social exchange. Specific skills, such as initiation and responsiveness, may also need to be specifically taught to young children.

Scripts have recently emerged as specific action plans that describe intervention steps in natural language. Scripts are viewed as effective ways of addressing behavior change because they (a) provide the "how to do it" in interacting with the child, (b) increase expectations that the individual intervening can be successful, (c) provide coaching and a clear way of providing feedback, and (d) are ethnically valid through their expression in natural or culturally specific languages (Barnett et al., 1993).

Self-regulation is an essential skill for learners identified as emotionally/behaviorally disordered. Graham, Harris, and Reid (1992) contend that self-regulation, if generalized, becomes a way

self-regulation self-instruction, goal-setting, and self-monitoring techniques to regulate his or her behavior

of proceeding for the learner. Academically, learning to self-regulate allows students to become more independent, increases their task engagement, and allows them to monitor and regulate their own performance. As students self-regulate, they learn to self-instruct, set goals, and self-monitor.

Self-regulation is, in itself, preventive discipline. Henley (1994) describes five foundations of self-regulation:

1. The student should control impulses in school in using instructional materials, moving in unstructured space, making classroom transitions, and resisting temptation of off-limit objects.

2. The student should be able to assess social reality by accommodating to classroom rules, organizing learning materials, accepting feedback, and appreciating the feelings of others.

3. The student should manage group situations by maintaining composure, appraising peer pressure, participating in cooperative activities, and evaluating effects of personal behavior.

4. The student should cope with stress by adapting to new situations, managing competition, tolerating frustration, and demonstrating patience.

5. The student should solve social problems by focusing on the present, learning from past experiences, recalling personal behavior, and resolving conflicts.

Self-managed learners require less external control, allowing teachers to spend more time on other aspects of curriculum and instruction (DiGangi & Maag, 1992). In their efforts to analyze the interaction between self-monitoring, self-evaluation/self-reinforcement, and self-instruction, Di Gangi and Maag reported that using a combination of these skills was most effective. Self-monitoring and self-evaluation/self-reinforcement, when used individually, were the least effective. The most effective component when used independently was self-instruction.

Kern, Dunlap, Childs, and Clarke (1994) suggest a classwide self-management program in working with learners identified as emotionally/behaviorally disordered. In this program, students record every 5 minutes whether they were in seat and working. Data showed significant increases in time-on-task and decreases in disruptive behavior. Teacher observations and parallel recordings for behavior reflected high accuracy levels between teachers and students.

In their review of the research on self-monitoring as a behavior management technique, Webber, Scheuermann, McCall, and Coleman (1993) reported that self-monitoring was found to be successful with students of various ages and in various settings. Specifically, self-monitoring increased attention to task, positive classroom behaviors, and some social skills. In addition, inappropriate classroom behavior was shown to decrease. Self-monitoring apparently has the additional benefit of enhancing the likelihood that positive classroom behaviors will generalize to other settings.

◊◊ Summary Points

- The steps of behavioral intervention are (a) selecting the target behavior, (b) collecting and recording baseline data, (c) identifying reinforcers, (d) implementing interventions and collecting and recording intervention data, and (e) evaluating the effect of the intervention.
- Functional assessment includes identifying the problem behaviors, setting priorities, and delineating operational definitions.
- Behavior management strategies grounded in the principles of reinforcement include positive reinforcement, extinction, punishment, differential reinforcement, shaping, contingency contracting, timeout, token economy, and modeling.
- Crisis intervention strategies are applied to respond immediately to behavior problems the student is confronting in the environment in which he or she is functioning.
- Scaffolding and scripts are useful in increasing the communicative competence of learners, thus increasing their socially proactive behaviors.

Select the most appropriate response.
1. During the initial stages of behavior change, behavior is reinforced
   a. on a fixed ratio.
   b. intermittently.
   c. continuously.
2. Generalization implies
   a. that each situation is unique to the learner.
   b. that the learner can be linked to a stimulus rather than a setting.
   c. multiple experiences.
3. Gathering baseline data allows
   a. practice in observing the target behavior.
   b. familiarity with the behavior in context.
   c. evaluation of the effectiveness of the intervention.
4. Naturalistic interventions are grounded in
   a. natural consequences.
   b. the natural systems in which learners interact.
   c. individual behaviors.
5. Keystone behaviors are those that
   a. are controlled by a single stimulus.
   b. are controlled by a prevalent reinforcer.
   c. are pivotal or prerequisite of other behaviors.
6. Scripts use
   a. various stimuli to increase generalization.
   b. various cues to increase discrimination.
   c. natural language.
7. Functional analysis
   a. emphasizes the functional relationships between events and the be-
      havior.
   b. identifies ways to increase discrimination.
   c. identifies ways for the teacher to implement an intervention more
      accurately.
8. Punishment
   a. has lasting long-term effects.
   b. is effective only short-term.
   c. is a naturalistic intervention.
9. In shaping
   a. lower level approximations of behaviors are sometimes reinforced to
      maintain them.
   b. successive approximations are reinforced.
   c. Intermittent reinforcement is provided to correct responses.

10. Self-regulation
    a. is less effective than other forms of behavioral intervention.
    b. is difficult to implement.
    c. becomes the student's way of proceeding.

Making the Language Your Own

Match each key word or phrase to its definition.

_____ 1. contingency contract   _____ 9. scripts

_____ 2. functional analysis   _____ 10. shaping

_____ 3. life-space interview   _____ 11. target behavior

_____ 4. positive reinforcement   _____ 12. self-regulation strategies
_____ 5. generalization
     _____ 13. baseline data
_____ 6. modeling
     _____ 14. discrimination
_____ 7. negative reinforcement   _____ 15. extinction

_____ 8. scaffolds

a. data collected before an intervention is implemented
b. an agreement between two or more parties that stipulates the responsibilities of the parties concerning a specific item or activity
c. ability to act in one way in one situation and in another way in a different
   situation
d. withholding of a reinforcer that has previously been reinforcing a behavior
e. identifying functional relationships between environmental events and the
   occurrence or nonoccurrence of a target behavior
f. behavior reinforced in the presence of one stimulus is exhibited in the
   presence of another
g. interviewing intervention built around an individual's direct life experience
h. the provision of an individual or group behavior to be imitated by the individual
i. strengthening of a behavior as a consequence of the removal of an
   already-operating aversive stimulus
j. presentation of a desirable reinforcer after a behavior has been exhibited
k. supports provided to enhance student functioning
l. personalized guidelines for intervention in natural language
m. self-instruction, goal setting, and self-monitoring
n. systematic, immediate reinforcement of successive approximations
o. specific behavior to be changed as a result of intervention

Theory Into Practice

1. Interview the principal of a local school. What is the process for referring individuals who are demonstrating behaviors which vary from their peers? Is there a form for documenting interventions? Is there a referral check sheet? How long does the referral process usually take?
2. Interview a parent of a child receiving special education services. What is his or her perception of the referral process?

◊◊ **References**

Anderson, M. G. (1992). The use of selected theatre rehearsal technique activities with African-American adolescents labeled "behavior disordered." *Exceptional Children, 59,* 132–139.

Axelrod, S. (1983). *Behavior modification for the classroom teacher.* New York: McGraw-Hill Book Co.

Barnett, D. W., & Carey, K. T. (1992). *Designing interventions for preschool learning and behavior problems.* San Francisco, CA: Jossey-Bass.

Barnett, D. W., Ehrhardt, K. E., Stollar, S. A., & Bauer, A. M. (1993). *PASSKey: A model for naturalistic assessment and intervention design.* Paper presented at the National Association of School Psychologists Annual Convention, Washington, DC.

Camp, B. W., & Bash, M. A. (1981). *Think aloud.* Champagne, IL: Research Press.

Caputo, R. A. (1993). Using puppets with students with emotional and behavioral disorders. *Intervention in School and Clinic, 29,* 26–30.

Carta, J. J., & Greenwood, C. R. (1985). Ecobehavioral assessment: A methodology for expanding the evaluation of early intervention programs. *Topics in Early Childhood Special Education, 5,* 88–104.

Clarizio, H. F., & Yelon, S. L. (1976). Learning theory approaches to classroom management: Rationale and intervention techniques. *Journal of Special Education, 1,* 267–274.

Demchak, M. (1993). Functional assessment of problem behaviors in applied settings. *Intervention in School and Clinic, 29,* 89–95.

DiGangi, S. A., & Maag, J. W. (1992). A component analysis of self-management training with behaviorally disordered youth. *Behavioral Disorders, 17*(4), 281–290.

Dunlap, G., Kern., L., de Perczel, M., Clarke, S., Wilson, D., Childs, K. E., White, R., & Falk, G. D. (1993). Functional analysis of classroom variables for students with emotional and behavioral disorders. *Behavioral Disorders, 18*(4), 275–291.

Evans, I. M., & Meyers, L. H. (1985). *Educative approach to behavior problems: A practical decision model for interventions with severely handicapped learners.* Baltimore: Brookes.

Gilliam, J. E. (1993). Crisis management for students with emotional/behavioral problems. *Intervention in School and Clinic, 28,* 224–230.

Graham, S., Harris, K. R., & Reid, R. (1992). Developing self-regulated learners. *Focus on Exceptional Children, 24*(6), 1–16.

Harris, K. R. (1982). Cognitive-behavior modification: Application with exceptional students. *Focus on Exceptional Children, 15*(2), 1–16.

Henley, M. (1994). A self-control curriculum for troubled youngsters. *Journal of Emotional and Behavioral Problems, 3*(1), 40–46.

Kern, L., Dunlap, G., Childs, K. E., & Clarke, S. (1995). Use of a classwide self-management program to improve the behavior of students with emotional and behavioral disorders. *Education and Treatment of Children, 17,* 445–458.

Lieber, J., & Beckman, P. J. (1991). Social coordination as a component of social competence in young children with disabilities. *Focus on Exceptional Children, 24*(4), 1–10.

Lloyd, J. W. (1980). Academic instruction and cognitive behavior modification: The need for attack strategy training. *Exceptional Education Quarterly, 1*(1), 53–63.

Long, N. J., & Newman, R. G. (1965). Managing surface behavior of children in school. In N. J. Long, W. C. Morse, & R. G. Newman (Eds.), *Conflict in the classroom: The education of emotionally disturbed children* (pp. 352–362). Belmont, CA: Wadsworth.

McIntyre, T. (1987). Classroom conferencing: Providing support and guidance for misbehaving youth. *Teaching: Behaviorally Disordered Youth, 3,* 33–35.

Meichenbaum, D. (1986). Cognitive-behavior modification. In F. H. Kanfer & A. P. Goldstein (Eds.), *Helping people change: A textbook of methods* (3rd ed., pp. 346–380). New York: Pergamon Press.

Morse, W. C. (1980). Worksheet in life space interviewing. In N. J. Long, W. C. Morse, & R. G. Newman (Eds.), *Conflict in the classroom* (4th ed.). Belmont, CA: Wadsworth.

Premack, D. (1959). Reinforcement theory. In D. LeVine (Ed.), *Nebraska Symposium on Motivation: 1965.* Lincoln: University of Nebraska Press.

Redl, F. (1959). The concept of life space interview. *American Journal of Orthopsychiatry, 29,* 1–18.

Redl, F., & Wineman, D. (1957). *The aggressive child.* New York: The Free Press.

Shea, T. M., Whiteside, W. R., Beetner, E. G., & Lindsey, D. L. (1974). *Micro teaching module: Behavioral interventions.* Edwardsville: Southern Illinois University.

Wahler, R. G., & Cormier, W. H. (1970). The ecological interview: A first step in outpatient child behavior therapy. *Journal of Behavior Therapy and Experimental Psychiatry, 1,* 279–289.

Walker, J. E., & Shea, T. M. (1995). Behavior management: A practical approach for educators. Upper Saddle River, NJ: Prentice Hall.

Webber, J., Scheuermann, B., McCall, C., & Coleman, M. (1993). Research on self-monitoring as a behavior management technique in special education classrooms: A descriptive review. *Remedial and Special Education, 14*(2), 38–56.

11 Supporting Behavior Change: Group Interventions

TO GUIDE YOUR READING

After you read this chapter, you will be able to answer these questions:

• What are the characteristics of teacher stance that prevent and ameliorate emotional/behavioral disorders?

• What classroom structures and management strategies are effective with learners identified as emotionally/behaviorally disordered?

• What strategies facilitate inclusion for learners identified as emotionally/behaviorally disordered?

◊ *We're going to be reviewing vocabulary and key ideas for the social studies test," Ms. Jones announced. "We're going to do 'inside-outside circles' in order to review. Let's count off to form our circles."*

The students began to count off. When they completed, Ms. Jones said, "Evens are our inside circle. Odds are our outside circle. We're going to start with our 'inside circle' being our questioners and the 'outside circle' being our answerers." Some of the students groaned. "As you all know, every five minutes we will switch."

Ms. Jones passed out vocabulary and key concept flash cards to the "inside circle" students. The students made two concentric circles, with the inside circle students facing the outside circle students. The inside students presented flash cards to their partners. After going through the three cards, the outside circle students moved to their right, facing a new partner.

People live in groups. Schools are based on groups of learners. Teachers of learners identified as emotionally/behaviorally disordered sometimes remark how charming certain learners may be in a one-to-one setting, yet how difficult they are to manage in a group. Yet using the group to create a community of learners is an asset to the education of learners identified as emotionally/behaviorally disordered. As Perls (1967) suggests, "in the group situation something happens that is not possible in the private interview" (p. 241).

This chapter presents several topics related to group interventions. First is teacher stance as it relates to the prevention and amelioration of emotional/behavioral disorders. This discussion includes a comparison of facilitative teacher stance and controlling and authoritarian teacher stance. Next, the reader is introduced to classroom structure and other management strategies effective with learners identified as emotionally/behaviorally disordered. This section includes a discussion of social skills curricula, levels systems, and the learning environment. The chapter concludes with a discussion of the inclusion of learners identified as emotionally/behaviorally disordered in the general education classroom and school.

◊◊ What Are the Characteristics of Teacher Stance that Prevent and Ameliorate Emotional/Behavioral Disorders?

A teacher's stance encompasses his or her personal posture toward self and others, as well as his or her theoretical orientation and instructional and management strategies (McGee, Menolascino, Hobbs, & Menousek, 1987). Teacher stance has a significant effect on students' social perceptions of the teacher, their classmates, and themselves. Evertson and Weade (1989) described the efficacy of a teacher stance that elicited and supported student participation. The effective teacher provided explicit rationales for activities, set and followed consistent routines for classroom interaction, and maintained sensitivity to students' needs in relation to the difficulty level of the lesson content.

The teacher's role in facilitating learning has emerged in qualitative studies conducted in general education classrooms. Rogers, Waller, and Perrin (1987) described the interactions of an "excellent" facilitative teacher as characterized by extended conversations with her students. The teacher's interactions were described as natural, spontaneous, sensitive, and individualized. Through facilitation, the teacher becomes less constraining and monitors the students' responses more carefully.

Mirenda and Donellan (1986) provided more specific contrasts between the communicative styles of facilitative and directive teachers. Facilitative teachers initiated fewer topics and initiated those topics through indirect questions, statements or comments. They rarely used direct questions to extend topics; Rather, they used statements, encouragements, and expansions.

Story (1985) reports that facilitative teachers provided for positive and close physical relationships, being on the same eye level when in discussion with students and touching the student to emphasize encouragement or enthusiasm. Verbal interactions were marked by encouragement, humor, and clarification strategies.

The "curriculum of control," often used to describe classrooms of students identified as emotionally/behaviorally disordered, is in stark contrast to facilitative teaching. As Nichols (1992) suggests, a controlling stance tends to generate the behaviors that placement in programs for learners identified as emotionally/behaviorally disordered is designed to ameliorate. Nichols contends that when teachers in a curriculum of control are having problems they rarely smile, whereas successful teachers look at their students when they talk to them, or quietly exchange everyday pleasantries. Morse (1994) agrees, noting that a common thread among gifted teachers is knowing their students and having a deep empathy for the stress in their lives.

Kohn (1993) argues that there are three alternatives to control: managing content, collaborating with students, and providing them with choice. In managing content, he suggests that teachers look at what the learners are being asked to do; if a learner does not comply to a request, consider the nature of the request. Collaboration involves mutual problem solving: teacher and student come to a mutual understanding of what constitutes inappropriate behavior. Kohn suggests that this most limited version of collaboration is the very least we owe a child. Regarding choice, Kohn contends that the more a student feels a part of the process, the more he or she is a part of the process. The more the student feels his or her view is solicited and taken seriously, the fewer problems there will be to deal with.

Teachers of learners identified as emotionally/behaviorally disordered must also project a stance that supports the reintegration of their students into general education. Schechtman, Reiter, and Schanin (1993) reported that teachers who viewed efforts to integrate learners with disabilities into the classroom as a personal and professional challenge were more likely to have favorable attitudes toward including that individual. Teacher's stance held greater significance in successful reintegration into general education than the amount of external school support teachers received. Rock, Rosenberg, and Carran (1995) indicate that a "positive reintegration orientation" (p. 254) was also significant to the success of learners identified as emotionally/behaviorally disordered in less restrictive settings.

◊◊ What Classroom Structures and Management Strategies are Effective with Learners Identified as Emotionally/Behaviorally Disordered?

Classroom structures used with learners identified as emotionally/behaviorally disordered include social skills curricula, levels systems, cooperative learning structures, and the learning environment, all of which are the antecedents of effective management. Management strategies include procedures, rules, space and facilities, schedules, cuing, and transitions.

Social Skills Curricula

As we have learned, students identified as emotionally/behaviorally disordered are often viewed by peers, teachers, parents, and others as socially incompetent. These students engage in behavior excesses, such as cursing, shouting, arguing, and disrupting. They have either not had the opportunity to learn or, given the opportunity, have not learned appropriate social skills (Carter & Sugai, 1989).

Fad (1990) identified three behavioral domains essential to learners with behavior problems if they are to function effectively in the general education classroom: peer relationships, work habits, and coping skills. To help students learn these skills, Fad suggests (a) identifying and assessing students' present level of skill, (b) setting priorities among the skills to be learned, (c) selecting effective instructional methods to teach the skills, and (d) evaluating and conducting follow-up assessment of the skills learned.

A **social skills curriculum** is designed to help learners increase their awareness and understanding of personal emotions, values, and attitudes through educational activities (Edwards & O'Toole, 1985; McGinnis, Sauerbry, & Nichols, 1985). These activities lead to improvement of the student's interpersonal problem-solving skills.

A frequently used social skills curriculum is the "Self-Control Curriculum for the Prevention of Behavioral and Learning Problems," commonly referred to as the "self-control curriculum," developed by Fagen, Long, and Stevens (1975). Designed as a preventive intervention for use with all children, the curriculum is based on the assumption that a common denominator for disruptive behavior is a lack of self-control. To function effectively, students must develop the capacity to control their behavior, even when frustrated. **Self-control** is defined as "one's capacity to direct and regulate personal action (behavior) flexibly and realistically in a given situation" (Fagen & Long, 1976, p. 2). An important objective of the curriculum is the reduction of students' anxiety over losing self-control by increasing the skills and confidence they have in the ability to regulate their impulsive behavior. Morse (1979) indicated that the self-control curriculum advocates inserting a cognitive pause between an impulse and its expression. It trains students to use cognitive processes to balance personal behavioral options in terms of their experiences and goals. This curriculum includes the integration of the eight skill clusters, which are selection, storage, sequencing and ordering, anticipating consequences, appreciating feelings, managing frustration, inhibition and delay, and relaxation.

In the self-control curriculum, the learning of each skill is accomplished through a variety of activities. The authors of the curriculum predict that, through learning the skills, the student's capacity to direct and regulate personal action in given situations will grow. Instructional activities are implemented in small devel-

social skills curriculum an intervention designed to help students increase their awareness and understanding of personal emotions, values, and attitudes through educational activities and, as a consequence, improve their interpersonal problem-solving skills

self-control the "capacity to direct and regulate personal action (behavior) flexibly and realistically in a given situation" (Fagen & Long, 1976)

Is everyone listening?

opmental steps and include positive feedback. Short, regular training sessions are advised.

Several social skills curricula are available in the literature. The practitioner must give careful consideration to the appropriateness of a particular program for the students with whom it is to be applied. Schumaker, Pederson, Hazel, and Mayen (1983) suggest five questions for teachers to address when selecting a social skills curriculum:

1. Does the curriculum promote social competence?
2. Does the curriculum respond to the learning characteristics of the students with whom it is to be applied?
3. Does the curriculum target the social skills deficits of the students with whom it is to be applied?
4. Does the curriculum provide training in situations as well as in skills?
5. Does the curriculum include instructional methodologies found to be effective with the population of students with whom it is to be applied?

Carter and Sugai (1989) developed a comprehensive procedure for the selection and analysis of social skills curriculum. They describe several programming issues that should be considered. First, they suggest that training occur in groups, yet be individualized to meet the needs of the students. Individualization may occur through varying levels of teacher assistance, reinforcers, accuracy criteria, and examples selected. Next, the program should require little additional training for the teacher and it should be affordable. Finally, the curriculum must provide for student assessment, progress monitoring, and maintenance and generalization training. Carter and Sugai designed a useful curriculum analysis checklist and decision-making grid.

Two important issues in social skills programming are maintenance and generalization. To increase the likelihood of the occurrence of maintenance and generalization, teachers should use multiple instructors and instruct in multiple settings. Responses should be varied so that they will be maintained in the natural environment. In addition, a variety of instructional strategies should be applied, including modeling, direct instruction, placing students in settings with other students who exhibit appropriate behavior, rehearsal and practice, shaping, prompting and coaching, and positive practice.

Nelson (1988) notes that according to research, a social skills curriculum does promote the acquisition of socially appropriate behaviors by students with disabilities. However, there is little research evidence that social skills instruction is effective over time and across settings. Zaragoza, Vaughn, and McIntosh (1991) analyzed 27 studies on the effects of social skills training on school-age children. They were somewhat optimistic with respect to the effects of social skills interventions with learners identified as emotionally/behaviorally disordered. When compared with nonparticipants, the participants felt better about themselves, and their teachers and parents felt better about them. In the majority of the studies, peers' feelings about the learners identified as emotionally/behaviorally disordered did not change.

Sabornie and Beard (1990) suggest that instruction in social skills for students with mild disabilities be provided on the basis of an individual's assessed needs. If the learner needs instruction, then that instruction should be structured and frequent. They suggest two approaches to instruction in social skills: (a) manipulation of antecedents and consequences of students' social behavior, and (b) application of a "packaged" curriculum.

levels system organi-
zational framework
within which various
behavior management
interventions are ap-
plied to change behavior

Levels Systems

A levels system is an organizational framework designed to change students' social, emotional, and academic behaviors (Bauer, Shea, & Keppler, 1986). Rather than an intervention technique or strategy derived from a single theoretical perspective, a levels system offers a structure within which various interventions may be applied. The interventions implemented within a levels system may range in theoretical construct from behavior modification (token economy, positive reinforcement, shaping, contingency contracting) to psychodynamic (group and individuals counseling, social skills curriculum, life-space interviewing).

The purpose of the levels system is to increase student responsibility for personal social, emotional, and academic performance. Students advance through the various levels as they show evidence of achievement and improved functioning. Expectations and rewards change as students demonstrate progress at each level. As students proceed through the levels, less controlled systems or less restrictive environments are imposed (Smith & Farrell, 1993).

Smith and Farrell (1993) suggest that levels systems are based on three underlying assumptions:

1. Combined techniques, such as token economies, contingency contracting, positive reinforcement, shaping, and fading should be used to assist students in changing their behavior.

2. Clearly defined expectations increase positive classroom interaction and classroom learning orientation.

3. Hierarchical systems provide a "ladder to success" (Walker & Shea, 1995) and facilitate generalization.

The advantages of a well-developed, individualized levels system include security, structure, and routine. The practitioner is delivered from the "me against them" stance, and structure and procedures enhance self-management.

Little research that supports the efficacy of levels systems has been generated. Scheuermann, Webber, Partin, and Knies (1994) and Scheuermann and Webber (1996) discussed several legal issues regarding the use of levels systems. From a legal perspective levels systems have been questioned because of (a) restrictions placed on access to the regular education setting; (b) a lack of individualization within the system; (c) restrictive procedures within the system, such as the requirement to proceed through each level; and (d) a lack of accountability and the use of punishment within the system.

Cooperative Learning Structures

Cooperative learning structures have expanded from early descriptions of group activities; they may now involve cooperative teaching and student-cooperative teams as well as the more traditional cooperative group activities.

"Cooperative teaching" refers to the educational approach in which general and special educators jointly teach academically and behaviorally heterogeneous groups of students in general education classrooms (Bauwens, Hourcarde, & Friend, 1989). Cooperative teaching is proactive; students with academic and/or learning difficulties can immediately receive instruction or curricular modifications early and intensively. Bauwens et al. describe three basic implementation options of cooperative teaching:

1. Complementary instruction, in which the general education teacher maintains the primary responsibility for teaching the specific subject matter in the instructional program, while the special educator assumes primary responsibility for the student's mastery of academic survival skills.

2. Team teaching, in which, at various times, each of the teachers assumes primary responsibility for specific types of instruction or portions of the curriculum.

3. Supportive learning activities, in which the general education teacher maintains responsibility for delivering the essential content of instruction, while the special educator is responsible for developing and implementing supplementary and supportive learning activities; both teachers are present and cooperatively monitor both essential content and supplementary activities.

Cooperative teaching may also occur in teams rather than pairs. A teaching team is an instructional arrangement of two or more members of the school or greater community who distribute among themselves planning, instructional, and evaluation responsibilities for the same students on a regular basis for an extended period of time (Thousand & Villa, 1990). Teams provide students with support from a variety of adults, all of whom are engaged in group problem solving (Vandercook & York, 1990). Cooperative teaching allows general and special educators to complement each other. Most general educators are skilled in large-group management and content, whereas special educators have expertise in analyzing and adapting instructional materials and strategies and developing IEPs (Bauwens, Hourcade, & Friend, 1989).

Bauwens et al. (1989) have identified three barriers to the implementation of cooperative teaching structures. First, a great deal of time must be spent on planning as a team. Second, cooperative working relationships must be in place. Finally, initial teacher perception of teaming as an increased work load must be overcome; teachers eventually assumed specific responsibilities based not only on their own unique areas of expertise, but also in their areas of interest, decreasing their concern regarding work load.

Student cooperative teaming (Gartner & Lipsky, 1990) provides unique opportunities for the improvement of all students. Through classwide tutoring teams, Gartner and Lipsky reported an increase in student opportunities to respond and to have those responses affirmed or corrected. Student cooperative teams were small and heterogenous (four to five students), using game formats for reviewing weekly instructional content. The cooperative goal structures were used in conjunction with systematic instructional strategies, and daily posting of teams' performance. In these groups, helping teammates learn the weekly content is described as the students' "job." Using materials, questions, and answers provided by the teacher, students take turns acting as tutor to their remaining teammates, the tutees.

Cooperative learning structures provide ways of organizing social interaction in the classroom (Kagan, 1989). Because they are independent of content, cooperative learning structures can be used across almost any subject area. Kagan contrasts cooperative learning with traditional teaching through the following example. In traditional teaching, the teacher usually asks a question, the students who wish to respond raise their hands, the teacher calls on one student, and the student attempts to state the correct answer. In a cooperative classroom, the teacher would form two groups. The teacher would have the students number off within their groups, and then ask a question. The teacher would ask the students to "put their heads together" to make sure that everyone on the team knows the answer. The teacher then calls a number and the students with that number can raise their hands to respond. This is a cooperative structure because if any student knows the answer, the ability of each student is increased. High achievers share answers because they know their number might not be called and they want their group to do well. Lower achievers listen carefully because they know their number may be called. Several of Kagan's structures for cooperative learning are presented in Table 11.1

Learning Environment

Variables related to the learning environment (antecedents to effective instruction) include rules; schedules; transitions; cuing; procedures for activities and classroom and nonclassroom space

Table 11.1 Sample Cooperative Learning Structures (Kagan, 1989)

Structure	Description	Functions
Round-robin	Students are in small groups; each student shares something with classmates.	Expressing ideas and opinions; equal participation
Corners	Teacher presents four alternatives; each student moves to a corner of the room. Students discuss within their corners, then listen to and paraphrase ideas from other corners.	Seeing alternatives; respecting different points of view
Pairs check	Students work in pairs within groups of four. Within pairs, students alternate—one solves a problem and the other coaches. After every two problems the pair checks to see if they have the same answer as other pairs.	Practice; helping, praising
Co-op Co-op	Students work in groups to produce a particular group product to share with the whole class; each student makes a particular contribution to the group.	Learning and sharing complex materials with multiple sources; presentation skills

and facilities; and the availability and use of space, materials, and equipment.

The effective program is planned and organized to facilitate instruction and management. Prior to the beginning of any school day or year, the practitioner must take into consideration a broad range of factors to enhance the probability that learning will occur. The teacher must develop procedures for: individual, small, and whole group activities; beginning and ending the school day or instructional period; transitions; housekeeping; interruptions; visitors; fire drills; and various other planned and unplanned activities.

Rules. According to Joyce, Joyce, and Chase (1989), a *rule* is "the specification of a relation between two events that may take the form of instruction, direction, or principle (p. 84)." The function of

rule "the specification of a relation between two events that may take the form of instruction, direction, or principle" (Joyce, Joyce, & Chase, 1989)

Our teacher really works with us.

a rule is to encourage appropriate behavior and prevent inappropriate behavior (Reith & Evertson, 1988). Teachers use various kinds of rules to organize for instruction and conduct. Rules are usually designed to apply to those activities and occurrences that are not governed by classroom and nonclassroom procedures.

Rules should be few in number. They should be brief and understandable to the students and positively stated. They should communicate expectations rather than prohibitions. Rules are best developed through the collaborative efforts of students and teacher (Thorson, 1996). When students are involved in developing rules, the rules become "our rules" rather than "the teacher's rules." When rules are set collaboratively, they may be changed only through discussion and consensus (Cheney, 1989).

Rules should be posted in a highly visible location in the classroom and reviewed with the students frequently (Blankenship, 1986). During the initial weeks of the school year, rules should be reviewed daily. Teachers should give students repeated examples of the behaviors that a student demonstrates when following the rules. Teachers are responsible for enforcing rules with fairness and consistency (Reith & Evertson, 1988).

Four or five rules are more than adequate to govern classroom behavior. They should be general in nature, but not so general as to be meaningless. Examples of general rules are:

• Be polite and helpful.

• Keep your space and materials in order.

• Take care of classroom and school property.

Some practitioners have certain highly specific rules. Examples are:

• Raise your hand before speaking.
• Leave your seat only with permission.
• Only one person in the restroom at a time.

Joyce et al. (1989) remind teachers that students whose behavior is rule governed (under control of reinforcers) may become insensitive to environmental conditions that make rule following inappropriate. To prevent the development of environmental insensitivity as a result of rule following, they suggest that students (a) be exposed to contingencies incompatible with specific rules, (b) be provided various tasks for meeting the objective of the rule, (c) be exposed to natural contingencies for appropriate behavior, and (d) be overtly aided to make transitions from rule-governed behaviors that were in effect in previous environments.

Schedules. Rosenshine (1977) found that student learning increases when teachers allocate considerable time for instruction and maintain a high level of task engagement. To develop an effective schedule, two important variables are considered: allocated time and engaged time (Shea & Bauer, 1987). Englert (1984) describes *allocated time* as the amount of time scheduled for a specific subject or activity. *Engaged time* is the amount of time students actually participate in the scheduled subject or activity. The literature indicates that generally half of the typical school hour is allocated to instruction, and most students are engaged only 70% to 80% of the time (Hollowood, Salisbury, Rainforth, & Palombaro, 1995). To increase engaged time, teachers must plan the schedule with care, begin and end activities on time, facilitate transitions from activity to activity, and assign scheduled activities as a first priority rather than engaging in spontaneous, alternative activities.

Scheduling is a dynamic process—a continuous and creative activity (Gallagher, 1988). Schedules must be revised throughout the school year in response to emerging student needs and changing behaviors, as well as the demands of the curriculum. The two most important kinds of scheduling are overall program scheduling and individual program scheduling.

Schedules are based on individual and group priorities. After determining priorities, the practitioner must fit available time, personnel, and materials and equipment into those priorities. Shea and Bauer (1987) suggested the step-by-step process for schedule development presented in Figure 11.1.

allocated time the amount of time scheduled for a specific subject or activity

engaged time the amount of time the students are actually participating in the subject or activity

1. Using each student's individualized education program or personal records as a data base, complete a 3-×-5 card for each goal for each student. On the card, write the student's name, current level of functioning, and short-term objectives with reference to the goal.
2. Group students by sorting cards by goals and functional levels.
3. Choose a specific schedule format. Reproduce the format on a standard sheet of paper. In the left-hand column, write the time periods available for scheduling.
4. Write the "given" activities (lunch, recess, art, music, speech therapy, physical education) on the schedule. Resource teachers must write the "givens" imposed by other teachers' schedules. Write the times needed for transitions. Write the times needed for data recording, communicating with others, and preparing for instruction.
5. Write group activities on the schedule. Adjust these until there are no conflicts with other scheduled activities.
6. Review and discuss the proposed schedule with others serving the students (general education teachers, special education teachers, therapists, parents, instructional specialists) to minimize conflicts.
7. Establish procedures for reevaluating the schedule.

Figure 11.1   Schedule Development Process

Two common schedule formats are the Premack principle schedule and the distributed-duties schedule. The Premack schedule is based on the presumption that behaviors that occur frequently and freely can be used as reinforcers for less frequently occurring behaviors. To apply this principle to scheduling, the teacher first marks each period of time with a plus (+) or a minus (−). The plus denotes behaviors that naturally occur at a high frequency level, and the minus sign denotes those that do not. It is suggested that the day begin and end with plus activities. The following is a partial Premack schedule.

+ 9:00   Free time to play and interact quietly
− 9:10   Return to seats for individual study during attendance, lunch count, and so on
+ 9:15   Circle or sharing time
− 9:35   First reading group, individual study for others
+ 9:55   Transition time, drinks, restroom
− 10:00   Second reading group, individual study for others
+ 10:20   Recess

The distributed-duties schedule (Bauer, 1980) is useful in programs in which paraprofessionals, volunteers, and other personnel are available to meet the needs of students. To use this schedule format, students are grouped homogeneously by functional level and individual goals and objectives. Next, they are grouped into the same number of groups as there are personnel available to service them during any given period of time. Each person assumes responsibility for a group's instruction during the available period. Personnel are assigned to groups on a rotating basis, as shown on the partial schedule that follows.

Group A *Jim/Betty/Mary*	*Group B* *Tara/Elmer/Mabel*	*Group C* *John/Tom/Dolores*
9:00	all students–group meeting	
9:20 spelling	reading	reading
9:40 numbers	basic concepts	math
10:00 reading	language arts	independent***
10:20	all students–recess	
10:40 music*	language arts**	spelling

*Betty to speech therapist
**Elmer to third grade
***John to psychologist

	Staff Assignments	
Annie B	Pam E	Bill W
Group A 9:00–10:00	10:00–12:00	P.M.
Group B 10:00–12:00	P.M.	9:00–10:00
Group C P.M.	9:00–10:00	10:00–12:00

Block scheduling is a strategy often used in inclusive settings to restructure the distribution of school resources, such as staff, space, and time (Snell, Lowman, & Canady, 1996). In working in blocks, students with disabilities are assigned to their grade level; assignments are balanced so that no teacher receives significantly more students with disabilities than another. Snell et al. also suggest that students with more extensive needs be assigned to teachers who had volunteered to have them and to those who had fewer students overall.

In a sample morning block, four base homeroom teachers, two special education teachers, two instructional assistants, and support staff are assigned to a grade or set of grades. Students work with teachers in small, teacher-directed groups, which may include writing lab, working on reading comprehension, language arts, or the reading-writing connection. When students are not working in teacher-directed groups, they attend the Extension Center. In the Extension Center all students receive enrichment and support, including journal writing, reading, library use, computer, group projects, cooperative learning, English as a second language, counseling, speech, or tutoring. The Extension Center is staffed by a variety of people, including special educators, Title I teachers, tutors, or support staff.

Another variable that must be considered when developing schedules is the length of time of the activity periods. As a rule, it is more effective to begin the school year with brief activity periods and gradually lengthen them as the year progresses; the students then learn the schedule and become more quickly involved in the learning process.

transitions the movement from one activity to another

Transitions.   *Transitions* are the movement from one activity to another. According to Rosenkoetter and Fowler (1986), transitions are complex activities that frequently result in classroom disruptions. They should be carefully planned to minimize the loss of instructional time. Effective transitions teach learners self-management skills.

In a study of 22 classes (15 general and 7 special education) for young children 4 and 5 years old, Rosenkoetter and Fowler (1986) found that on average, 18% of the school day was devoted to transitions. Special and general education classes differed with regard to the management of transitions. General education teachers used more cues than special education teachers. Special education teachers used children's names as cues; general education teachers used group names. Individual cues in the general education classroom were rare; when special education teachers used group cues, they would follow with individual cues. Special teachers employed one- and two-step directions; regular teachers employed three- and four-step directions. Special teachers often used proximity control. It was noted that in special education classes, children were frequently not held responsible for their materials and were not taught group movement.

Rosenkoetter and Fowler (1986) suggested several guidelines for special education teachers wishing to facilitate student transition when integrated into the general education classroom:

- Visit the general education classroom to determine the transition rules.

- Plan for transitions and use shaping to assist in the learning of appropriate behavior.

- Evaluate existing transition behaviors to determine if students need more or less assistance.

- Move from individual to group cues.
- Use a variety of cues.
- Teach lining-up and moving-in-line behaviors.
- Teach children how to ask for assistance.

According to Shea and Bauer (1987), teachers may use the following activities to facilitate transitions:

- Model appropriate transition behaviors.
- Signal or cue the beginning and ending of activities.
- Remediate transition difficulties such as slowness and disruptiveness.
- Observe student performance during transitions and, if the student is having difficulties, repeat the rules and practice until they are firmly established behaviors.
- Reinforce quick and quiet transitions.

Effective transitions are essential to maximize engaged time in the classroom.

Cuing. Cuing is the process of using symbols to communicate essential messages between individuals. The use of cuing reduces interruptions in ongoing activities, and the symbols facilitate structure and provide routine (Legare, 1984; Olson, 1989). Cuing is a proactive, preventive behavior management intervention (Slade & Callaghan, 1988). Various cues or help signs can be used in the classroom. Such cues are most effective if developed collaboratively by students and teacher at the beginning of the school year. Among the many cues that may be implemented are the following:

cuing the process of using symbols to communicate essential messages between individuals

- Students place a sign or flag in a holder at their work station when assistance is needed.
- Students write their names on the chalkboard when assistance is needed.
- Students take a ticket (as in the supermarket deli) when assistance is needed.
- Students use a cardboard symbol such as the letter "R" for restroom, "P" for pencil, "W" for water in place of frequently asked questions.
- Teachers use traffic signals to control noise levels (red means too loud, yellow means caution, green means noise level okay).
- Teacher turns lights on and off to signal the beginning and ending of activities.

In addition, teachers may wish to use body language, hand signals, smiles and frowns, and schedules as cues. The design and use of cues in the classroom is limited only by the imagination of the teacher and students. Of course, cues should not be used in lieu of appropriate verbal communication.

Procedures.   The teacher is responsible for developing a variety of classroom and nonclassroom procedures to facilitate instruction and appropriate behavior (Walker & Shea, 1995; Emmer, Evertson, Clements, & Worsham, 1997; Evertson, Emmer, Clements, & Worsham, 1997).

Teachers should establish classroom procedures for the following: the care of students' desks and storage areas; the number of students permitted in various areas of the room at one time; the use of the drinking fountain, sink, pencil sharpener, restroom, and other shared facilities; the use and care of common and personal instructional materials; and students' and teachers' personal space and possessions.

Outside of the classroom, procedures are needed for the use of nonclassroom space and facilities such as restrooms, drinking fountains, offices, library, media rooms, and resource rooms. Procedures must be established for activities such as students' leaving the classroom and the movement of individual students and groups within the school building. Playground activity procedures must facilitate fair play and safety, and maximize enjoyment. Special procedures are frequently needed for the lunchroom because of the large number of students in the facility and the limited time and space available.

The practitioner must also develop procedures for a variety of individual, small group, and whole group activities. Procedures are developed for the conduct of discussions, the answering of questions during class, talking among students, out-of-seat behavior, and so on. The teacher instructs students about the cues and prompts he or she will use to attain student attention. Procedures are developed for making assignments to work groups, assigning home study, distributing supplies and materials, turning in and returning work, and completing missing assignments. Students should know what they are expected to do when they have completed assignments and have unscheduled time available.

During small group activities, students should know the cues the teachers uses to begin and end, what materials to bring to group, and behavioral expectations. Students who are not in a particular small group must know what is expected of them during other students' small group activities.

Students working individually must know how to obtain their work, where they are to work, what work to do, how to signal for assistance, and what to do when their work is completed.

It is wise to establish standard procedures for beginning and ending the school day and each period. Students should know the procedures for reporting after an absence, tardiness, and early dismissal. Procedures should be established for the selection and duties of helpers. These duties should be shared by all students. Finally, procedures are needed for conduct during interruptions and delays; fire, tornado, and earthquake drills; and other infrequent and unplanned occurrences.

Space, materials, and equipment.   At the beginning of the school year, practitioners should plan for the use of space, materials and equipment.

Walls and bulletins boards are valuable spaces that can be used to display materials such as rules, schedules, seasonal and topical items, calendars, study assignments, housekeeping assignments, charts, and maps. It is prudent not to overdecorate; space should be reserved for student work and current items. Students can profit from helping plan displays. Materials on display should be changed periodically so that students will not become desensitized to them.

The use of floor space will vary with the size of the room, the number and characteristics of students, and the activities to be conducted. The room must be arranged to insure that the teacher can observe all areas in which students are working and recreating and that the students will be able to see the teacher and work materials that are being used for instruction. Students desks and tables should be arranged away from high traffic areas. If tables are used instead of individual desks then space for storage of student materials must be planned.

Space must be available for learning centers (reading, mathematics, science, and so on), if they are used. Centers that generate a high degree of activity and noise should not be located near centers that require a high degree of student concentration. All needed materials and equipment should be located in the appropriate center.

Teachers must plan where common items such as plants, pet cages, fish tanks, bookcases, and storage cabinets will be located. The teacher's desk, file cabinet, and other equipment must be located where they are easily accessible yet do not interfere with activities. Every effort should be made to maintain traffic lanes in the classroom to prevent confusion as students move about the room. If the classroom is serving students with physical disabilities or visual impairments, free traffic lanes must be maintained at all times and accessible space made available.

The teacher must plan for the storage and use of the various kinds of supplies, materials, and equipment that are used in the classroom. These include everyday supplies and materials, infrequently used supplies and materials, student supplies and materials, teacher supplies and materials, and personal items of students and teacher.

Everyday supplies and materials such as pencils, paper, duplicating materials, and chalk should be stored in an easily accessible location. The teacher may wish to store these items where they are available to students. Student instructional materials such as texts, workbooks, dictionaries, and study guides may be stored in students' desks, bookcases, or filing trays and cabinets. Infrequently used items such as seasonal and topical items should be stored in the back of cupboards. When not in use, equipment such as overhead projectors, record players, and movie projectors should be stored in a safe place but should be easily accessible to electrical outlets.

Students should have a private place for personal items such as clothing, gym shoes, lunch boxes, and prized possessions. The teacher must have private space for his or her briefcase, and other personal items as well as personal instructional supplies, materials, and equipment. It is essential that the personal and private space of all, students and teacher, not be violated.

◊◊ What Strategies Facilitate Inclusion for Learners Identified as Emotionally/Behaviorally Disordered?

inclusion the philosophy that all students, regardless of disability, are a vital and integral part of the general education system; special needs services addressing the IEP goals and objectives of students with disabilities that may be rendered in the general education classroom

Inclusion is the philosophy that all students, regardless of disability, are a vital and integral part of the general education system. Schwartz (1996) contends that the goal of inclusion is not just about measured behaviors; it is about belonging and participating in a community of one's peers, and being supported to succeed in an accepting, yet challenging, environment. The goals of inclusive settings are to (Stainback & Stainback, 1990):

• Meet the unique educational needs of all students within the same classroom.

• Help all students feel welcome and secure through the development of friendships and/or peer supports.

• Challeng every student to go as fast and as far as possible to fulfilling potential.

- Develop and maintain a positive classroom atmosphere that is conducive to learning for all students.
- Arrange the physical and organizational characteristics of the classroom to accommodate each student.
- Provide each student with the ancillary services he or she needs.

Tomlinson (1995) provides several rules of thumb for differentiating instruction within inclusive classrooms. First, teachers should be clear on key concepts and generalizations or principles that give meaning and structure to the topic, chapter, unit, or lesson being planned. All lessons should be engaging and should emphasize critical thinking. In addition, there should be a balance between student-selected and teacher-assigned tasks and working arrangements.

Tomlinson (1995) also provides several strategies for managing a differentiated classroom:

- Have a strong rationale for differentiating instruction based on student readiness and interest.
- Allocate slightly shorter time to a task than the attention span of the students who are working on the task.
- Use an anchor activity to free up time for more individualized assistance. Begin by teaching the whole class, then have half the class work on an anchor activity while the other half engages in different content-based activities.
- Create and deliver instructions carefully.
- Have a home base; beginning and ending classes or lessons from a home base enables students to use materials more effectively.
- Design a way for students to get help when the teacher is occupied.
- Give students as much responsibility for their learning as possible.

Vandercook and York (1990) indicate that in an inclusive classroom, there should be clear understandings among the adults as well as the students. The goals for including the student should be clear to all involved, and the roles of any additional support persons should also be very clear. Students should be empowered to be active participants in the classroom, with support personnel doing things with, instead of for, the individual.

When general education teachers were asked how they adapted their classrooms for inclusion, two areas emerged from their responses: structural arrangements and instructional arrangements (Ysseldyke, Thurlow, Wotruba, & Nania, 1990). In their structural arrangements, teachers reported that they used another adult in the room, but did not vary their grouping. The most frequent methods of instruction were direct instruction, followed by cooperative groups, discovery learning, and independent work. In adapting instruction, the two most common adaptations were (a) holding the students accountable for their performance and for working to the best of their abilities, and (b) altering instruction so that the students could experience success.

As inclusive classrooms become more common, new roles for teachers emerge. Ferguson, Meyer, Jeanchild, Juniper, and Zingo (1992) describe an "inclusion facilitator" who works as (a) a broker, locating resources and matching them in a way that will not deter the formation of natural supports; (b) an adaptor, developing and suggesting accommodations; and (c) a collaborator, working closely with the other teacher. The three kinds of support that emerged for the inclusion facilitator included teaching support, both in the planning of teaching and the actual teaching; prosthetic support, or providing strategies to support what was happening in the classroom; and interpretive support, or providing explanations regarding the individual's disability, styles, and strengths.

Developing social relationships between students in inclusive settings is an additional challenge. In their analysis of the efforts of general education teachers in facilitating social interactions in their inclusive classrooms, Salisbury, Gallucci, Palombaro, and Peck (1995) identified five themes. First, cooperative learning groups were helpful, in that they decreased competition among students. Collaborative problem solving was also helpful, as teachers worked with the students to capitalize on discussions of interpersonal issues that, if solved by an adult alone, may yield less understanding and social knowledge. Peer tutoring, and roles for each student were essential, as was structuring time and opportunity for the students to make connections on their own.

◊◊ Summary Points

- The teacher's stance has a significant impact on interactions within the classroom.
- Social skills curricula may support learners in developing the peer relationships, work habits, and coping skills required in general education classrooms.

- Levels systems may offer a structure within which various interventions may be applied; legal issues regarding levels systems must be considered before implementation.
- Effective programs facilitate instruction through managing variables within the learning environment, including rules, schedules, transitions, cues, and procedures.
- Inclusive classrooms require collaboration among students, support personnel, and teachers.

◊   **Self-Evaluation**

Select the most appropriate response.
1. Facilitative teachers initiated
   a. more direct questions toward their students.
   b. fewer topics with their students.
   c. positive reinforcement systems with their students.
2. A controlling teacher stance generates
   a. undesirable behaviors among learners identified as emotionally/behaviorally disordered.
   b. passive-aggression among learners identified as emotionally/behaviorally disordered.
   c. an orderly classroom.
3. Teacher stance is
   a. more significant than teacher preparation.
   b. more significant than external school supports.
   c. less significant than external school supports.
4. In order to function effectively in general education classrooms, learners identified as emotionally/behaviorally disordered must
   a. respond to facilitative teachers.
   b. develop peer relationships and coping skills.
   c. manage their aggression.
5. Two essential issues in social skills programming are
   a. individualization and group work.
   b. teaching and practice.
   c. maintenance and generalization.
6. Levels systems are helpful in that they
   a. Have been supported in the courts.
   b. eliminate the need for individualization.
   c. offer a structure within which various interventions may be applied.
7. Cooperative learning structures are
   a. most effective for drill and practice.
   b. independent of content.
   c. effective in eliminating aggression.

8. Student learning increases when teachers
   a. allocate considerable time for instruction and maintain a high level of task engagement.
   b. employ levels systems.
   c. engage in social skills curriculum training daily.
9. Allocated time
   a. is synonymous with engaged time.
   b. surpasses engaged time.
   c. increases when a social skills curriculum is employed.

Making the Language Your Own

Match each key word or phrase to its definition.

_____ 1. rule   _____ 6. engaged time

_____ 2. allocated time   _____ 7. levels system

_____ 3. self-control   _____ 8. social skills curriculum

_____ 4. inclusion   _____ 9. transitions

_____ 5. cuing

a. the amount of time scheduled for a specific subject or activity
b. the process of using symbols to communicate essential messages between individuals
c. organizational framework within which various behavior management interventions are applied to change behavior
d. the amount of time students are actually participating in the subject or activity
e. the philosophy that all students, regardless of disability, are a vital and integral part of the general education system
f. the specification of a relation between two events that may take the form of instruction, direction, or principle
g. the capacity to direct and regulate personal behavior
h. an intervention designed to help students increase their awareness and understanding of personal emotions, values, and attitudes through educational activities
i. the movement from one activity to another

Theory into Practice

1. Select one of the social skills curricula discussed in this chapter. Evaluate the curriculum using the selection questions of Schumaker et al. (1983) and the programming issues of Carter and Sugai (1989).
2. Observe a classroom in which a levels system is employed. Are restrictions placed on access to general education? Is there individualization within the system? Are restrictive procedures in place within the system? Is punishment used?

◊◊ References

Bauer. A. M. (1980). Head teacher's handbook. St. Louis: Special School District of St. Louis County, Missouri.

Bauer, A. M., Shea, T. M., & Keppler, R. (1986). Levels systems: A framework for the individualization of behavior management. *Behavioral Disorders, 12,* 28–35.

Bauwens, J., Hourcade, J. J., & Friend, M. (1989). Cooperative teaching: A model for general and special education integration. *Remedial and Special Education, 10*(2), 17–22.

Blankenship, C. S. (1986). Managing pupil behavior during instruction. *Teaching Exceptional Children, 19,* 52–53.

Carter, J., & Sugai, G. (1989). Social skills curriculum analysis. *Teaching Exceptional Children, 22*(1), 36–39.

Cheney, C. O. (1989, August). First time in the classroom? Start off strong! *Exceptional Times, 4.*

Edwards, L. L., & O'Toole, B. (1985). Application of self-control curriculum with behavior disordered students. *Focus on Exceptional Children, 17*(8), 1–8.

Emmer, E. T., Evertson, C. M., Clements, B. S., & Worsham, M. E. (1997). *Classroom management for secondary teachers* (4th ed.). Boston: Allyn and Bacon.

Englert, C. S. (1984). Measuring teacher effectiveness from the teacher's point of view. *Focus on Exceptional Children, 17,* 1–14.

Evertson, C. M. & Weade, R. (1989). Classroom management and teaching style: Instructional stability and variability in two junior high English classrooms. *Elementary School Journal, 89,* 379–393.

Evertson, C. M., Emmer, E. T., Clements, B. S., & Worsham, M. E. (1997). Classroom management for elementary teachers (4th ed.). Boston: Allyn and Bacon.

Fad, K. (1990). The fast track to success: Social-behavioral skills. *Intervention in School and Clinic, 26,* 39–43.

Fagen, S. A., & Long, N. J. (1976). Teaching children self-control: A new responsibility for teachers. *Focus on Exceptional Children, 7*(8), 1–10.

Fagen, S. A., Long, N. J., & Stevens, D. J. (1975). *Teaching children self-control: Preventing emotional and learning problems in the elementary school.* Columbus, OH: Merrill.

Ferguson, D. L., Meyer, G., Jeanchild, L., Juniper, L., & Zingo, J. (1992). Figuring out what to do with the grownups: How teachers make inclusion work for students with disabilities. *Journal of the Association for Persons with Severe Handicaps, 17,* 218–226.

Gallagher, P. A. (1988). *Teaching students with behavior disorders* (2nd ed.). Denver: Love.

Gartner, A., & Lipsky, D. K. (1990). Students as instructional agents. In W. Stainback & S. Stainback (Eds.), *Support networks for inclusive schooling* (pp 81–98). Baltimore: Brookes.

Goldstein, A. P., Spafkin, R. P., Gershaw, N. J., & Klein, P. (1983). Structured learning: A psychoeducational approach for teaching social competencies. *Behavioral Disorders, 8*(3), 161–170.

Hollowood, T. M., Salisbury, C. L., Rainforth, B., & Palombaro, M. M. (1995). Use of instructional time in classrooms serving students with and without severe disabilities. *Exceptional Children, 61*(3), 242–253.

Joyce, B. G., Joyce, J. H., & Chase, P. N. (1989). Considerations for the use of rules in academic settings. *Education and Treatment of Children, 12,* 82–92.

Kagan, S. (1989). The structural approach to cooperative learning. *Educational Leadership, 217,* 12–15.

Kohn, A. (1993). *Punished by rewards: The trouble with gold stars, incentive plans, A's, praise, and other bribes.* New York: Houghton Mifflin.

Legare, A. F. (1984). Using symbols to enhance classroom structure. *Teaching Exceptional Children, 17,* 69–70.

McGee, J. J., Menolascino, F. J., Hobbs, D. C., & Menousek, P. E. (1987). *Gentle teaching.* New York: Human Science Press.

McGinnis, E., Sauerbry, L., & Nichols, P. (1985). Skillstreaming: Teaching social skills to children with behavior disorders. *Teaching Exceptional Children, 17*(3), 160–167.

Mirenda, P., & Donellan, A. (1986). Effects of adult interaction style versus conversational behavior in students with severe communication problems. *Language, Speech, and Hearing Services in the Schools, 17,* 126–141.

Morse, W. C. (1979). Self-control: The Fagen-Long curriculum. *Behavioral Disorders, 4,* 83–91.

Morse, W. C. (1994). The role of caring in teaching children with behavior problems. *Contemporary Education, 66*(3), 42.

Nelson, C. M. (1988). Social skills training for handicapped children. *Teaching Exceptional Children, 20,* 19–23.

Nichols, P. (1992). The Curriculum of Control: Twelve reasons for it, some arguments against it. *Beyond Behavior, 3*(2), 3–5.

Olson, J. (1989). Managing life in the classroom: Dealing with the nitty gritty. *Academic Therapy, 24*, 545–553.

Perls, F. (1967). Group vs. Individual therapy. In P. L. Newcomer, (Ed.), *Readings in emotional disturbance* (pp. 249–252). Austin, TX: Pro-ed.

Reith, H., & Evertson, C. (1988). Variables related to the effective instruction of difficult-to-teach children. *Focus on Exceptional Children, 20*, 1–8.

Rock, E. E., Rosenberg, M. S., & Carran, D. T. (1995). Variables affecting the reintegration rate of students with serious emotional disturbance. *Exceptional Children, 61*(3), 254–268.

Rogers, D. L., Waller, C. B., & Perrin, M. S. (1987). Learning more about what makes a good teacher good through collaborative research in the classroom. *Young Children, 34*, 34–39.

Rosenkoetter, S. E., & Fowler, S. A. (1986). Teaching mainstreamed children to manage daily transitions. *Teaching Exceptional Children, 19*, 20–23.

Rosenshine, B. (1977). Review of teaching variables and student achievement. In G. D. Borich & K. S. Fenton (Eds.), *The appraisal of teaching: Concepts and process.* Menlo Park, CA: Addison Wesley.

Sabornie, E. J., and Beard, G. H. (1990). Teaching social skills to students with mild handicaps. *Teaching Exceptional Children, 23*(1), 35–38.

Salisbury, C. L., Gallucci, C., Palombaro, M. M., & Peck, C. A. (1995). Strategies that promote social relations among elementary students with and without severe disabilities in inclusive schools. *Exceptional Children, 62*(2), 125–137.

Schechtman, Z., Reiter, S., & Schanin, M. (1993). Intrinsic motivation of teachers and the challenge of mainstreaming: An empirical investigation. *Special Services in the Schools, 7*(1), 107–121.

Scheuermann, B., & Webber, J. (1996). Level Systems: Problems and solutions. *Beyond Behavior, 7*(2), 12–17.

Scheuermann, B., Webber, J., Partin, M., & Knies, W. C. (1994). Levels systems and the law: Are they compatible? *Behavioral Disorders, 19*(3), 205–220.

Schumaker, J. B., Pederson, C. S., Hazel, J. S., & Mayen, E. L. (1983). Social skills curricula for mildly handicapped adolescents: A review. *Focus on Exceptional Children, 16*(4), 1–16.

Schwartz, I. S. (1996). Expanding the zone: Thoughts about social validity and training. *Journal of Early Intervention, 20*(3), 204–205.

Shea, T. M., & Bauer, A. M. (1987). Teaching children and youth with behavior disorders (2nd ed.). Upper Saddle River, NJ: Prentice Hall.

Slade, D., & Callaghan, T. (1988). Preventing management problems. *Academic Therapy, 23,* 229–235.

Smith, S. W., & Farrell, D. T. (1993). Levels system use in special education: Classroom intervention with prima facie appeal. *Behavioral Disorders, 18*(4), 251–264.

Snell, M., Lowman, D. K., & Canady, R. L. (1996). Parallel block scheduling: Accommodating students' diverse needs in elementary schools. *Journal of Early Intervention, 20*(3), 265–278.

Stainback, S., & Stainback, W. (1990). Facilitating support networks. In W. Stainback & S. Stainback (Eds.), *Support networks for inclusive schooling* (pp. 25–36). Baltimore: Brookes.

Story, C. M. (1985). Facilitator of learning: A microethnographic study of the teacher of the gifted. *Gifted Child Quarterly, 29*(4), 155–158.

Thorson, S. (1996). The missing link: Students discuss school discipline. *Focus on Exceptional Children, 29*(3), 1–12.

Thousand, J. S., & Villa, R. A. (1990). Sharing expertise and responsibilities through teaching teams. In W. Stainback & S. Stainback (Eds.), Support networks for inclusive schooling (pp 151–166). Baltimore: Brookes.

Tomlinson, C. A. (1995). *How to differentiate instruction in mixed-ability classrooms.* Alexandria, VA: Association for Supervision and Curriculum Development.

Vandercook, T., & York, J. (1990). A team approach to program development and support. In W. Stainback & S. Stainback (Eds.), *Support networks for inclusive schooling* (pp 95–122). Baltimore: Brookes.

Walker, J. E., & Shea, T. M. (1995). *Behavior management: A practical approach for educators.* Upper Saddle River, NJ: Prentice Hall.

Ysseldyke, J. E., Thurlow, M. L., Wotruba, J. W., & Nania, P. (1990). Instructional arrangements: Perceptions from general education. *Teaching Exceptional Children, 22*(4), 4–8.

Zaragoza, N., Vaughn, S., & McIntosh, R. (1991). Social skills interventions and children with behavioral problems: A review. *Behavioral Disorders, 16*(4), 260–275.

12 Preventing Emotional/Behavioral Disorders

TO GUIDE YOUR READING

After you read this chapter, you will be able to answer these questions:

- What is prevention?
- What is the role of early intervention in the prevention of emotional/behavioral disorders?
- What is the role of conflict resolution in the prevention of emotional/behavioral disorders?
- What is the role of family intervention in the prevention of emotional/behavioral disorders?
- What is the role of violence prevention in schools?
- In what preventive efforts can teachers engage to mitigate the impact of contemporary social problems on children and youth?

◊ *The number of children and youth younger than 18 years of age who were arrested for murder increased 158% between 1985 and 1994.*

◊ *The number of children without health insurance is anticipated to increase 40% between 1992 and 2002. (Children's Defense Fund, 1997)*

◊ *The current United States infant mortality rate is 8.5 deaths for every 1,000 live births—the highest among Western industrialized nations.*

This final chapter focuses on the important topic of prevention of emotional/behavioral disorders. After a thorough review and discussion of the literature on the treatment and education of learners identified as emotionally/behaviorally disordered presented in the previous 11 chapters, it appears that the best approach to this most serious of contemporary social problems is prevention. In this chapter, we review several interventions that can be implemented to keep emotional/behavioral disorders from occurring. The chapter concludes with a discussion of the teacher's role in the prevention of emotional/behavioral disorders.

The contemporary professional literature, as well as popular literature, informs us that a significant percentage of the population is at-risk for emotional/behavioral disorders, as well as other social problems. ***At-risk*** is not a precise category of disability such as learning disability, developmental disability, or emotional/behavioral disorder. Rather, it represents a set of presumed dynamics that could place an individual in danger of negative future events (McWhirter, McWhirter, McWhirter, & McWhirter, 1993). McWhirter et al. describe "at-risk" as a continuum, beginning with minimal risk, in which an individual has favorable demographics, such as positive family, school, and social interaction; and limited stressors. Next is high risk, which includes negative family, school, and social interaction; numerous stressors; negative attitudes and emotions; and skill deficiencies. Finally, there is imminent risk, which includes the development of gateway or threshold behaviors and activities. A large number of those who are at-risk are inner-city children who live in poverty, and are exposed to the many challenges of inner-urban life. Human service agencies may contribute to and compound the problems of at-risk populations by engaging in ***turfism*** or the guarding of areas of professional expertise and services from encroachment by others, rather than providing an integrated services network (Fredericks, 1994).

at-risk a set of presumed dynamics that could place an individual in danger of negative future events (McWhirter et al., 1993)

turfism guarding areas of professional expertise and services from encroachment by others

◊◊ What Is Prevention?

Prevention is the interventions engaged in to keep emotional/ behavioral disorders from occurring. The most commonly used definition of prevention describes three levels of activity: primary, secondary, and tertiary (Caplan, 1964). *Primary prevention* focuses on the population at large. It is concerned with eliminating the causes of emotional/behavioral disorders and reducing the incidence of the development of emotional/behavioral disorders. *Secondary prevention,* in Caplan's structure, is aimed at reducing the duration of cases of individuals with emotional/behavioral disorders. The goals of secondary prevention are to reduce the intensity and/or duration of emotional/behavioral disorders in order to prevent more serious emotional/behavioral disorders in the future. *Tertiary prevention* is directed at reducing the likelihood that individuals with emotional/behavioral disorders will develop more serious problems. Its aim is to reduce the residual effects of emotional/behavioral disorders.

Apter (1982) provides a strong rationale for prevention. First, mental health services are expensive, and with increased incidence of emotional/behavioral problems as well as increased medical costs, these services are becoming even more expensive. In addition, mental health care is not always effective, nor is it universally available. The mental health system has too few professionals to serve the needs of the community. An additional need for prevention emerges from the history of mental health services reaching too few people too late.

Currently, two major prevention-focused programs are being developed: programs related to reducing stress in the community and programs related to building individual capacity to withstand stress. Community prevention efforts include support to families, community education, and the utilization of community strengths. Individual strategies include supporting the development of competence in children, identifying and building on the specific strengths of each child, providing basic social behaviors to each child, and building competence in individual adults (Apter, 1982).

Prevention is a primary means of managing behavior. Curwin and Mendler (1988) suggest that there are several stages of prevention: (a) increasing teacher self-awareness, (b) increasing student self-awareness, (c) expressing genuine feelings, (d) discovering and recognizing alternatives, (e) motivating students, (f) establishing social contracts with the class, and (g) implementing social contracts. Curwin and Mendler feel that by providing structure and direction, as well as demonstrating flexibility, teachers can prevent many behavior problems. In their emphasis on

prevention interventions engaged in to keep emotional/behavioral disorders from occurring

primary prevention prevention strategies aimed at the population at large

secondary prevention prevention efforts to reduce the intensity and/or duration of problems in the future

tertiary prevention prevention efforts directed at reducing the likelihood that problems will become more serious

prevention, they contend that teachers should use a problem reso-lution process that includes individual student contracts to pre-vent behavior problems. These contracts should begin with a dis-cussion of preventive procedures with the student and the development of a mutually agreeable plan for problem resolu-tion. Teachers and students then monitor the plan and revise it as necessary.

◊◊ What Is the Role of Early Intervention in the Prevention of Emotional/Behavioral Disorders?

early intervention
services provided to in-fants and toddlers, birth through age 3, and their families

Early intervention has both a legal and a colloquial definition. Legally, *early intervention* are those services provided to infants and toddlers (birth through 3 years of age) and their families in re-sponse to Individuals with Disabilities Education Act (IDEA) man-dates. These early intervention services are provided through the implementation of an Individualized Family Service Plan (IFSP). Colloquially, early intervention is used to refer to services provided to families before their children attain school age. Independent of the definition used, the goal of early intervention is to optimize the learning potential and daily well-being of the child and his or her family (Dunst, Trivette, & Deal, 1988).

Ramey and Ramey (1992) found significant long-lasting (through age 12) differences between children who received intensive early intervention and a control group. Significantly fewer children failed a grade or had tested intelligence quotient of more than one stan-dard deviation below the mean.

Kauffman (1989) suggests that the strongest predictor of appro-priate behavior in children is the quantity and quality of caregiver supervision. Zirpoli and Melloy (1997) suggest several other vari-ables related to the development of appropriate behavior in young children. Consistency, they indicate, is significant in that it builds an understanding and expectations between child and caregivers. The educational environment also may have an influence on the behavior of young children. Variables in the environment related to the behavior of young children include (Zirpoli, 1995):

- Social density, or the number of children in the setting. Crowded settings are related to reduced responseness on the part of care-givers.

- Physical layout. The setting should be safe, and the design of the setting should limit the number of young children in each area.

- Appropriate use of materials, including calming activities as well as stimulating materials.

- Effective scheduling, including routines, short time segments, active play and group times, as well as passive and quiet activities.
- Staffing qualifications and ratios.

In the Community Integration Project, a demonstration project, Bruder (1993) found eight characteristics of effective service delivery within early childhood programs:

1. A program philosophy of inclusive early childhood services. An inclusive program is a place where everyone belongs, is accepted, and supports and is supported by peers in the course of having his or her individual educational needs met (Stainback & Stainback, 1990).

2. A consistent and ongoing system for family involvement. Services must (a) be based on the premise that the family is the enduring and central force in the life of the child, and as such, services should be responsive to the lifestyles, values, and priorities of the family; (b) document the concerns, resources, and priorities of families; (c) communicate effectively with families; and (d) provide services within the context of families.

3. A system of team planning and program implementation. In transdisciplinary teams, members share roles and cross professional service boundaries systematically and communicate on a regular planned basis.

4. A model and system for collaboration and communication with other agencies that provide services to young children with disabilities and their families.

5. A well-constructed Individualized Educational Plan or Individualized Family Service Plan that dictates the intervention content for each participating child. Individualized goals should be functional and embedded in daily activities and routines engaged in by the child.

6. Integrated delivery of educational and related services. By capitalizing on the child's interests, preferences, and actions, emphasis is placed on the child's initiations rather than on an individual service provider's choices; interventions then encourage the acquisition of generalizable and functional skills.

7. A consistent and ongoing system for training and staff development. All staff members, including administrative personnel, must be part of the training effort.

8. A comprehensive system for evaluating the effectiveness of the program. Evaluation should be multidimensional.

Helping families helps children.

An ongoing tension exists between early childhood education personnel and early childhood special education personnel. Bredekamp (1993) suggests that this tension may be grounded in misconceptions about developmentally appropriate practice. She suggests, according to the National Association for the Education of Young Children, that developmentally appropriate means both age appropriate and individually appropriate. In addition, the almost exclusive use of teacher-directed instruction is not appropriate for any child because it denies the opportunity for social interaction. She argues that programming must be individually appropriate: a program must assess and plan for children's individual needs and interests. Bredekamp suggests six elements of best practice in early childhood special education that could be integrated into the early childhood education knowledge base. These elements are summarized in Table 12.1.

In inclusive early childhood education settings, Cavallaro, Haney, and Cabello (1992) suggest strategies that capitalize on the developmental opportunities available within integrated preschool settings without compromising child choice. These strategies include:

• Attention and responsiveness to children by responding both to the children's interests and to their intent.

Table 12.1   Elements of Best Practice in Early Childhood Special
Education (Bredekamp, 1993)

Individually appropriate practice	Early childhood education strongly values the individual child but has been less systematic in ensuring that the individual child's needs are met in relation to program goals.
Early intervention	Early intervention should include interactive teaching, a continuum of possible teaching behaviors from nondirective to directive, with the mediating behaviors of facilitating, supporting, and scaffolding.
Family-centered services	As the child is perceived less at-risk, focus on family weakens in early childhood.
Advocacy	Early childhood educators need to join in advocating for young children with special needs.
Transition	Transition is challenged due to practices in kindergarten and primary grades.
Interdisciplinary approaches	They are necessary in early childhood education.

- Environmental structuring strategies, including selecting materials to facilitate engagement and interaction, structuring activities to promote interaction, providing choices, maintaining adult proximity, and facilitating peer proximity.
- Adult mediation strategies, including questioning, encouraging and commenting; behavioral, metacognitive, and reflective modeling; responsive prompting; fine-tuning; and providing feedback.
- Peer mediation strategies, including modeling and peer mediated training.

◊◊ What Is the Role of Conflict Resolution in the Prevention of Emotional/Behavioral Disorders?

Conflict, a condition of disagreement or disharmony, has a negative connotation. However, Johnson and Johnson (1996) argue that conflict in the school environment is not only inevitable, but also desirable, if managed constructively without physical or verbal violence, so that children and youth can learn to be peacemakers. They contend that conflicts have value when they:

conflict a condition of disagreement; disharmony

- Focus attention on problems that need solutions.
- Clarify students' identity and values.

- Highlight patterns of behavior that are not successful.
- Help students understand other students and their values.
- Strengthen relations by increasing confidence that participants can resolve disagreements.
- Resolve the small tensions that naturally occur when interacting with others.
- Release anger, anxiety, insecurity, and sadness.
- Clarify students' commitments and values.
- Stimulate students' interests and actions.

   Johnson and Johnson (1996) describe their "Teaching Students to be Peacemakers Program" as a schoolwide cooperative effort. A 12-year spiral program in which students learn increasingly sophisticated negotiation and mediation strategies, it focuses on teaching students to be peacemakers. There are six steps in the program. The first step involves creating a cooperative context. As a problem-solving approach, the program requires students to recognize their interdependence. Next, students are taught to recognize when conflict is occurring and when it is not occurring. They learn specific procedures for negotiating agreements and for mediation and have opportunities to practice these procedures. Johnson and Johnson urge that peer mediation programs be in place and that training in negotiation and mediation procedures occur weekly throughout the students' school career. They suggest that when students are taught how to negotiate and are given opportunities to mediate their peers' conflicts, they are provided the tools needed for self-regulation and self-monitoring; judging what is appropriate, given the situation and the other person's perspective; and how to behave accordingly.

   Disruptive behaviors may occur more often when students are asked to perform or complete tasks when they lack the skills necessary for success (Denny, DePaepe, Gunter, Jack, and Shores, 1994). Occurrences of disruptive behavior, in this study, decreased dramatically when direct instruction and feedback were provided. It was found, however, that teachers supplied only information students needed to complete assigned tasks about 20% of the time.

◊◊ What Is the Role of Family Interventions in the Prevention of Emotional/Behavioral Disorders?

Historically, therapeutic interventions for children and youth identified as emotionally/behaviorally disordered have been based on the premise that mental illness is caused by family factors

(Terkelsen, 1983). As a result, prevention efforts often focus on the family. *Family intervention* includes strategies that target family interactions to change behavior of family members.

family intervention strategies that target family interactions to change behavior of family members

Patterson (1986) describes a model of interaction for families engaged in patterned exchanges of aversive behaviors. In these families, interaction sequences of relatively trivial behaviors were the learning base for family members' high-amplitude aggressive behaviors. Escape-avoidant behaviors (attack-counterattack-positive outcome) may occur hundreds of times a day. Children move from being noncompliant to physically assaultive, beginning with behaviors such as whining, yelling, and temper tantrums, as a substitute social skill. As other family members begin to use these skills in response, the likelihood for violence increases. As the child becomes more skillfully coercive, he or she becomes even more difficult to discipline. Presumably, training parents to use more effective discipline would reduce this behavior.

Family-focused interventions for students at-risk for emotional/behavioral disorders vary depending on family structure, family interaction patterns, and other family characteristics (Lambie & Daniels-Mohring, 1993). Lambie and Daniels-Mohring suggest seven different types of interventions that may assist in prevention:

1. Emotional support, which may involve simply listening (Lambie, 1987). In emotional support, the professional provides the family with a sense of being understood and cared about.

2. Resource identification, which may include making information available, such as information related to parents' and children's rights, procedures, and services.

3. Technical assistance, which involves professionals suggesting that families employ at-home management strategies or use training techniques; professionals may also make suggestions directly to the parents.

4. Referral, which may include referral to counseling or therapy, or to medical or financial services.

5. Normalization, which is an intervention in which professionals help children view their behavior as being within normal limits.

6. Reframing, an intervention sometimes used with normalization, offers an alternative interpretation of behavior or events that changes the meaning of the behavior for the family.

7. Contextualization, which is similar to reframing. In contextualization, professionals work with families to interpret behavior in and through the context in which it occurs. Professionals help parents understand the contextual factors related to their behavior.

In a study by Soderlund, Epstein, Quinn, Cumblad, and Petersen (1995), parents reported persistent needs even though their general feelings about the services that they had received were positive. They indicated that they needed additional information about community services, needed to be able to find recreational activities, and needed assistance in locating transition programs and alternative schooling for their children.

◊◊ What Is the Role of Violence Prevention in the Schools?

Violence in our schools has increased significantly during the past 10 years. Curwin (1994) argues that violence is now more random and senseless when compared to violence in the past. In response to this change, Curwin suggests that students be actively taught *violence prevention,* or efforts aimed at decreasing the engagement of individuals in aggressive activity. Students should be taught alternatives to violence; the making of effective choices; and modeling of appropriate expressions of anger, frustration, and impatience. In addition, children must be taught values.

violence prevention efforts aimed at decreasing the engagement of individuals in aggressive activity

The role of television viewing in the violent behavior of children has been postulated for many years. Gadow and Sprafkin (1993) conducted a 10-year study of the relationships between children's television viewing habits and aggressive acts, and the effects of a "viewing skills curriculum." They reported that children identified as emotionally/behaviorally disordered viewed relatively large amounts of violent material, preferred aggressive characters, and were more likely to believe fictional content as true. However, it was not more likely for them to behave aggressively following aggression-ladened viewing. Although students did increase their knowledge of television viewing following the implementation of a "viewing skills curriculum," their actual viewing behavior did not change.

Brendtro and Long (1994) suggest that a conflict cycle is at work among individuals engaged in violence. They suggest that in these individuals, stressful situations evoke irrational beliefs, such as, "everyone is against me." These irrational, biased beliefs trigger feelings of distress, such as fear or anger, which in turn drive defensive behavior, such as avoidance or aggression. In relationships, the individual's behavior then provokes reciprocal reactions from others, such as counteraggression.

In order to break this cycle, Brendtro and Long (1994) suggest primary prevention activities, for example, preventing broken relationships, teaching children self-discipline, and teaching *conflict resolution,* or activities engaged in to find an answer or solution to a disagreement or disharmony. They also suggest early intervention in which children and parents are both targeted for mentoring and encouraged to disengage from punitive cycles. School bullying, which often results in moving resources to the front line, should be addressed. Finally, they suggest restoring social bonds by fostering attachment, achievement, and autonomy.

The more effective teachers are at empowering children, the less violence the children will initiate (Haberman, 1994). Haberman suggests that children living in poverty, in addition to having violence present in their daily lives, have a lack of trust that makes them suspicious of motives and actions of adults. A sense of hopelessness characterizes the urban life of older children and adults in poverty, as well as frustration with the many bureaucracies with which they must engage. The culture of authoritarianism that pervades poverty leads to frustration, which is expressed as violence.

Haberman (1994) suggests that if the harshest punishments available to teachers and schools can be ignored or even laughed at by students then teachers are not justified in believing they can coerce, force, demand, or require students to comply and learn. He contends that most teachers do not know alternatives to coercive teaching, that they were never taught these alternatives in their own preparation, or that they themselves were socialized by power relationships. A teacher's strength is an inner quality demonstrated by an ability to share authority with children whom most people are unwilling to trust. Teachers must self-analyze their prejudices, and learn to treat everyone with respect and dignity.

A contrasting view of intervening to control violence is "getting tough with violence" offered by Kauffman (1994). He suggests that schools stop aggressive behavior early and when it does occur provide effective consequences for it. Students should have restricted access to instruments of aggression. In addition, he suggests that effective instruction in violence prevention should be provided. Recommendations for decreasing violence in schools are summarized in Figure 12.1.

◊◊ In What Preventive Efforts Can Teachers Engage to Mitigate the Impact of Contemporary Social Problems on Children and Youth?

Effective discipline may, in itself, prevent emotional/behavioral disorders. Smith and Rivera (1995) suggest several principles for effective discipline. The climate of the school and classroom should

conflict resolution
activities engaged in to find an answer or solution to a disagreement or disharmony

Students must believe they are competent in making decisions.

be positive; it should provide a foundation for a positive learning environment. Prevention of, rather than reaction to, discipline problems should be emphasized. Collaborative relationships with parents and other professionals for dealing with disciplinary concerns and promoting a positive learning climate should be established. Interventions should match the behavior problems, and an evaluation system that frequently monitors student progress should be in place.

The issue of "hope" is important for children who are at-risk. Curwin (1994) has two basic suggestions for instilling hope. First, students must believe they are competent in the subjects they are learning. Teachers should help students gain confidence in themselves and their ability to learn by insuring that the students achieve at least one meaningful learning objective each day. Second, learning tasks should not be too easy; simple tasks can be perceived by students as condescending, babyish, and not worth doing and have a negative impact on the students' perceptions of themselves as learners.

- Provide prenatal and early childhood programs for at-risk populations.
- Expand parent educational and family support programs.
- Provide violence prevention programs such as conflict resolution and peer mediation.
- Provide and integrate family support services that affect children, including schools, child care, and health care.
- Restrict everyone's access to guns; reform the gun industry, with stronger criminal liabilities for illegal sales.
- Reduce and reform instances of violence presented to the public as entertainment.
- Educate families about the risk of maintaining firearms at home.
- Encourage the use of effective alternatives to incarceration for youth when appropriate, and the use of effective rehabilitation programs.
- Expand interventions that place caring adults in the lives of young adults.
- Prevent teen pregnancy, including outreach to young males.
- Enforce zero tolerance for gun possession at school.
- Support programs that reduce violence in families by making homes safer for all family members.

Figure 12.1 Recommendations of the National Summit on Youth and Violence (1994) for decreasing violence in schools

Jones (1993) suggests that developing an effective classroom and school management plan must address five questions:

1. Does the plan treat students with dignity?
2. Does your response to student behavior include an educational component, that is, does it teach students new skills?
3. Does the program require and support an environmental analysis?
4. Is the response to rule violations clear to everyone?
5. Is there a sequential response to rule violation?

Suicide

One of the most difficult challenges confronting teachers is responding appropriately to suicide ideations and attempts and suicide among students. Most school-based suicide prevention programs deal with identifying signs of depression and suicidal ideation. Preventive efforts attempt to help students succeed in school, grow emotionally, and achieve their personal potential (Putnam, 1995).

McGee and Guetzloe (1988) offer several suggestions for working with an individual who may be suicidal:

- Always consider suicide threats or gestures as serious.
- Convey to the student that you consider suicide threats as serious but do not make the student feel guilty.
- Encourage the student to use his or her existing social support systems including parents, friends, school personnel, or a community counseling or mental health personnel.
- Recognize that to an adolescent the loss of a romantic relationship may represent the end of all hope for a loving relationship.
- Remove anything in the immediate environment that could be used as a weapon.
- Mention events that may be coming up to elicit the individual's interest and motivate involvement.
- Make sure that students have the telephone number of a crisis center, the suicide hotline, or a member of school staff.
- Tell the student that you cannot keep his or her suicidal statements secret; as a responsible professional you must report to the appropriate school personnel.
- Ask the student for a commitment that he or she will not harm himself or herself and that if he or she feels any kind of suicidal impulse, he or she will call a teacher, a counselor, or hotline worker.

Drug and Alcohol Use and Abuse

Putnam (1995) describes several programs for the prevention of alcohol and other drug use. "Students Against Drunk Driving" or SADD, for example, is a club to promote the nonuse of alcohol and other drugs by peers and their parents, particularly when driving. Individuals write a "contract for life" in which the individual agrees to call for help or transportation if in a situation where he or she has been drinking and needs to go home. SADD uses strategies such as posters, presentations, and speakers.

The "Just Say No Club" also advocates the nonuse of alcohol and other drugs, as well as training in the skills needed to say "no" to peers and others and to support others in their efforts to say "no." Adventure-based programs, including canoeing, camping, mountain climbing, sailing, and hiking, may be used to fill the adolescent's need for adventure and risk-seeking behaviors without the use of alcohol or other drugs. Mini-courses and wellness days, as well as activities to increase positive school climate, are also used to prevent drug and alcohol use.

Adolescent Pregnancy

Approximately 1 million American adolescent girls become pregnant each year. Of these girls, approximately one third have abortions, one in seven miscarries, and slightly over half have children. The annual cost of adolescent motherhood plus the costs of other disadvantages faced by adolescent mothers may be between 13 and 19 billion dollars (Children's Defense Fund, 1997).

The National Campaign to Prevent Teen Pregnancy, which began in 1996, aims to reduce teen births through enlisting the media, supporting state and local actions, and disseminating effective programs. The Campaign identified several likely causes of the high pregnancy rates among American teens, including the lack of negative consequences for male partners, the absence of forceful messages that teens should not be parents, mass glorification of sex, influences of childhood sexual abuse, sexual exploitation by older men, earlier onset of puberty, lack of accessibility to family planning services, and insufficient information about sexuality and contraception provided to children and adolescents.

Prevention programs emphasize the need to provide comprehensive youth development programs, and education on sexuality and contraception.

◊◊ Summary Points

- Prevention is usually described as three levels of activity: primary, secondary, and tertiary prevention.
- Two major prevention-focused programs emerging include reducing stress in the community and building individual capacity to withstand stress.
- Early intervention can make significant, long-lasting differences in the lives of very young children identified as emotionally/behaviorally disordered.
- Providing students with opportunities and training to mediate their own conflicts increases their ability to self-regulate and self-monitor.
- Family intervention efforts vary depending on family characteristics.
- Students must be actively taught alternatives to violence.
- Through effective discipline, teachers can mitigate the impact of contemporary social problems on their students.

Self-Evaluation ◊

Select the most appropriate response.

1. "At-risk" is
   a. a legal category of disability.
   b. overused to the point of banality.
   c. a set of dynamics.
2. Human service agencies
   a. emphasize interagency collaboration.
   b. provide adequate services to at-risk families.
   c. are underfunded for their prevention efforts.
3. Tertiary prevention aims to
   a. reduce the residual effects of emotional/behavioral disorders.
   b. reduce the number of individuals with emotional/behavioral disorders.
   c. reduce service costs of individuals with emotional/behavioral disorders.
4. Early intervention services
   a. have short-term effect on families.
   b. have been documented by few longitudinal studies.
   c. have made significant long-lasting differences for children.
5. Among young children, the strongest predictor of appropriate behavior is
   a. parents' skills.
   b. structure of the program.
   c. the quantity and quality of caregiver supervision.
6. The tensions between early childhood education and early childhood special education may be grounded in
   a. the need for children with disabilities to have one-on-one instruction.
   b. misconceptions about developmentally appropriate practice.
   c. the inability to engage in developmentally appropriate practice while implementing IEPs.
7. Conflict in the school environment
   a. rarely occurs in well-structured programs.
   b. is highly disruptive.
   c. is valuable for students in learning peacemaking.
8. Disruptive behavior among students may be related to
   a. demands to complete tasks for which they do not have the skills.
   b. family factors.
   c. poor mediation skills.
9. Historically, interventions have been based on the premise that
   a. mental illness is caused by family factors.
   b. poverty and at-risk designations are linked.
   c. boys are more likely to have emotional/behavioral disorders than girls.
10. Teachers whose students initiate less violence
    a. use mediation techniques.
    b. empower their students.
    c. provide clear contingencies for aggression.

Making the Language Your Own

Match each key word or phrase to its definition.

_____ 1. conflict   _____ 7. tertiary prevention

_____ 2. turfism   _____ 8. conflict resolution

_____ 3. primary prevention   _____ 9. family intervention

_____ 4. at-risk   _____ 10. prevention

_____ 5. early intervention   _____ 11. violence prevention

_____ 6. secondary prevention

a. prevention strategies aimed at the population at large
b. disharmony
c. dynamics that could place an individual in danger of negative future events
d. efforts aimed at decreasing the engagement of individuals in aggressive activity
e. guarding areas of professional expertise and services
f. interventions engaged in to keep emotional/behavioral disorders from occurring
g. efforts directed at reducing the likelihood that problems will increase in intensity
h. activities engaged in to find an answer or solution to a disagreement
i. strategies that target family interactions
j. services provided to infants and toddlers
k. efforts to reduce the intensity and/or duration of problems in the future

Theory into Practice

1. Contact a community agency. What services does the agency provide? Which of these services are preventive in nature?
2. During your television viewing for one week, log the commercial spots related to public information or prevention. Who funds these spots? What were the targets of these spots?

◊◊ **References**

Apter, S. (1982). *Troubled children, troubled systems.* New York: Pergamon.

Bredekemp, S. (1993). The relationship between early childhood education and early childhood special education: Healthy marriage or family feud? *Topics in Early Childhood Special Education, 13*(3), 258–273.

Brendtro, L. K., & Long, N. J. (1994). Violence begets violence: Breaking conflict cycles. *Journal of Emotional and Behavioral Problems, 3*(1), 2–7.

Bruder, M. B. (1993). The provision of early intervention and early childhood special education within community early childhood programs: Characteristics of effective service delivery. *Topics in Early Childhood Special Education, 13*(1), 19–37.

Caplan, G. (1964). *Principles of preventive psychiatry.* New York: Basic Books.

Cavallaro, C. C., Haney, M., & Cabello, B. (1992). Developmentally appropriate strategies for promoting full participation in early childhood settings. *Topics in Early Childhood Special Education, 13*(3), 293–307.

Children's Defense Fund. (1997). *The state of American children yearbook 1997.* Washington, DC: Author.

Curwin, R. L. (1994). Teaching at-riskers how to hope. *The Education Digest, 60*(2), 11–15.

Curwin, R. L. (1995). A humane approach to reducing violence in schools. *Educational Leadership, 52*(5), 72.

Curwin, R. L., & Mendler, A. N. (1988). *Discipline with dignity.* Alexandria, VA: Association for Supervision and Curriculum Development.

Denny, R. K., DePaepe, P. A., Gunter, P. L., Jack S. L., & Shores, R. E. (1994). A case study of the effects of altering instructional interactions on the disruptive behavior of a child identified with SBD. *Education and Treatment of Children, 17,* 435–444.

Dunst, C. J., Trivette, C., & Deal, A. (1988). *Enabling and empowering families: Principles and guidelines for practice.* Cambridge, MA: Brookline Books.

Fredericks, B. (1994). Integrated service systems for troubled youth. *Education and Treatment of Children, 17,* 387–416.

Gadow, K. D., & Sprafkin, J. (1993). Television "violence" and children with emotional and behavioral disorders. *Journal of Emotional and Behavioral Disorders, 1*(1), 54–63.

Haberman, M. (1994, Spring). Gentle teaching . . . in a violent society. *Educational Horizons,* 131–135.

Henley, M. (1994). A self-control curriculum for troubled youngsters. *Journal of Emotional and Behavioral Problems, 3*(1), 40–46.

Johnson, D. W., & Johnson, R. T. (1996). Peacemakers: Teaching students to resolve their own and schoolmates' conflicts. *Focus on Exceptional Children, 28*(6), 1–11.

Jones, V. (1993). Assessing your classroom and school-wide management plan. *Beyond Behavior, 4*(3), 9–12.

Kauffman, J. (1994). Violence and aggression of children and youth: A call for action. *Preventing School Failure, 38*(3), 8–9.

Kauffman, J. M. (1989). *Characteristics of behavior disorders of children and youth* (4th ed.). Upper Saddle River, NJ: Prentice Hall.

Lambie, R. (1987). *Working with families of children with handicaps.* Richmond: Virginia Department of Education.

Lambie, R., & Daniels-Mohring, D. (1993). *Family systems within educational contexts.* Denver: Love.

McGee, K., & Guetzloe, E. (1988). Suicidal emotionally handicapped students: Tips for the classroom teacher. *The Pointer, 32,* 7–10.

McWhirter, J. J., McWhirter, B. T., McWhirter, A. M., & McWhirter, E. H. (1993). *At-risk youth: A comprehensive response.* Pacific Grove, CA: Brooks/Cole.

National Summit on Youth Violence (1994). *Breaking the cycle of violence.* Bloomington, IN: National Educational Service Foundation.

Patterson, G. (1986). Performance models for antisocial boys. *American Psychologist, 41*(4), 432–444.

Putnam, M. L. (1995). Crisis intervention with adolescents with learning disabilities. *Focus on Exceptional Children, 28*(2), 1–24.

Ramey, C. T., & Ramey, S. L. (1992). Effective early intervention. *Mental Retardation, 30,* 337–345.

Smith, D. D., & Rivera, D. P. (1995). Discipline in special education and general education settings. *Focus on Exceptional Children, 27*(5), 1–14.

Soderlund, J., Epstein, M. H., Quinn, K. P., Cumblad, C., & Petersen, S. (1995). Parental perspectives on comprehensive services for children and youth with emotional and behavioral disorders. *Behavioral Disorders, 20*(3), 157–170.

Stainback, S., & Stainback, W. (1990). *Support networks for inclusive schooling.* Baltimore: Brookes.

Terkelsen, K. G. (1983). Schizophrenia and the family: Adverse effects of family therapy. *Family Process, 22,* 191–200.

Zirpoli, T. J. (1995). *Understanding and affecting the behavior of young children.* Upper Saddle River, NJ: Prentice-Hall.

Zirpoli, T. J., & Melloy, K. J. (1997). *Behavior management: Applications for teachers and parents.* Upper Saddle River, NJ: Prentice Hall.

◇ ◇

Answer Key

Chapter 1
Self-Evaluation

1. a	**6.** c
2. a	**7.** b
3. b	**8.** c
4. c	**9.** c
5. b	**10.** c

Making the Language Your Own

1. b	**6.** i
2. a	**7.** h
3. e	**8.** g
4. c	**9.** f
5. d	

Chapter 2
Self-Evaluation

1. b	**6.** a
2. a	**7.** c
3. c	**8.** c
4. b	**9.** a
5. c	**10.** c

Making the Language Your Own

1. j	**4.** b
2. a	**5.** c
3. i	**6.** g

7. d	**9.** e
8. f	**10.** h

Chapter 3
Self-Evaluation

1. b	**5.** c
2. b	**6.** a
3. a	**7.** f
4. b	**8.** e

Making the Language Your Own

1. d	**4.** c
2. b	**5.** h
3. a	**6.** g

Chapter 4
Self-Evaluation

1. c	**6.** b
2. c	**7.** b
3. c	**8.** b
4. b	**9.** a
5. b	

Making the Language Your Own

1. b	**5.** f
2. e	**6.** g
3. a	**7.** c
4. d	

Chapter 5
Self-Evaluation

1. c	**6.** c
2. a	**7.** c
3. b	**8.** c
4. c	**9.** c
5. b	**10.** c

Making the Language Your Own

1. b	**4.** c
2. d	**5.** e
3. a	

Chapter 6
Self-Evaluation

1. c	**6.** c
2. c	**7.** c
3. b	**8.** c
4. c	**9.** b
5. c	**10.** b

Making the Language Your Own

1. d	**5.** e
2. c	**6.** b
3. h	**7.** a
4. f	**8.** g

Chapter 7
Self-Evaluation

1. c	**6.** a
2. c	**7.** a
3. c	**8.** c
4. b	**9.** b
5. b	**10.** b

Making the Language
Your Own

1. e	**5.** c
2. a	**6.** d
3. g	**7.** b
4. f	

Chapter 8
Self-Evaluation

1. c	**6.** c
2. c	**7.** a
3. c	**8.** b
4. a	**9.** a
5. a	**10.** c

Making the Language
Your Own

1. e	**5.** a
2. c	**6.** b
3. d	**7.** g
4. h	**8.** f

Chapter 9
Self-Evaluation

1. b	**3.** b
2. a	**4.** c

5. b	**8.** b
6. c	**9.** c
7. a	**10.** b

Making the Language
Your Own

1. b	**6.** d
2. c	**7.** g
3. e	**8.** j
4. h	**9.** i
5. f	**10.** a

Chapter 10
Self-Evaluation

1. c	**6.** c
2. c	**7.** a
3. c	**8.** b
4. b	**9.** b
5. c	**10.** c

Making the Language
Your Own

1. b	**9.** l
2. e	**10.** n
3. g	**11.** o
4. j	**12.** m
5. f	**13.** a
6. h	**14.** c
7. i	**15.** d
8. k	

Chapter 11
Self-Evaluation

1. b	**3.** c
2. b	**4.** b

5. c	**8.** b
6. c	**9.** a
7. c	**10.** b

Making the Language
Your Own

1. f	**6.** d
2. a	**7.** c
3. g	**8.** h
4. e	**9.** i
5. b	

Chapter 12
Self-Evaluation

1. c	**6.** b
2. c	**7.** c
3. a	**8.** a
4. c	**9.** c
5. c	**10.** b

Making the Language
Your Own

1. b	**7.** k
2. e	**8.** h
3. a	**9.** i
4. c	**10.** f
5. j	**11.** d
6. g	

Name Index

Subject Index